Electrical Spectrum and Network Analyzers

Electrical Spectrum and Network Analyzers

A Practical Approach

Albert D. Helfrick
Consulting Engineer
Kinnelon, New Jersey

Academic Press, Inc.
Harcourt Brace Jovanovich, Publishers
San Diego New York Boston London Sydney Tokyo Toronto

Academic Press, Inc.
San Diego, California 92101

United Kingdom Edition published by
Academic Press Limited
24–28 Oval Road, London NW1 7DX

Library of Congress Cataloging-in-Publication Data

Helfrick, Albert D.
Electrical spectrum and network analyzers: a practical approach / Albert D. Helfrick.
p. cm.
Includes bibliographical references and index.
ISBN 0-12-412031-8
1. Spectrum analysis. 2. Spectrum analyzers. I Title.
TK7879.4.H45 1991
621.382--dc20 90-49831
CIP

PRINTED IN THE UNITED STATES OF AMERICA
91 92 93 94 9 8 7 6 5 4 3 2 1

Contents

Preface

This book fills the gap between the texts that provide all there is to know about the theory of spectrum analysis and the glorified instruction books. For most engineers and technicians, what is most necessary for the effective use of the spectrum analyzer is the knowledge of how the instrument operates. The physical basis for the displayed spectra, the Fourier and fast Fourier transforms, and the rigorous theoretical foundations of spectral analysis are often beyond what is needed to make effective use of the spectrum analyzer. On the other hand, knowledge of the internal structure of an instrument helps in understanding the proper operation of that instrument.

This text presents some theory and some theoretical circuits, but primarily it provides a view of practical circuits and useful operational techniques. Insight into some of the more specialized analyzers is presented so that the student will appreciate the wide use of spectral analysis. The main thrust, however, is the use of spectral analysis for radio frequency measurements. The operational techniques described in this book go beyond those provided in the typical instruction manual. Because operational techniques are generic and thus applicable to any spectrum analyzer, techniques that extend beyond just the operation of an analyzer are given. Use of the spectrum analyzer for troubleshooting is discussed as well as numerous accessories that make the analyzer more valuable.

The tracking generator, one of the more useful of these accessories, is covered as is the network analyzer, a practical extension of the spectrum analyzer–tracking generator combination. In some modern instruments both functions are contained in a single instrument. Therefore, to keep the text modern and complete, the network and spectrum analyzers are covered in a similar fashion.

Above all, this is a textbook. There are end-of-chapter review questions, an extensive bibliography, and practical circuits that may be constructed and investigated.

Albert D. Helfrick

1

Spectra and Spectrum Analysis

1.1

Waveforms: A Review of Basics

The first application of electricity was the transmission of energy. Long before anyone dreamed of transmitting voices and pictures through space, solving equations with a computer, probing the human body, and a variety of other things electrical energy can do, electric lights and motors dominated the use of electricity. A lamp or motor operating from a battery represents the conversion of chemical energy to electrical energy, transmitted through the interconnecting wires and converted to either mechanical motion in the case of the motor, or heat and light in the case of a lamp. Battery operation is an example of an unvarying transfer of energy. A steady current flows, and the illumination from the lamp or the motion of the motor is steady.

The advantages of alternating current were known and debated with the advocates of direct current during the early days of commercial electrical energy generation. Alternating current was easier to generate and distribute, while direct current was better suited to power and control electric motors. In the very early days of commercial electricity generation, motors and illumination constituted the vast majority of electrical energy use, thus making the advantage of direct current significant.

The amount of energy transmitted per second is the product of the current in the interconnecting wire and the electrical potential (voltage) between the wires. The rate of energy flow is called power and is simply

$$P = EI \tag{1-1}$$

where P is the power of a circuit, E is the circuit voltage, and I is the circuit current. This equation is, of course, Ohm's law.

Since the current and voltage provided by a battery are constant, and this refers to a perfect battery that does not slowly go dead, the circuit voltage and current in Eq. (1-1) are constants.

When the electrical current or voltage or both vary over time, Eq. (1-1) must reflect this fact and may be written as

$$P(t) = E(t)I(t) \tag{1-2}$$

This equation is the same as (1-1) except that it is acknowledged that the power $P(t)$, voltage $E(t)$, and current $I(t)$ are possibly not constant but rather are functions of time t.

One example of a time-varying voltage that would produce a time-varying current and power is a battery that does, indeed, go dead. In this case, the battery voltage would drop as the load consumed the stored energy; and as the voltage dropped the rate of power transfer would decrease.

Whatever is the nature of the battery slowly going dead, it happens only once and, unless the battery is recharged, never repeated. There are time-varying mathematical functions that are repeated on a regular basis, such as the sine and cosine functions. These functions have the form

$$v(t) = V \sin(\omega t + \phi) \tag{1-3}$$

where $v(t)$ is the time-varying voltage, V is the peak value of the voltage, ω is the angular frequency, t is the independent variable, and ϕ is a constant.

This function is periodic, which means that it is repeated indefinitely. This can be represented mathematically as

$$v(t + nt_0) = v(t + n/f_0) = v(t) \tag{1-4}$$

where n is any integer, t_0 is the period of the function, and f_0 is the frequency.

1.2 The Fourier Transform

Whenever electrical voltage or current in a circuit varies over time, the energy of the voltage or current becomes distributed over a band of frequencies. The variation of the voltage or current can be of a complex nature in perhaps a completely random fashion, or the variation can be of a simple nature where the pattern is repeated. An apparently random waveform can have a complex pattern that is repeated.

Where the variation is simple and repetitive, the distribution of energy over frequency is simple. When the variation is complex, the energy distribution is likewise complex. The sine function in Eq. (1-3) is about as simple as a repetitive waveform can be. The "band" of frequencies around which the energy is distributed is only one frequency, f.

The mathematical *function* that describes the energy distribution of a time-varying quantity as a function of frequency is the *spectrum* of the quantity. The most important mathematical *operator* that translates a time-varying function to the frequency-dependent function is called the Fourier transform. A Fourier transform exists for practically any function—periodic, random, or single occurrence. Even the example of the dying battery supplying a load has a Fourier transform.

The Fourier transform can be defined for any two variables. Because time and frequency are so important in the understanding of electronics, the discussion of Fourier transform in this text will refer only to the conversion of a time-varying function to the counterpart frequency function. These two variables are also the basis for what is called a domain. The time domain refers to analysis, calculation, and measurement using time as the independent variable. The frequency domain refers to analysis, calculation, and measurement with frequency as the independent variable. Time domain measurements are made with an oscilloscope, and frequency domain measurements are made with a spectrum analyzer.

1.3 The Fourier Series

A special case of the Fourier transform is the Fourier series, which is the result of taking the Fourier transform of a periodic function. The general form of the Fourier series is

$$F(f) = \frac{a_0}{2} + \sum_{n=1}^{\infty} (a_n \cos n\omega t + b_n \sin n\omega t) \tag{1-5}$$

where $F(f)$ is the frequency-dependent Fourier series, n is an integer from one to infinity, ω is the angular frequency of the waveform, and a_n and b_n are constants. The waveform described by the Fourier series has a basic frequency of $2\pi/t$, where t is the period of the repetitive waveform.

For an odd function, that is, a function where $f(x) = -f(-x)$, all the coefficients of the cosine terms in the Fourier series become zero; for an even function where $f(x) = f(-x)$, the coefficients for the sine terms become zero.

Therefore, for odd or even functions the Fourier series may be simplified by eliminating either the sine or cosine series and writing a series of only one set of terms. This would take the form

$$F(f) = \sum_{n=1}^{\infty} b_n \sin n\omega t \tag{1-6}$$

for an odd function and

$$F(f) = \frac{a_0}{2} + \sum_{n=1}^{\infty} a_n \cos n\omega t \tag{1-7}$$

for an even function.

The constants may be evaluated by

$$\begin{aligned} a_n &= \frac{2}{T}\int_{-T/2}^{T/2} f(t)\cos\frac{2n\pi t}{T}\,dt \\ b_n &= \frac{2}{T}\int_{-T/2}^{T/2} f(t)\sin\frac{2n\pi t}{T}\,dt \end{aligned} \qquad (1\text{-}8)$$

where t is the period of the function $f(t)$.

The Fourier transform uniquely defines a function. A Fourier transform can be worked "in reverse" to find the only mathematical function the transform represents. This is called the inverse Fourier transform and converts a frequency domain equation to the time domain.

As a simple example, the Fourier series for a simple sine function will be calculated.

Because the sine function is an odd function, only sine terms will be present in the Fourier series, and thus the series is of the form

$$F(f) = \sum_{n=1}^{\infty} b_n \sin n\omega t \qquad (1\text{-}9)$$

The constants b_n are evaluated by

$$b_n = \frac{2}{T}\int_{-T/2}^{T/2} \sin\omega t \sin\frac{2n\pi t}{T}\,dt \qquad (1\text{-}10)$$

Evaluating b_1, the following is obtained:

$$\begin{aligned} b_1 &= \frac{2}{T\omega}\int_{-T/2}^{T/2} \sin^2\omega t(\omega\,dt) \\ &= \frac{2}{T\omega}\left[\frac{\omega t}{2} - \frac{1}{2}\sin\omega t\cos\omega t\right]_{-T/2}^{T/2} = 1 \end{aligned} \qquad (1\text{-}11)$$

The other constants are evaluated by

$$b_n = \int_{-T/2}^{T/2} \sin\omega t \sin n\omega t\,dt = 0 \qquad \text{for} \quad n \neq 1 \qquad (1\text{-}12)$$

As it can be seen, the Fourier series for a simple sine function contains only one term, the actual function itself.

As a second example, consider the function of Fig. 1-1. This function is that which would be obtained if a cosine function of unity amplitude were half-wave rectified with a perfect diode. The cosine function was chosen because a half-wave rectified cosine function is an even function and will allow a simpler calculation. The cosine and sine functions are the same except for a 90° phase

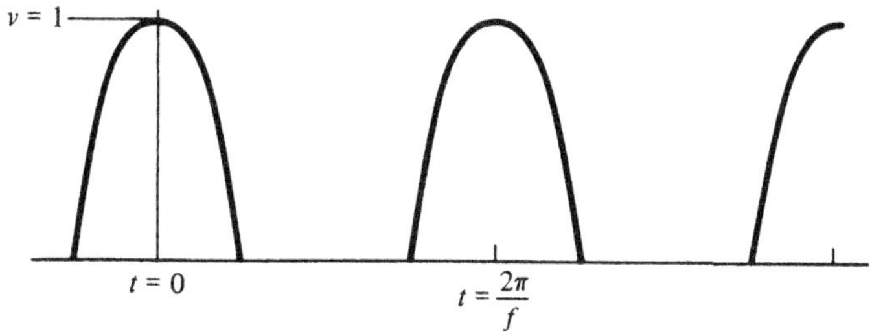

Figure 1-1
A half-wave rectified cosine function contains only the positive values of the cosine; elsewhere the function is zero.

difference. Calculating the Fourier series for the cosine function will produce the same Fourier coefficients as for the series for a half-wave rectified sine function.

The form of the Fourier series will be as shown in Eq. (1-7). It is only necessary to calculate the coefficients.

The first coefficient is

$$\begin{aligned} a_0 &= \frac{2}{T}\int_{-T/4}^{T/4} \cos\frac{2\pi t}{T}\,dt = \frac{2}{T}\left[\frac{T}{2\pi}\sin\frac{2\pi t}{T}\right]_{-T/4}^{T/4} \\ &= \frac{1}{\pi}\left[\sin\frac{\pi}{2} + \sin\frac{\pi}{2}\right] = \frac{2}{\pi} \end{aligned} \tag{1-13}$$

The general formula for the coefficient (which is derived from evaluating the other coefficients and which is beyond the scope of this text) is

$$a_n = a_0 \left| \frac{\cos n\frac{\pi}{2}}{1-n^2} \right|$$

Therefore:

$$a_0 = \frac{1}{\pi}, \quad a_1 = \frac{1}{2}, \quad a_2 = \frac{2}{3\pi}, \quad a_3 = 0, \quad a_4 = \frac{-2}{15\pi} \tag{1-14}$$

From this formula it may be seen that the rectified cosine function has only even harmonics with rapidly decreasing amplitude as the harmonic number becomes greater. Also note that there is a constant term, sometimes referred to as a DC term, which represents the average value of the waveform. It is a well-known fact that the half-rectified sine or cosine wave has a DC value, as DC voltage is generated by half-wave rectifying a sinusoid and filtering the result.

The Fourier series produces a sum of terms of like kind. In other words, if the Fourier series were calculated for a voltage waveform, the resulting Fourier series would include terms representing voltages. Often the relative powers are needed from a voltage waveform, which is not unusual. The relative powers of a Fourier series are equal to the voltage coefficients squared, divided by the circuit impedance. Since the amplitude of the sinusoid is set to one for simplicity, the impedance will be assumed to be 1 Ω. As an example, the relative power levels of the rectified cosine function are shown in Table 1-1. This is calculated by taking the equivalent RMS value for each term of the Fourier series, except the DC term, which is the same as the RMS value, and squaring it.

The sum of the powers of each Fourier component should be the same as the calculated power of the waveform. In this case, with a half-rectified cosine of peak amplitude 1 and an assumed impedance of 1 Ω, the power is half the power of an unrectified cosine wave, which is ¼ W. Therefore, the sum of the powers in Table 1-1 should be ¼ W. The actual sum of the above is 0.24978 W. The remainder 0.00022 W would be forthcoming from the higher harmonics, which are not calculated. However, it is interesting to note that 99.9% of the power of this waveform is contained in the DC value, the fundamental, and only two of the existing harmonics.

Circuits are analyzed by providing an input signal and observing how the output is related to the input. The relationship is unique to the circuit and is called the transfer function of the circuit. As an example,

$$E(t) = A \sin(2\pi f t) \tag{1-15}$$

is a time-domain stimulus, where time t is the independent variable and f and A are constants.

A transfer function is a mathematical function that describes the treatment of a time-dependent equation when the function is used as a stimulus for a circuit being analyzed. Figure 1-2 shows an integrator using an operational amplifier. The transfer function of this circuit would be

$$V_{\text{out}} = \frac{-1}{RC} \int_0^T V_{\text{in}}\, dt \tag{1-16}$$

where $V_{\text{in}}(t)$ is the input stimulus as a function of time and V_{out} is the output

Table 1-1

Frequency	Relative power
0, DC	0.101
Fundamental	0.125 (0 dB)
Second harmonic	0.0225 (−7.4 dB)
Third harmonic	0
Fourth harmonic	0.0009 (−21.4 dB)
Sixth harmonic	0.000083 (−31.8 dB)

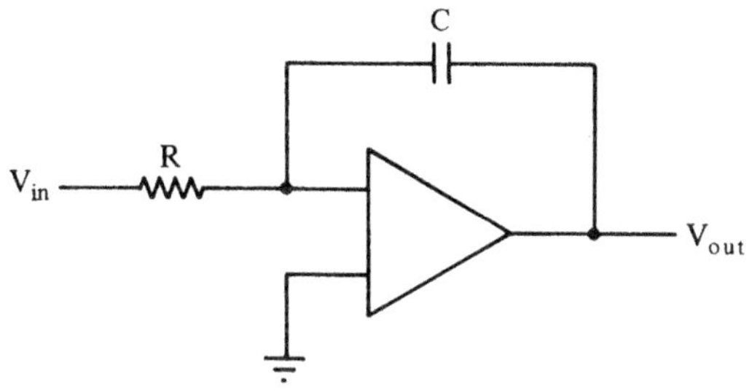

Figure 1-2
An integrator using an operation amplifier.

result as a function of time, R and C are the circuit parameters, and T is the elapsed time from when the integrating capacitor is discharged.

Equation (1-16) will describe the output signal of the circuit of Fig. 1-1 as a result of a time-varying stimulus.

As an example, use the simple sine function described above and apply that to the circuit of Fig. 1-1 and the transfer function.

Substituting the time-dependent Eq. (1-15) into the transfer function of Eq. (1-16), the output signal becomes

$$V_{out} = \int_0^T A \sin \pi f t \, dt = \frac{-A}{2\pi f} \cos 2\pi f t + C \tag{1-17}$$

If the integrator circuit were to be analyzed first mathematically by the process just performed and then verified by actual measurements, the stimulus would be supplied from a signal generator and the verification would be performed by viewing the resultant waveform with an oscilloscope.

Now, look at an electronic circuit from a frequency-domain standpoint. For more complex waveforms, the Fourier series will provide a series of sine functions at the basic frequency of a time-dependent signal plus harmonics. Each term of the series has only two parameters that may be varied by a circuit, the amplitude of the series component and the phase angle.

Using the example integrator, the amplitude of each Fourier series component will be reduced by an amount equal to $1/2\pi f$ and the phase angle is varied by exactly $\pi/2$ radians. Therefore, for an input of $A \sin(2\pi f t)$ the output is

$$\frac{A}{2\pi f} \cos \pi f t \tag{1-18}$$

This refers to any sine input; therefore, each component of the complex signal that is represented by the Fourier series will be affected by Eq. (1-18). The higher order harmonics will be attenuated more than the lower order harmonics or the fundamental.

1.4 Measuring Spectra

The oscilloscope is the well-known analysis tool for the time domain. The oscilloscope provides a display of the variation of a voltage (or current when used with a current probe) as a function of time.

The spectrum analyzer provides the basic analytical tool for frequency-domain analysis. The oscilloscope provides the complete time-domain picture of the input voltage. The spectrum analyzer is missing some important information.

The Fourier series described in Eq. (1-5) included both the sine and cosine terms. For a measuring instrument to distinguish sine functions from cosine functions of the same frequency, the instrument must be phase sensitive. The conventional spectrum analyzer does not preserve phase information and provides only the magnitude of the harmonics of the signal.

The spectrum analyzer is a powerful tool without the phase information being present. In most cases the phase information is not of importance.

Some spectrum analyzers determine the spectrum by mathematical means, using a computer. These spectrum analyzers are capable of calculating the complete Fourier series, both sine and cosine terms; but even these analyzers display the resultant spectrum using the vector sum of a_n and b_n.

The inverse Fourier transform is capable of reconstructing a signal to the time domain from the Fourier series. Since the spectrum analyzer does not preserve the phase information, it is not possible to reconstruct the time domain function from the spectrum as determined by the analyzer. As an example of the possible ambiguity, consider the spectrum obtained from the integrator previously described when it is stimulated with a complex period function. A spectrum analyzer would display the effects of the reduction in amplitude of the higher order harmonics of the input waveform. However, the fact that each frequency component has been phase shifted by exactly 90 degrees would not be indicated. Since there are circuit elements other than an integrator that could affect the amplitude in the same way as an integrator for some signals but not the phase, the spectrum analyzer could not be used to completely characterize the transfer function of any electronic circuit. The network analyzer, which is discussed later in this text, does preserve phase information and will uniquely characterize any electronic circuit.

1.5 Standards for Spectrum Analyzers

Standardization in the electronics industry has extended from units of measure to terminology. Electronics, being a relatively new science, has avoided some of the pitfalls that have befallen other disciplines. As an example, the only system of measurement used in electrical and electronic science has been metric. With a few exceptions, most notably in magnetics, the units of measurement have been MKS. (Oersted and gauss are the notable uses of CGS units in electrical measurement.) Compare this to the confusion of the measurement of length as used throughout the world. In common use are light years, statute miles, nautical miles, kilometers, leagues, fathoms, furlongs, meters, yards, feet, inches, centimeters, mils, microns, angstroms, and so on.

To insure that a spectrum analyzer is not confusing to the operator who regularly uses such an instrument, a complete set of terms relative to spectrum analyzers has been published by the Institute of Electrical and Electronics Engineers (IEEE) so that all spectrum analyzers throughout the world carry the same nomenclature and thus an engineer or scientist will understand the operation of the instrument regardless of the manufacturer. The IEEE standard will be used throughout this text.

The IEEE definitions will be outlined and explained in this chapter; however, it will be advantageous to refer to these definitions for clarification when covering the material in later chapters. The definitions are presented here in alphabetical order.

Baseline clipper A method of reducing the intensity of the baseline by blanking the lower portion of the noisy baseline trace. This would be necessary when a spectrum to be viewed is weak or dim and the illumination of the bright baseline would obscure the spectrum. This is particularly useful when photographing the display and the bright baseline would cause an overexposure of the film.

Center frequency The center-span frequency. Some spectrum analyzers may be capable of switching the frequency display from center to start frequency.

Deflection factor The amount of deflection of the spectrum display for a change of input amplitude. For example, a 10-dB change of input will provide a one-division change of display. This would indicate a logarithmic display. For a linear display, a 10-to-1 change of input, 20 dB, must provide a 10-to-1 change of the display. For linear displays the deflection factor is an absolute, such as 1 mV per division.

Display flatness The variation of displayed amplitude for a constant level input for a specified frequency range.

Display frequency The frequency of the center or left side of the display as indicated by the analyzer.

Display reference level A designated vertical position from which the displayed level is referenced. Unlike an oscilloscope, where the display reference (often called ground reference) is placed anywhere on the screen using the position control, spectrum analyzer reference level is usually the top of the screen. This is done to avoid confusion. In an oscilloscope, the baseline, that is, the oscilloscope trace with no input is set with the position control to correspond to the reference line. In the case of a spectrum analyzer, the baseline is a function of the noise level of the analyzer, which is a function of the intermediate frequency (IF) bandwidth. As the parameters of the spectrum analyzer are changed, the baseline will be raised or lowered. Typically a spectrum analyzer display will be labeled as zero at the top and −10 dB, −20 dB, etc., down from the top.

Display law The mathematical law that governs the display. This was alluded to in the definition of deflection factor. There are three forms of display law: linear, power, and logarithmic. A linear display is one in which the display has a linear relationship to input voltage such as 1 μV per division. With a linear display, the bottom of the display is zero and the top is the reference level. As an example, for an eight-division display, where the deflection factor is 1 μV per division, the reference level, the top of the display, is 8 μV.

A power display, also called a square-law display, is one in which the display deflection is a function of the square of the input voltage. Because power is proportional to the square of voltage, the display has a linear relationship to the input power. The bottom of the display is zero and the top is the reference. As an example, if a 10-division display has a deflection factor of 1 mW per division, the bottom of the display is zero and the top is 10 mW.

A logarithmic display, which is the most popular, presents a deflection that is proportional to the logarithm of the input voltage or power. In this case, the bottom of the display is never zero but is a constant fraction of the top of the display. As an example, for an eight-division display where the deflection factor is 10 dB per division, the bottom of the display is $1/10^4$ of the voltage of the top. This is also one $1/10^8$ of the power represented by the top. Usually the noise level of the spectrum analyzer is greater than the bottom of the display.

Dynamic range The ability of a spectrum analyzer to display multiple simultaneous signals without generating spurious displays.

Harmonic dynamic range is the ability of the analyzer to measure the level of the fundamental and the harmonics of a signal to within a specified accuracy.

Nonharmonic dynamic range is the ability of the analyzer to measure the level of two independent signals without the generation of spurious signals.

Display dynamic range is the ratio of two nonharmonically related signals that may be simultaneously *displayed* without the generation of spurious signals. This dynamic range is different than nonharmonic dynamic range in that it is possible to view two signals that do not produce visible spurious signals where one or more of the measured signals is off the display.

Envelope display A display that is produced when the resolution of the analyzer is greater than the individual frequency components, thus not resolving them but producing an envelope that encompasses these frequency components. This form of display occurs when the spectrum of pulse-modulated signals is measured and is often called a "dense" display.

Free-running sweep This refers to a frequency sweep that does not require a source of synchronization. After a sweep has occurred, retrace occurs and the sweep begins again. See triggered sweep.

Frequency drift This is the gradual long-term frequency drift of the display of a spectrum analyzer. This drift could also be specified as a function of some other external parameter, such as temperature or line voltage.

Frequency linearity The deviation from a straight-line relationship of frequency to X-axis position of a spectrum analyzer display. As an example, consider a spectrum analyzer that is displaying the frequency range from 10 to 20 MHz in 10 divisions, which is a deflection factor of 1 MHz per division. If any input frequency does not fall exactly on the indicated X-axis, the deviation is the frequency error. As an example, assume the worst-case error occurs at a frequency of 15 MHz where an input of exactly 15 MHz falls on an indicated frequency of 14.5 MHz. The error is 0.5 MHz from a total displayed range of 10 MHz, or 5%.

Frequency response This is the peak-to-peak variation of the displayed amplitude over the entire frequency range of the spectrum analyzer. This is distinguished from the display flatness in that the displayed amplitudes need not all be present in the display simultaneously.

Frequency span The total frequency range displayed. This can be represented as frequency per division or frequency. Generally, spectrum analyzers have 10 major X-axis divisions and the total frequency span is 10 times the per-division span.

Full span, max span A mode of operation of the spectrum analyzer where the full frequency range of the analyzer is displayed.

Hum sidebands A term originally used to describe sidebands that were generated within the spectrum analyzer appearing on displayed signals that were separated from the desired response by the fundamental and harmonics of the power-line frequency. In modern spectrum analyzers, sidebands are more likely generated by the fundamental and sidebands of the switching rate of a switching power supply and the reference frequency of a phase-locked loop frequency-stabilization system. These sidebands are more accurately called internally generated sidebands.

Impulse bandwidth A theoretical rectangular bandwidth that has an area equal to the integrated voltage envelope of the spectrum analyzer's IF filter. The amplitude of a displayed wideband signal is proportional to the impulse bandwidth of the IF filter.

Intermodulation rejection The difference in level between two equal-amplitude signals and the intermodulations produced by those two signals.

Internal trigger, or video trigger The triggering of the spectrum trace from the input signal. This is usually reserved for zero span when the spectrum analyzer display presents the time domain of the demodulated input signal.

Line display The display produced when the displayed spectrum has frequency components greater than the resolution bandwidth. Thus each spectral component is displayed. This is the opposite of envelope display.

Line trigger Triggering the start of the spectrum trace from the power-line frequency. This is done to prevent wavering of the display due to frequency modulation of the input signal from power-line sources.

Maximum safe input power The maximum input power that may be applied to the spectrum analyzer without causing damage to the unit. Both the peak and average power must be taken into consideration. High peak powers may damage sensitive devices such as the input mixer while having a very low average power and causing no significant power dissipation in such items as the input attenuator. It must also be understood that in some spectrum analyzers, no DC level is permitted, since the analyzer is DC-coupled. Even a small amount of DC voltage can cause heavy current flow and possible damage.

Noise sidebands A broadening of the spectrum display due to the effects of internally generated noise present on the local oscillators. Noise sidebands are specified as dBc/Hz, which means decibels below the peak of the displayed carrier per hertz of bandwidth.

Noise Bandwidth The theoretical rectangular bandwidth having an area equal to the integrated area under the power envelope of the spectrum analyzer's IF filter. The amplitude of the display of a random noise signal is proportional to the noise bandwidth.

Residual frequency modulation Frequency modulation applied to one or more of the internal oscillators which causes frequency modulation to appear on the signal being analyzed. This is similar to noise sidebands but may be specified for periodic frequency modulation rather than random noise. Residual frequency modulation is specified as the peak-to-peak frequency deviation in hertz.

Residual response An internally generated response that would be present with no input. This does not include the response at zero frequency.

Resolution The ability of the spectrum analyzer to display individual signals. Generally, resolution is measured when two responses of equal level merge with a 3-dB notch.

Resolution, optimum Because of the effects of the sweep time on the apparent bandwidth of the spectrum analyzer, there is an optimum resolution which is given by:

$$R_0 = \sqrt{\frac{\text{Frequency Span}}{\text{Sweep Time}}}$$

Resolution bandwidth The width of the spectrum analyzer's response relative to either a 3-dB or 6-dB point down from the peak of the response.

Scanning velocity The sweep rate in frequency divided by time.

Sensitivity The ability of the spectrum analyzer to display low-level signals. This will be a strong function of the IF bandwidth and the setting of IF and RF attenuators. Often this is specified as a signal 3 dB above the average noise level of the analyzer and is called input signal level sensitivity.

Sensitivity, equivalent input noise The level of the internally generated noise of a spectrum analyzer. This is also a function of IF bandwidths.

Shape factor The ratio of bandwidth of the 6- to 60-dB bandwidth of the analyzer IF filters.

Single sweep The mode of operation where a single trace is produced from either a manual push-switch or from a triggering source. This is often used when photographing the spectrum to prevent multiple displays.

Spurious response, "spur" A display of a signal that does not exist at the spectrum analyzer input. These responses are either generated from the interaction of the input signal with internal circuits of the spectrum analyzer or between signals within the spectrum analyzer and input signal, or from internal signals alone.

Video filter A filter after the detected output of the IF amplifier. This is helpful in removing noise from displays.

Zero pip A response due to the local oscillator of the spectrum analyzer being equal to the first IF; it corresponds to zero frequency.

Zero span A mode of operation of the spectrum analyzer that reduces the span to zero. In this mode of operation, the spectrum analyzer functions as a radio receiver. The display of the spectrum analyzer may then be used to display the time variation of the demodulated output.

2

Methods of Spectrum Analysis

2.1 Overview

There are as many types of spectrum analyzers as spectrum types. The numerous types of spectra in the physical world include optical spectra, which describe the colors that constitute a particular light and are measured with a spectrometer or specialized instruments such as a gas chromatagraph. Nuclear spectra, the distribution of the energies of the emissions of a nuclear event, are measured with a pulse-height analyzer. Vibration from moving machinery is displayed with a vibration analyzer, and so on.

Not all spectra are the energy of a signal as a function of frequency. As an example, a nuclear spectrum would be the number of events that occurred as a function of energy. This would be an indication of the type of nuclear event that is taking place. In the electronics world, however, a spectrum is the energy of a signal as a function of frequency. The electronic spectrum analyzer must separate the various frequency components and measure the energy at a selected frequency component. The result is displayed on an oscilloscope screen, a computer output, or by some other suitable method.

There are two basic approaches to electronic spectrum analysis. The older and still often-used method is to provide a filter or filters to separate the spectral components. A newer method digitizes the waveform to be analyzed and a computer performs a Fourier transform resulting in the calculation of the spectral components.

Various names are given to the two basic approaches. When the filter method is used, the signal to be analyzed must be present while the analysis is being made. Because of this, the method is often called the "real-time" method.

In the computer method, almost universally the mathematical tool used to calculate the spectrum is a Fourier transform, usually a special form called the fast Fourier transform, FFT, which is particularly suited to computers. Thus, the digital method of spectrum analysis is often called an FFT analyzer.

In the case of digitizing the waveform, the analysis may be performed at any time and may take as much time as desired, which allows very substantial analysis. The disadvantage is that the signal must be accurately digitized, which limits this technique to low frequencies with present technology. The digital method or Fourier method is limited to the lower radio frequencies, whereas the filter or real-time technique can perform spectrum analysis to the highest reaches of the radio frequency spectrum.

2.2 The Parallel Filter Analyzer

The simplest arrangement of the filter method of spectrum analysis is shown in Fig. 2-1. In this example, a number of filters are used to separate the spectral components of the signal to be analyzed. The output of each filter is rectified, which provides an indication of the amplitude of the signal that passed through the filter. The rectified amplitudes are sequentially displayed to represent the spectrum of the input signal.

This rudimentary method, in spite of serious shortcomings, is used as a spectrum analysis tool. Several serious problems are associated with the method. First, if an accurate spectral display is desired, a large number of filters are required. The passband of the filters must be broad enough so that a spectral component does not "fall between the cracks" and not be registered. When the passbands of the filters overlap, which would prevent a spectral component from falling between the cracks and being lost, there is an additional problem. If a spectral component were between the center frequencies of two adjacent filters where some energy was able to pass through each filter, the result would appear to be two spectral components when in fact it was only one component at a frequency between the filter passbands. Because of this inability to separate spectral components that are close in frequency, this type of spectrum analyzer is used for signals where there are no closely spaced spectral components, or where it is not necessary to resolve closely spaced spectral components should they exist.

There is a significant advantage to this type of analyzer in that a spectrum can be rapidly measured; just as soon as the signal propagates through the filter and is rectified, the spectrum is determined. This quick spectrum determination is needed in military electronic warfare systems where the "signature" or spectrum of a radar or other transmission must be determined very quickly. On the other hand, the parallel filter method of spectrum analysis may be used when

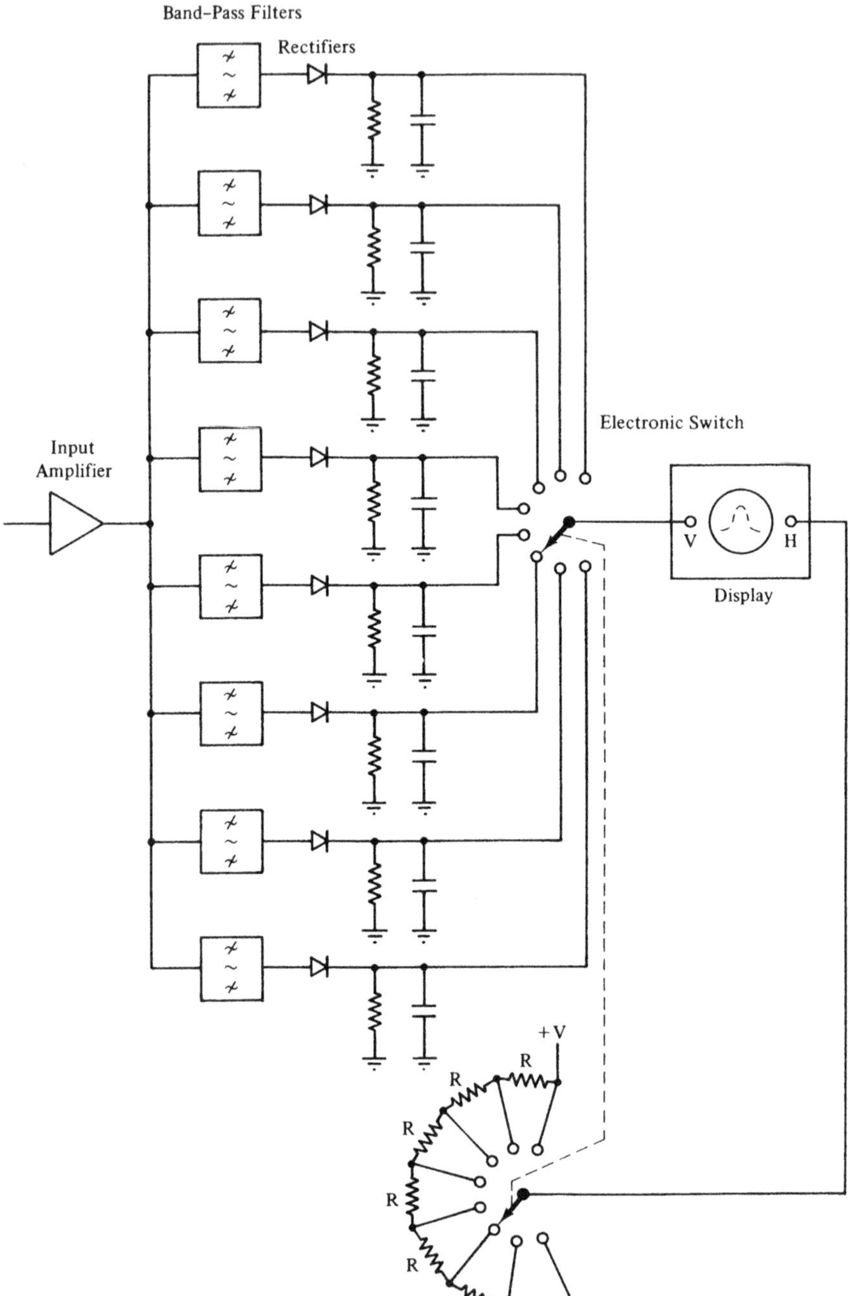

Figure 2-1
A block diagram of the parallel filter method of spectrum analysis. Each filter is tuned to a portion of the spectrum to be analyzed and the detected level is sequentially displayed.

great resolution is not required, such as the investigation of vibration in large machines or the measurement of the acoustics of a room.

2.3
The Superheterodyne Analyzer

The use of a filter to separate the components of a signal by frequency is an attractive idea, but the main disadvantage of the parallel filter type of analyzer is the large number of filters required. If all the frequencies of a spectrum to be analyzed were converted to a common frequency, the input spectrum could be analyzed by the use of only one filter. To do this, the input spectrum is converted to a common frequency by using a mixer and a local oscillator much like a superheterodyne receiver. The frequency of the local oscillator is electronically varied so that the entire frequency range to be analyzed will eventually be converted to the filter's center frequency. Like the superheterodyne receiver, the filter frequency is called the intermediate frequency, or the IF, of the analyzer. As in the parallel filter spectrum analyzer, the output of the filter is rectified and displayed.

Because the local oscillator allows only one frequency component to be analyzed at any time, there are interactions with the rate at which the local oscillator is tuned and the spectrum displayed. This will be discussed in a later chapter.

Figure 2-2 shows a simplified block diagram of a superheterodyne type of spectrum analyzer. The input frequency is converted to an IF by the local oscillator. The majority of the gain of the spectrum analyzer is obtained at the IF and is indicated by the amplifier following the IF filter.

As in any superheterodyne receiver, the image must be eliminated from the input to prevent spurious responses; it is removed from the desired input frequency by twice the IF.

In the conventional superheterodyne receiver, a bandpass filter is employed at the input of the receiver where the center frequency of the filter is the tuned frequency of the receiver. In the mechanically tuned receiver, the local oscillator tuning capacitor and the input filter were connected to a common tuning shaft.

The spectrum analyzer is electronically tuned; and although it is possible to tune both the local oscillator and the input filter electronically, this is undesirable for a number of reasons.

One reason for not employing a tuned circuit in the input of a spectrum analyzer is the large tuning range required of the tuned circuit. A spectrum analyzer covering the range of 1 to 100 MHz would require a 100-to-1 tuning range of the input filter, and this is essentially impossible. (There are special broadband tuned circuits such as a YIG resonator, but these are found only in some microwave analyzers. Even these devices are not capable of a tuning range of 100.)

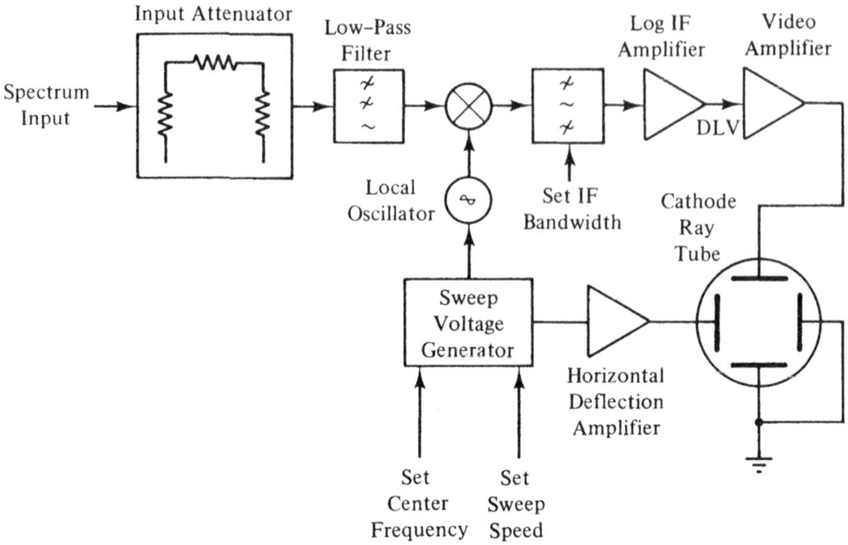

Figure 2-2
The block diagram of a simple single-conversion, superheterodyne type of spectrum analyzer.

Another reason for not employing an electronically tuned input filter is that the filter may generate spurious signals from the electronically tuned reactances.

A simple solution to this dilemma is to choose an IF above the highest input frequency so that the image frequency range, likewise, falls above the highest input frequency. Thus, a low-pass filter with a cutoff frequency above the highest input frequency but below the image frequency range will eliminate the image frequency range without tuning the filter.

An an example, consider a spectrum analyzer with an input frequency range from near-zero to 500 MHz. The term "near-zero" will be used throughout this text. It is not possible for the heterodyning type of spectrum analyzer to analyze frequencies to zero or DC. The reasons behind this will be discussed at a later point. Assume the IF is 700 MHz. The local oscillator frequency range is from 700 to 1200 MHz, which will convert the near-zero-to-500-MHz range to an IF of 500 MHz. The image frequency range is from 1400 to 1900 MHz; it is easily eliminated with a low-pass filter with a cutoff frequency of, perhaps, 600 MHz. It would not be desirable to set the cutoff frequency at exactly 500 MHz because the cutoff frequency usually refers to the 3-dB frequency, which would have an undesirable effect of depressing the high-frequency end of the spectrum analyzer input by up to 3 dB.

It would be a desirable characteristic of the input filter to reject the IF as well, since any energy at the IF that passes through the mixer will cause spurious responses.

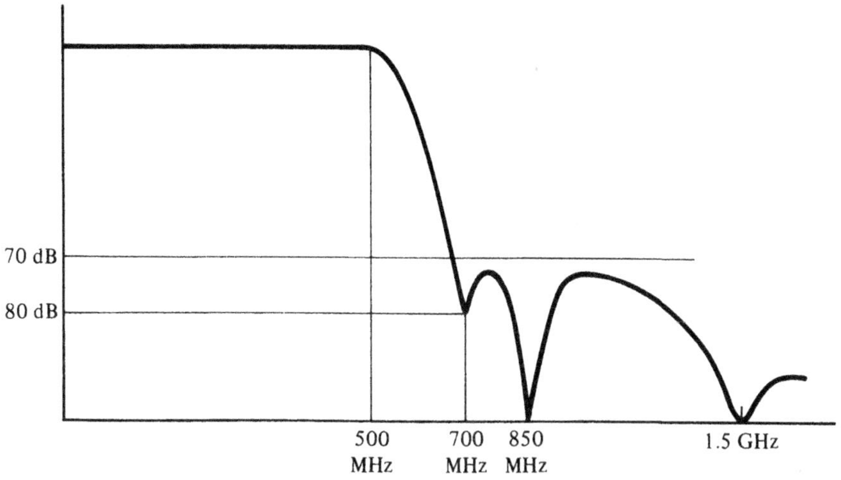

Figure 2-3
The passband of an elliptical low-pass filter showing the deliberate setting of a null at the spectrum analyzer's IF.

Figure 2-3 shows a typical passband of a spectrum analyzer input filter using the example of a near-zero-to-500-MHz analyzer. The schematic of the realization of this filter is shown in Fig. 2-4. This realization is generated with a filter design called elliptical, which is characterized by a passband that has a rise before the cutoff, a very sharp cutoff, and additional passbands above the cutoff frequency. These spurious passbands usually have an attenuation considerably greater than the main passband. However these spurious passbands allow signal levels greater than the ultimate attenuation of the filter. Between the spurious passbands there are deep nulls of great attenuation. These can be used to good advantage by designing the filter so that the nulls occur at specific frequencies such as an IF. To prevent the amplitude rise before the cutoff frequency from

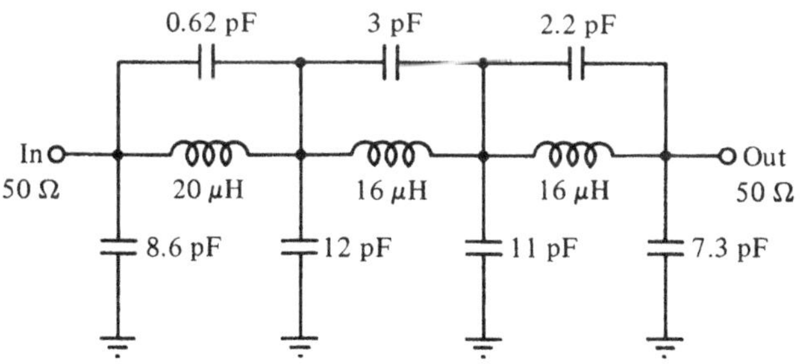

Figure 2-4
The actual hardware realization of the filter passband shown in Fig. 2-3. Notice the filter is not symmetrical.

destroying the frequency response of the spectrum analyzer, the rise in amplitude is set to be above the highest input frequency of the analyzer, which for the foregoing example is 500 MHz. Thus, the rise is centered around 600 MHz, so that there is very little effect at 500 MHz yet there is a deep null at the IF of 700 MHz. The first spurious passband occurs at about 900 MHz, which is not in the image frequency range. There are other spurious passbands, but at the image frequency range the filter attenuation is great and successfully eliminates the image frequency band.

2.3.1 Determining the Internal Frequencies

The local oscillator covers the frequency range from the IF to the IF plus the upper frequency range of the analyzer. For the example spectrum analyzer, the IF was 700 MHz and the highest input frequency was 500 MHz, resulting in a local oscillator frequency range of 700 to 1200 MHz.

For a conventional varactor-tuned oscillator, the rule of thumb for the maximum tuning range is two to one. If the oscillator's inductor were resonated only with the varactor, this would require a varactor capacitance ratio of four to one. Because the oscillator contains other capacitances, deliberate and parasitic, the actual capacitance tuning ratio required of the varactor diode is much greater than four to one. The tuning range of a varactor diode is dependent on the construction of the diode, especially on the way the charges are distributed in the depletion region. Hyper-abrupt varactor diodes are available with tuning ratios greater than 10, but these diodes have problems with temperature stability, Q, and tuning linearity. Therefore, it is desirable to limit the frequency tuning ratio of the local oscillator to less than two for spectrum analyzer applications.

Using the limit of two for the tuning range of the local oscillator, the minimum frequency for the IF can be calculated. The tuning ratio of the local oscillator is defined as

$$F_h/F_l = 2 \tag{2-1}$$

where F_h is the high-frequency limit and F_l is the low-frequency limit.

The lowest frequency of the local oscillator occurs when "zero" frequency occurs and results in

$$F_l = F_{IF} \tag{2-2}$$

where F_{IF} is the intermediate frequency.

Substituting this into Eq. (2-1), the relationship of the IF to the local oscillator high-frequency limit is given by

$$F_h - 2F_{IF} \tag{2-3}$$

The input frequency range is the difference between the high and low local-oscillator frequencies and is

$$F_h - F_l = F_{IF} \tag{2-4}$$

Therefore, for the minimum IF, the input frequency range is from zero to the IF. The image frequency range is from $2F_{IF}$ to $2F_{IF} + (F_h - F_l)$. This would require the input low-pass filter to have an infinite cutoff at the high-frequency end to reject the IF, which is impossible. It is necessary, therefore, to provide an IF greater than the highest input frequency. In addition, this has the advantage of reducing the tuning ratio of the local oscillator. An acceptable IF is about 1.5 times the highest input frequency.

2.3.2 Log IF Amplifiers

Like a superheterodyne radio receiver, the majority of the system gain of a spectrum analyzer is obtained at the IF. But unlike a radio receiver, the signal present in the IF amplifier is not demodulated to remove the information. Only the signal level is of importance.

Most spectrum analyzers are capable of distinguishing signals that are quite disparate, especially in level. A display of the spectrum of a signal or several unrelated signals may include spectral components whose power levels differ by a million to one or more. If power were the vertical axis of a spectrum display when disparate levels were displayed simultaneously, the larger of the two signals would be so much larger than the smaller of the two signals that the smaller components would go unnoticed. Displaying voltage, which is proportional to the square root of power, would reduce a million-to-one power difference to a thousand-to-one voltage difference. This would be an improvement, but even a thousand-to-one difference would be difficult to see.

The usual method of categorizing signals when there is a large difference in levels is to use the concept of decibels. A decibel is given as

$$\text{dB} = 10 \log P_1/P_2 \tag{2-5}$$

where P_1 and P_2 are two power levels.

Notice that a decibel notation does not indicate an absolute power but only the ratio of two powers. To use decibel notation for the representation of absolute power, a reference is chosen and the signal to be described is compared to the reference. As an example, a very common reference, and practically the only reference used for spectrum analysis, is 1 mW. Powers represented by decibel notation referenced to 1 mW are called dBm, the m indicating the reference is one milliwatt. To convert a power to dBm, the following relationship is used:

$$P_{(\text{dBm})} = 10 \log \frac{P}{1 \times 10^{-3}} \tag{2-6}$$

where P is the power to be expressed in watts.

Using a decibel display, powers divergent by 60 dB, to use the previous example, represent a difference of only six 10-dB divisions.

The output of the IF amplifier not only represents the signal level but, additionally, provides a logarithmic output; which is to say, the output voltage is proportional to the log of the input signal power.

Some electrical devices have a logarithmic relationship between two parameters of the device. The best known of the simple electronic devices is the common diode, where the voltage across a diode is proportional to the log of the current through the diode. Although the simple diode can be used to convert signal levels to logarithms, it suffers from several almost insurmountable problems when required to handle a large dynamic range such as that in a spectrum analyzer.

Spectrum analyzers use a "log IF" where an output voltage is proportional to the logarithm input voltage or power. The output of the log IF amplifier is called the detected log video, or DLV. The most common type of log IF is obtained by a technique of successive limiting and detection.

Figure 2-5 shows an example of a six-stage successive-limiting log IF amplifier. Six identical amplifiers are cascaded, and each amplifier output is rectified and summed. There is nothing special about the amplifiers except that each amplifier has a predictable limiting threshold.

For ease of explanation, assume the rectified voltage from the output of any amplifier to be equivalent to the RMS value of the amplifier output. If this were not so, the gain of the summing amplifier could be adjusted so the output would be equal to the sum of the RMS values of the amplifiers. This also assumes the detector diode providing the output is in the linear region and a sine wave is the input to the log amplifier, which in a spectrum analyzer is usually the case. The DLV output of the amplifier is equal to

$$V_{out} = nV_s + V_{in}(G + G^2 + G^3 + \cdots + G^{k-n}) \qquad (2\text{-}7)$$

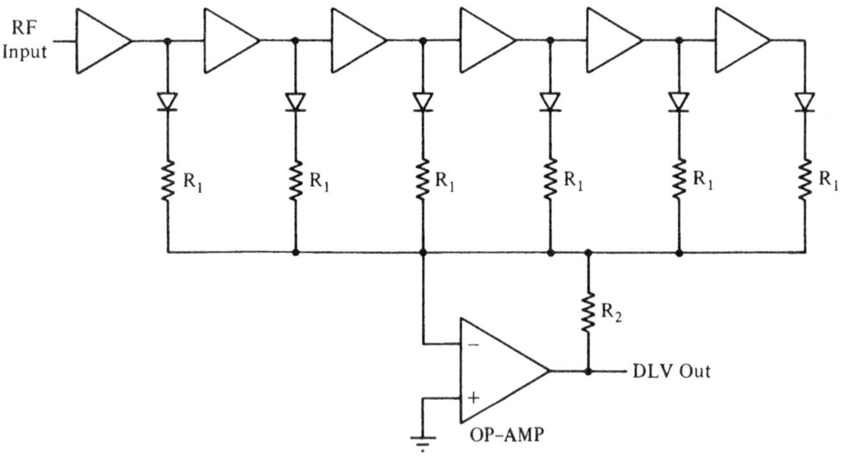

Figure 2-5
An example of a six-stage successive approximation log amplifier.

where V_{out} is the DLV, V_{in} is the input voltage, V_s is the output saturation voltage, n is the number of amplifiers in saturation, G is the gain of each amplifier (which is the same for each amplifier), and k is the total number of amplifiers in the log amplifier.

Looking at Eq. (2-7) it can be seen that the output is equal to a fixed amount for each amplifier in saturation due to the term nV_s and the sum of the outputs from the amplifiers not in saturation.

The gain of the circuit is

$$\frac{dV_{out}}{dV_{in}} = (G + G^2 + G^3 \cdots + G^{k-n}) \tag{2-8}$$

This is to be expected, since those amplifiers not in saturation provide gain while those in saturation provide only a constant term to Eq. (2-7). The concept of gain in this sense relates a DC output and an AC input, not in the usual sense of a linear amplifier.

Investigating Eq. (2-7) will provide a calculation of the breakpoints. Any breakpoint occurs when the last amplifier to enter saturation has an input level of V_s/G. The stage just preceding the stage that entered saturation has an input voltage of V_s/G^2. This is true for any stage that has just entered saturation, regardless of the number of amplifiers in the chain, as the gains of the amplifiers are identical. When the input signal is increased by a factor of G, the voltage input to the amplifier stage just preceding the saturating stage will be V_s/G, which is the level that will just produce saturation in that amplifier stage. Therefore, every time the input signal is increased by a *factor* of G a new amplifier stage will enter saturation. Notice that a new amplifier enters saturation every time the signal is increased by a factor of G, not when the signal is increased by G. Increasing a signal by a constant factor is the same as increasing the signal by a constant number of decibels, which is the desired result.

To determine the output voltage for the breakpoints consider the input voltage V_{in} for a number of amplifiers in saturation.

$$V_{in}(n) = \frac{V_s}{G^{k-n+1}} \tag{2-9}$$

Substituting this into Eq. (2-7) yields

$$V_{out}(n) = V_s(n + G^{n-k} + G^{n-k+1} + G^{n-k+2} + \cdots + G^{-1}) \quad 1 \le n \le k \tag{2-10}$$

To gain an understanding of the accuracies possible with this scheme, we will investigate the transfer function for a practical six-stage log amplifier using amplifiers with a 1 V V_s and a gain of 12 dB. Equation (2-9) is used to calculate the values of $V_{in}(n)$ for n between 1 and 6; these values are shown in Table 2-1. This is a rather easy task, as only the first level needs to be calculated and the subsequent points are simply 12 dB higher.

Table 2-1

$V_{in}(1)$	=	1.00 mV	−47 dBm
$V_{in}(2)$	=	3.98 mV	−35 dBm
$V_{in}(3)$	=	15.8 mV	−23 dBm
$V_{in}(4)$	=	63.0 mV	−11 dBm
$V_{in}(5)$	=	250 mV	+1 dBm
$V_{in}(6)$	=	1.00 V	+13 dBm

The corresponding V_{out} values are calculated to obtain a plot of the log amplifier. This can be done very simply by solving Eq. (2-10) for the six values of n, as shown in Table 2-2.

Notice that the values of V_{out} fit the equation $V_{out}(n) = mn + b$ for $m = 1$ and $b = 0.33$. The error is zero for $n = 1, 2,$ and 3; the error is 0.2% for $n = 4$; 1.1% for $n = 5$; and 5.5% for $n = 6$. This demonstrates the increasing error as more stages enter saturation.

When all the amplifiers are in saturation, theoretically there will be no further increase in output level for an increase in input level. In practice, the amplifiers do not enter saturation abruptly but somewhat gradually, which would allow some range beyond +13 dBm. Likewise, for levels below −47 dBm, the output level will decay to zero, but not necessarily in a strictly linear fashion, due to the nonlinearity of the diode rectifiers; this will allow some range below −47 dBm. Thus the total range of the six stages is somewhat more than 60 dB.

The discussion of the log IF amplifier has been centered on the location of the breakpoints between the straight-line segments. No calculation of the error between the breakpoints was made. However, the log function is a well-behaved function and does not have any wild excursions. It would be expected that a straight-line segment between two points separated by only 12 dB, as in the example, would not deviate far from the actual value.

The error could be calculated by taking the equation of the successive limiting log output and subtracting it from the theoretical output. The difference would be the error, which could be investigated by taking derivatives and locating the points of largest error.

A much simpler method is to make a computer plot of both the theoretical

Table 2-2

$V_{out}(1)$	=	1.33 volts
$V_{out}(2)$	=	2.33 volts
$V_{out}(3)$	=	3.33 volts
$V_{out}(4)$	=	4.31 volts
$V_{out}(5)$	=	5.25 volts
$V_{out}(6)$	=	6.00 volts

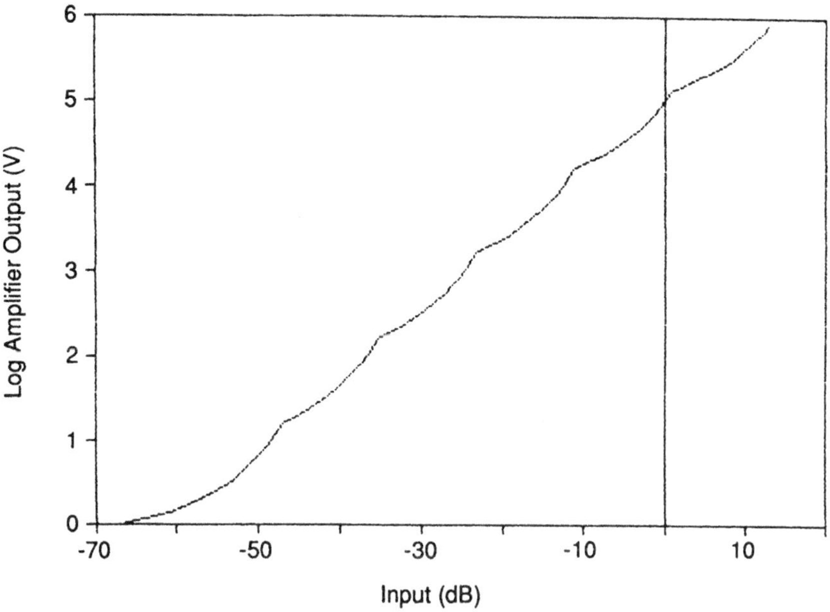

Figure 2-6
A computer-generated plot of the calculated output of a successive approximation log amplifier. A perfect log amplifier would produce a straight line.

log transfer function and the output of the successive limiting amplifier and find the maximum error by inspection. Figure 2-6 shows a spreadsheet-generated plot; it can be seen that the error is very small.

2.3.3 Multiple-Conversion Superheterodyne Analyzers

The spectrum analyzer shown in the block diagram of Fig. 2-2 is a single-conversion superheterodyne type, and the entire selectivity of the analyzer is obtained from the one and only filter. As a practical matter, this filter cannot be made sufficiently narrow in bandwidth to provide a bandwidth suitable for a spectrum analyzer. Using the example of Fig. 2-2, for an IF of 700 MHz, a bandwidth of a few hundred kilohertz would be about the minimum. Even achieving this degree of selectivity would involve circuit Qs of thousands, which would imply cavity resonators or surface acoustic wave (SAW) devices. Providing a near-zero to 500-MHz spectrum analyzer with a selectivity of a few hundred kilohertz minimum would be insufficient. To achieve narrower selectivity than this, at least a second IF, at a lower frequency, is required.

Figure 2-7 shows a spectrum analyzer using a second stage of frequency conversion to provide a second IF much lower than the first and thus providing

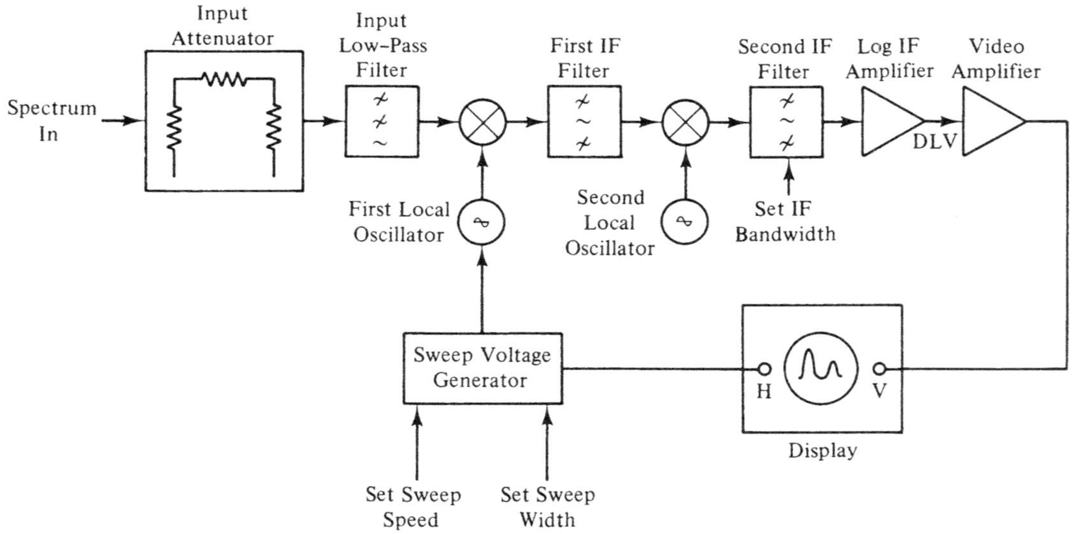

Figure 2-7
A block diagram of a dual-conversion spectrum analyzer.

the opportunity to achieve a narrower selectivity. Since the ultimate selectivity of the spectrum analyzer is not dependent on the first IF filter, extremely high Q resonators are not required.

The approach to the first IF filter cannot be handled with total abandon; it is necessary to eliminate the image response of the second frequency conversion. Referring to the previous example, assume the spectrum analyzer of Fig. 2-2 were changed to that of Fig. 2-7 and the second IF were chosen to be 455 kHz to take advantage of standard filters. This is an attractive idea except the image is either at 700.91 MHz, if the second local oscillator is at 700.45 MHz, or at 699.09 MHz if the second local oscillator is at 699.55 MHz. In either case the image frequency is only 910 kHz from the desired center frequency, which represents one part in about 770. It is necessary for the image to be suppressed by as much as possible to prevent spurious responses, which would require resonators that would be nearly impossible to manufacture. In fact, it would be easier to improve the selectivity of the spectrum analyzer by increasing the Q of the first IF filter than to eliminate the image frequency for a too-low second IF.

The second IF should be on the order of one-twentieth to one-tenth of the first IF to achieve a reasonable image rejection.

Returning to the example spectrum analyzer, a second IF of 45 MHz would be a reasonable frequency where standard monolithic crystal filters could be employed.

Although a vast improvement in selectivity can be made from the 700-MHz first IF to the 45-MHz monolithic crystal filter, the minimum bandwidth of the 45-MHz filter may not be sufficiently narrow. The minimum bandwidth of a crystal filter at 45 MHz is on the order of 10 kHz or so, and this may not be sufficient. Therefore, a third frequency conversion may be made.

For this conversion, the same cautions concerning the image suppression are necessary. For the example of a 45-MHz second IF, a 455-kHz third IF could be possible, as many crystal filters for 45-MHz applications have excellent image rejection at 910 kHz, twice the IF, from the desired center frequency.

There is no theoretical limit to the number of conversions that may be made to increase the selectivity of the spectrum analyzer. There are practical limitations, however.

First, each frequency conversion requires more hardware, local oscillators, mixers, and filters.

Second, every time a frequency conversion takes place there is yet another local oscillator that, if not properly shielded, can cause a spurious response in the spectrum analyzer by making its way into an amplifier, or even in the front end of the analyzer. To prevent this from occurring, each oscillator must be carefully shielded, which requires even more hardware.

Third, the lack of frequency stability or frequency accuracy of any of the conversion oscillators adds to an inaccurate or unstable spectrum display. This often requires a crystal oscillator, which is not difficult if the oscillator frequency is relatively low, such as below 100 MHz. In the case of the example in Fig. 2-7, the second local oscillator is near 700 MHz, and a crystal cannot be used without frequency multipliers. This generates even more potential spurious responses. There are justifiable reasons to not use a crystal oscillator for some of the frequency conversions.

In spite of the foregoing, most spectrum analyzers have two or three and, occasionally, four frequency conversions.

2.3.4 Local Oscillators

The voltage-controlled oscillator, VCO, used as the local oscillator for a spectrum analyzer can take one of many popular forms. The simplest, and quite serviceable, is a conventional varactor-tuned L-C oscillator using either a bipolar or a field-effect transistor as the gain element.

Figure 2-8 shows a typical bipolar varactor-tuned oscillator. There are many types of varactor-tuned oscillators based on any of the classic L-C oscillators; the example shown here is the Colpitts.

Two varactor diodes are used in series. This prevents the AC voltage present across the oscillator inductor from causing the diodes to conduct and thus create a current path that dissipates the circulating energy in the tuned circuit, reducing the circuit Q. When two diodes are placed in series, even though one

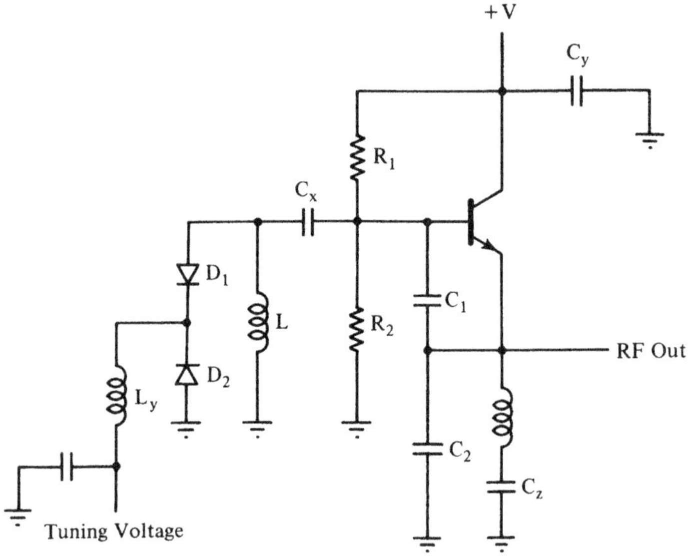

Figure 2-8
Schematic of a voltage-tuned Colpitts oscillator using two varactors in series to prevent conduction.

diode may be forward biased, the second diode is reverse biased and prevents a current path. The result is reasonably equivalent to a single varactor diode with the same characteristics of the single diode but with half the capacitance.

Understanding the tuning characteristics of the VCOs used in a spectrum analyzer requires an understanding of varactor diodes.

A varactor diode is a simple application of a reverse-biased junction diode where the capacitance of the depletion region is used. The depletion region, which is lacking free carriers, is essentially an insulator or dielectric. The P type and N type materials that comprise the diode's junction possess a relatively large number of free carriers. Therefore, the insulating depletion region is bounded by two conducting regions and thus is a capacitor. The width of the depletion region is dependent on the applied reverse bias and, therefore, the capacitance of the diode is a function of the applied reverse bias.

A relatively good approximation of the capacitance of a varactor diode as a function of applied reverse bias voltage may be described as

$$C = \frac{K}{(V_r + V_d)^n} + C_c \tag{2-11}$$

where C_c is the case capacitance of the diode, V_r is the reverse bias voltage, V_d is the diffusion voltage of the diode, and K is a parameter that is dependent on the manufacture of the diode and can be calculated from parametric measurements. The exponent n sets the tuning range of the diode and is a function of the grading of the diode junction. The value of n is typically 0.5 for an alloy diode, 0.33 for a diffused diode, and 0.75 for a hyper-abrupt junction.

The equivalent circuit of a varactor diode includes more than the junction capacitance, as shown in Fig. 2-9. Part (a) of Fig. 2-9 shows the complete equivalent circuit of the varactor diode. The resistance R_s is the series resistance due to the bulk resistivity of the diode. The resistance R is due to the reverse resistance of the diode, which is a function of the applied reverse bias; C_c is the case capacitance of the diode, which is due to the metallic ends of the case that mounts the diode chip: C_j is the actual junction capacitance, which is a function of the applied voltage; L_s is the series inductance, which is due to the leads of the diode.

Generally, for high Q diodes, the value of R_s is very low while R is quite high, and R may be eliminated from the equivalent circuit. Special care is taken in the manufacture of diode cases to minimize the series inductance, and in many cases this inductance may be ignored for calculations. Figure 2-9(b) shows a high-frequency equivalent circuit, while Fig. 2-9(c) shows a low-frequency equivalent circuit of the varactor diode.

The operating frequency of the oscillator is set by the total circuit capacitance and the inductance. In the oscillator shown, as well as in most other oscillators, the total circuit capacitance is a combination of the varactor capacitance plus the parasitic capacitances of the circuit. These capacitances include the input

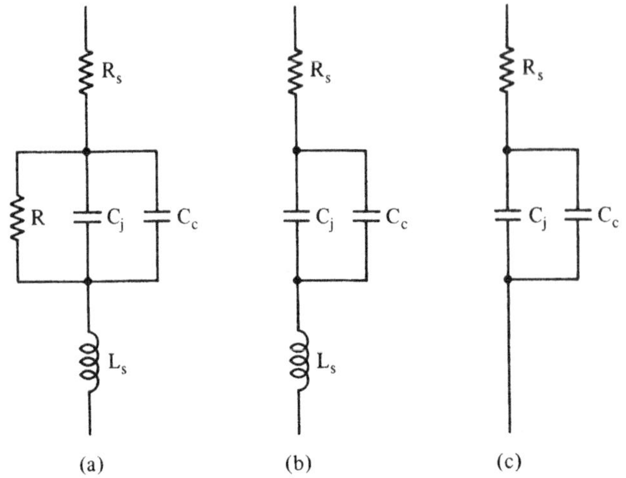

Figure 2-9
Three equivalent circuits of a varactor diode, depending on the frequency.

capacitance of the transistor, the distributed capacitance of the coil, the capacitance of the printed circuit board, and the capacitance of the varactor diode.

To achieve the maximum tuning range of the oscillator, the parasitic capacitances of the oscillator must be reduced to a minimum; this requires attention to each source of parasitic capacitance. In the case of the transistor, use of a small-geometry transistor, essentially a high-frequency transistor, will result in the minimum capacitance (C_{bc}, C_{be}). The disadvantage of this is the increased cost and the danger of undesired parasitic oscillations at very high frequencies.

For the case of the distributed capacitance of the inductor, special inductors using flat conductors to minimize the interwinding capacitance may be used.

For the case of the printed-circuit (PC) board, careful layout and microstrip techniques may be employed.

The reduction of parasitic inductance is as important as the reduction of parasitic capacitance. Low-inductance transistor and diode packages are used to minimize these effects.

To gain an insight into the tuning range of a varactor-tuned oscillator, the equivalent circuit of the oscillator of Fig. 2-8 is shown in Fig. 2-10. Using the equivalent circuit, the oscillating frequency as a function of all the circuit capacitances and the deliberate reactances as well as the parasitic reactances are used in the calculation. The resonant frequency is

$$\omega = \frac{1}{2\pi\sqrt{\left[\frac{(C_1 + C_{be})C_2}{C_1 + C_{be} + C_2} + C_{bc} + \frac{C_v}{2}\right]L}} \tag{2-12}$$

In the equivalent circuit, it is assumed that the parasitic reactances have been reduced to a minimum such that the lead inductance of the transistor and diode, the PC board capacitance and inductance, and other even smaller reactances can be ignored. Several characteristics of the oscillator are to be determined. First the relationship of the oscillation frequency to the tuning voltage is desired. Second, the tuning ratio of the oscillator can be obtained from the frequency–voltage relationship by substituting the lowest and highest tuning voltages and taking the ratio.

To determine the tuning function of the oscillator, the equation for the varactor diode capacitance as a function of reverse bias is substituted into Eq. (2-12) and produces

$$\frac{1}{2\pi\sqrt{C'L + \dfrac{K}{(V_R + V_D)^n}\left(\dfrac{L}{2}\right)}} \tag{2-13}$$

where C' is the composite of all the fixed capacitances in the equation.

It would be nice to have a linear frequency–voltage relationship, but this is not always possible. A linear voltage–frequency relationship implies that the derivative

$$\frac{d\omega}{dV_R} = \frac{1}{8\pi}\,\frac{nKL}{\left[C'L + \dfrac{KL}{(V_R + V_D)^n}\right]^{3/2}(V_R + V_D)^{n+1}} \tag{2-14}$$

is a constant. It is not necessary that (2-14) be a constant for all values of tuning voltage but for a useful portion of the varactor voltage.

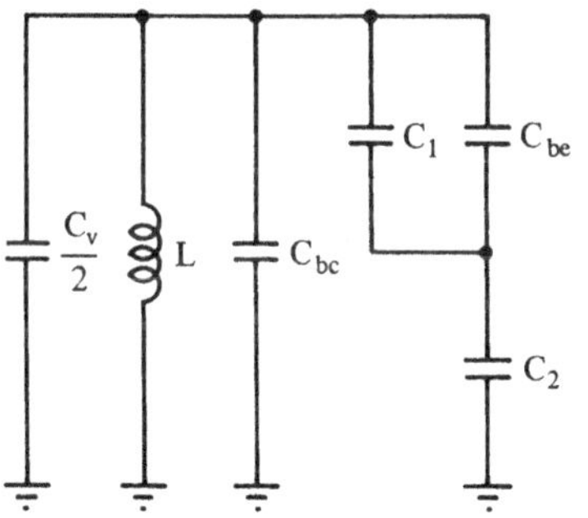

C_{bc} is the base–collector capacitance.
C_{be} is the base–emitter capacitance.
C_v is the varactor capacitance.

Figure 2-10
The equivalent circuit of the tuned circuit of the oscillator in Fig. 2-8.

To calculate what characteristics of the varactor diode would produce linear tuning, assume that the external capacitances are kept to a very low value, so that C' is considerably smaller than K. With this restriction,

$$\frac{d\omega}{dV_R} \cong \frac{1}{4\pi} \frac{nKL}{\left[\frac{KL}{(V_R + V_D)^n}\right]^{3/2} (V_R + V_D)^{n+1}}$$

$$= \frac{n}{4\pi\sqrt{KL}} (V_R + V_D)^{(n/2)-1} \tag{2-15}$$

For Eq. (2-15) to be a constant, n must be equal to 2; this produces the result

$$\frac{d\omega}{dV_R} = \frac{1}{4\pi\sqrt{KL}} \tag{2-16}$$

Although no diodes have a value of n this great, the closer to this value a diode is, the more linear the tuning will become.

The other important consideration of a VCO is the tuning range. To determine the tuning range, it is necessary to substitute the values into the equations and ascertain that the diode will produce the necessary range.

As an example, the VCO range of 700 to 1200 MHz will be used with a hyper-abrupt junction diode with the relatively high n value of 1.0.

The ratio of the high VCO frequency F_H to the low frequency F_L is equated to the minimum and maximum capacitances as

$$\frac{F_H}{F_L} = \sqrt{\frac{C' + C_{vL}}{C' + C_{vH}}} \tag{2-17}$$

where C_{vL} is the low-frequency varactor capacitance and C_{vH} is the high-frequency varactor capacitance.

Substituting the frequencies for the example synthesizer, the following is obtained.

$$\frac{1200 \text{ MHz}}{700 \text{ MHz}} = 1.7 = \sqrt{\frac{C' + C_{vL}}{C' + C_{vH}}} \tag{2-18}$$

If the varactor diode has a case capacitance of 0.5 pF and the circuit capacitance, which represents C', is 5.0 pF, the following is obtained.

$$1.7 = \sqrt{\frac{5.5 \text{ pF} + C_{VL}}{5.5 \text{ pF} + C_{VH}}}; \qquad 2.9 = \frac{5.5 \text{ pF} + C_{VL}}{5.5 \text{ pF} + C_{VH}} \tag{2-19}$$

There are two inherent limitations for the varactor voltage. First is a value near zero, as the diode will begin to conduct and will no longer provide capacitance but becomes a low resistance instead. The other limit is the maximum voltage that will not produce breakdown of the diode. For the investigation at hand the values of 3 and 30 V would represent reasonable values for common varactor diodes.

Using Eq. (2-11) for C_{vL} and C_{vH} with the values of 3 and 30 V, respectively, the following is obtained.

$$C_{vH} = \frac{k}{30.7}; \qquad C_{vL} = \frac{k}{3.7} \tag{2-20}$$

Substituting the results of (2-20) into (2-19) and solving for k produces

$$10.5\ \text{pF} + \frac{2.9k}{30.7} = \frac{k}{3.7}; \qquad k = 59\ \text{pF} \tag{2-21}$$

In addition to the oscillator shown in Fig. 2-8, there are three stages of buffering to prevent pulling of the oscillator frequency from large input signals feeding through the first mixer. The tuning range of the first local oscillator of a typical spectrum analyzer can approach two-to-one, as previously explained, which implies that the buffer amplifiers following the VCO must be broad band. It is important that the first mixer of the spectrum analyzer receive a reasonably constant level of local oscillator energy, but not such that an automatic leveling circuit would be required. In addition to the buffering, the local oscillator would receive careful shielding to prevent the generation of spurious signals.

One type of oscillator that deserves special treatment, as it is used in many spectrum analyzers, is the YIG oscillator. YIG, yttrium iron garnet, is a ceramic substance that has unique ferromagnetic properties. Like many ferromagnetic materials, YIG molecules have magnetic moments that are normally randomly aligned. When this material is placed in a uniform magnetic field, the molecules align in the direction of the applied uniform field. These molecules are like spinning tops and, like tops, tend to precess around their axes. The frequency of precession is dependent on the size and type of material used and is directly proportional to the applied magnetic field. This relationship is given as

$$F = \gamma H_0 \tag{2-22}$$

where H_0 is the applied magnetic field and gamma is the constant of proportionality called the gyromagnetic ratio.

Achieving frequency stability of the YIG oscillator requires that the magnetic field strength in which the YIG sphere is immersed be equally stable. This requires the mechanical structure of the oscillator to be constructed of mechanically stable material, typically a mixture of 48% nickel and 52% iron.

Energy can be coupled into and out of the YIG material if the applied frequency of the energy is precisely that of the precession frequency. Since the precession frequency is a function of the applied uniform magnetic field, the resonant frequency of the YIG sphere may be tuned electronically.

As shown in Fig. 2-11, a small coil surrounding the YIG sphere provides the method of coupling energy into and out of the YIG sphere. The RF field is applied perpendicular to the static magnetic field, which tends to force the magnetic dipoles normally aligned to the applied static magnetic field to precess. This results in an equivalent circuit consisting of a parallel resonant circuit with a small series inductance due to the inductance of the coupling loop.

The resonant frequency of the YIG sphere can be set by varying the strength of the uniform magnetic field. Unlike varactor-tuned oscillators, where the tuning ratio is limited by the capacitance of the varactor at the highest reverse voltage, the YIG resonant frequency can be set by a magnetic field that can span several octaves.

A second very useful property of YIG resonators is their very high Q. This is in comparison to the relatively low Q of a varactor-tuned oscillator, especially an oscillator with a broad tuning range. Lack of Q in an oscillator produces phase noise that can destroy the selectivity of the spectrum analyzer. This will be discussed in more detail later.

YIG resonators are made from highly polished spheres of a diameter of about 0.25 mm. The sphere is placed in a uniform magnetic field as shown in Fig. 2-11. The coupling coil couples the energy into and out of the sphere.

Figure 2-12 shows a YIG oscillator. In this circuit the YIG resonator is connected in the emitter of the oscillator, which provides the equivalent of a negative resistance to sustain oscillation. Feedback is achieved through the capacitances of the oscillator transistor, which tend to be small. This prevents the

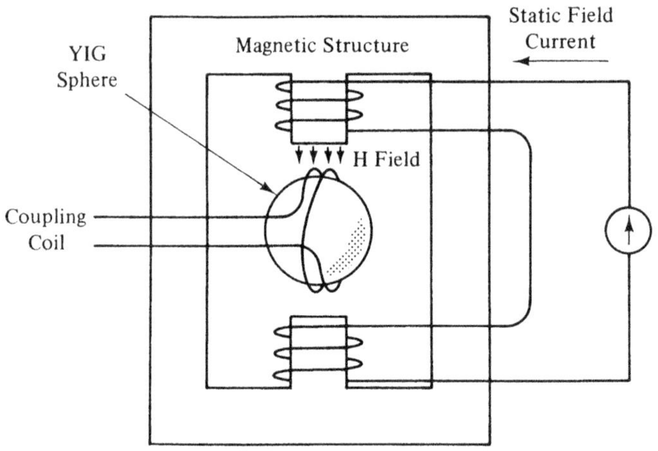

Figure 2-11
Details of a YIG resonator showing the sphere and the magnetic structure.

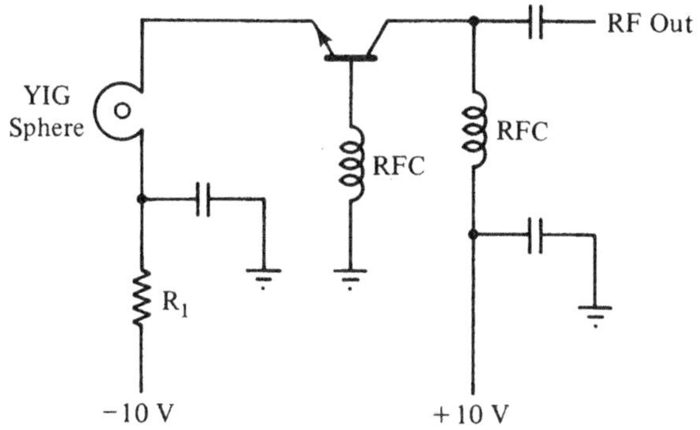

Figure 2-12
Schematic of a negative resistance YIG oscillator.

loading of the transistor from destroying the Q of the YIG sphere and increasing the phase noise of the oscillator.

Bipolar YIG oscillators as shown in Fig. 2-12 are made for frequencies as high as 20 GHz. For higher frequency ranges, GaAs FET oscillators may be used.

A very useful characteristic of the YIG oscillator is the inherent linear relationship between the magnetic field and the frequency of oscillation. This results in a linear relationship between the applied current and the frequency. This is because the frequency of oscillation is directly proportional to the applied magnetic field and does not involve distributed capacitance or other parasitic reactances.

2.3.5 Frequency Linearizers

A linear relationship between the tuning voltage in a varactor-tuned oscillator or the field current in a YIG oscillator is necessary to insure that the frequency of the display tracks the deflection voltage, resulting in a linear display of frequency. The linearity of frequency as a function of applied current in a YIG oscillator can be quite good—on the order of 0.05%. A varactor-tuned oscillator, on the other hand, is difficult to make linear and consequently is not very linear at all. It is necessary to "bend" or linearize the tuning voltage applied to the varactor diode in the oscillator to achieve acceptable linearity.

Generally, the tuning sensitivity, that is, the change in frequency per change in tuning voltage, decreases at greater varactor voltages or at the higher frequency range of the oscillator. To maintain a constant tuning sensitivity, the applied tuning voltage must be shaped such that the gain of the shaper is greater at higher frequencies.

Figure 2-13 shows a typical tuning curve for a varactor-tuned oscillator.

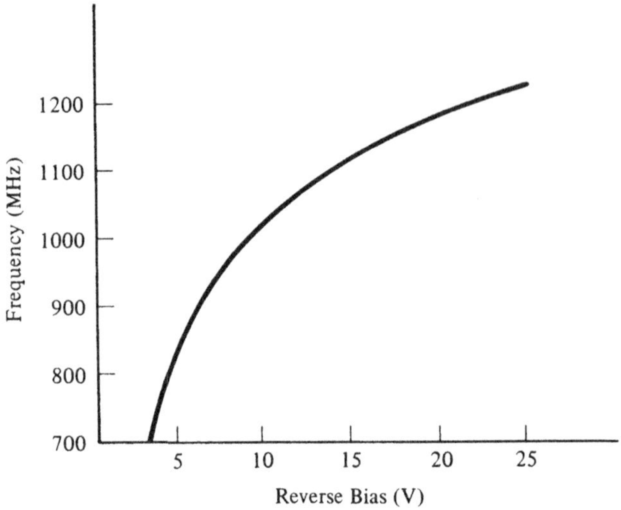

Figure 2-13
Typical relationship between the tuning voltage and the frequency of a varactor-tuned oscillator.

The tuning curve begins to flatten at its higher frequency end, which is indicative of the reduction of tuning sensitivity. The amount of flattening depends on the oscillator topology and the type of varactor diode used. The hyper-abrupt diodes tend to have a tuning curve that is closer to being linear. For good linearity, that is, on the order of 0.5%, a linearizing circuit is required.

What a linearizing circuit does is provide a transfer function that is the opposite of the tuning curve. That is, if the tuning curve flattens at the high-frequency end, the linearizing circuit expands the input voltage at the high-frequency end. This can be achieved in a number of ways; one suitable circuit is shown in Fig. 2-14.

Because the nonlinearity of a VCO does not follow any simple mathematical function such as a logarithm or simple polynomial, a simple circuit element such as a diode cannot be used to create the linearizing circuit. A linearizing circuit uses a number of straight-line segments where the slope and intercept of each straight-line segment can be individually set to create any arbitrary function, such as the circuit of Fig. 2-14.

In this example, the breakpoint, that is, where each line segment begins, is set by the adjustment of R_A through R_F. The slope of the line segment is adjusted by the resistors R_G through R_L. As each breakpoint is reached, the gain of the op-amp circuit is increased by virtue of the reduction of the feedback (and resulting increase of gain). As a diode conducts, the feedback path from the op-amp output to the summing junction is reduced by shunting the current through the diode to the relatively low impedance of the voltage divider.

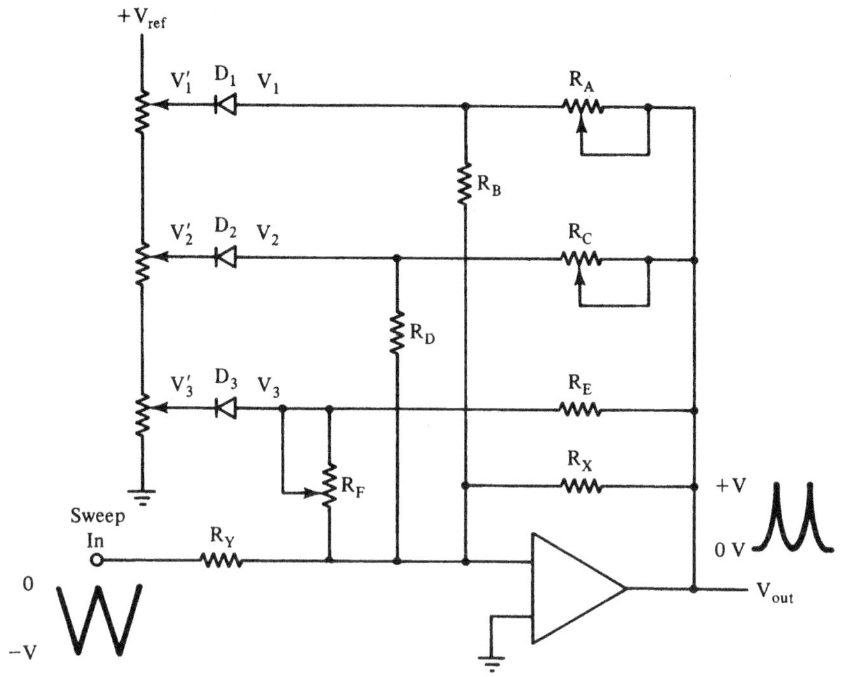

Figure 2-14
A frequency linearizer circuit for a varactor-tuned oscillator.

To calculate the gain and transfer function of the shaper, consider first the situation where none of the diodes are conducting. This occurs where V_{out} is less than V_1, V_2, or V_3. More specifically, V_{out} is less than

$$\begin{aligned} V_{out} &< V_1(R_A + R_B)/R_B \\ V_{out} &< V_2(R_C + R_D)/R_D \\ V_{out} &< V_3(R_E + R_F)/R_E \end{aligned} \tag{2-23}$$

where $V_1 = V_1' - V_0$; $V_2 = V_2' - V_0$; and $V_3 = V_3 - V_0$. V_0 is the on voltage of the diode.

For this level of V_{out}, the gain of the amplifier is

$$\frac{V_{out}}{V_{in}} = \frac{(R_A + R_B)(R_C + R_D)(R_E + R_F)R_X}{(R_A + R_B + R_C + R_D + R_E + R_F)R_Y} \tag{2-24}$$

In this situation, the gain is set by the paralleled combination of $(R_A + R_B)$, $(R_C + R_D)$, $(R_E + R_F)$, and R_X divided by R_Y. When the output reaches a threshold set by

$$V_{out} > \frac{V_1(R_A + R_B)}{R_B} \tag{2-25}$$

the diode D_1 conducts and stops the feedback path through R_E and R_F. The gain is higher as one of the parallel resistances is removed from the feedback path. This will occur again at a threshold of

$$V_{out} > \frac{V_2(R_C + R_D)}{R_D} \tag{2-26}$$

In this case D_2 conducts and the feedback path through R_D and R_E is severed. This increases the gain further.

At a threshold of

$$V_{out} > \frac{V_3(R_E + R_F)}{R_E} \tag{2-27}$$

diode D_1 conducts and the gain increases further to a value of R_X/R_Y.

Notice that the thresholds which determine the breakpoints of the shaper amplifier are a function of the resistances R_A through R_E. To minimize the effect of these resistors, R_A, R_C, and R_E are considerably greater than R_B, R_D, and R_E, respectively.

The resistances R_A, R_C, and R_E are adjustable to set the slope of the shaper above the associated threshold.

In spite of the restrictions placed on the resistor values, the variable resistances interact and it is necessary to have an adjustment procedure for setting the shaper.

2.3.6 IF Filters

The resolution of the spectrum analyzer is set by the IF filters. A filter is required for each frequency conversion in the spectrum analyzer to remove the image. However, many of the frequency conversions involve very high frequencies, where a narrow filter would be difficult to make. For this reason, the actual resolution of the analyzer is usually set by the filters in the lowest frequency IF amplifier.

Several bandwidths are available and are switched either with a PIN diode, other type of electronic switch, or by a relay or mechanical switch.

Depending on the IF and the bandwidth required, the IF filter may use one of several technologies. For moderate and wide bandwidths, a conventional L-C filter may be used. For narrow bandwidths, crystal filters may be used.

The shape of the filter is critical for good spectrum analyzer operation. Unlike a radio receiver or other radio-frequency communications equipment, the IF filter does not require sharp skirts and excellent "adjacent channel" rejection. Filters with very sharp skirts, indicating high-Q elements within the filter, suffer from ringing as the analyzer is swept through a signal. A gradual skirted filter such as a Gaussian filter is desired for the IF filter in a spectrum analyzer.

A Gaussian filter has a bandpass with the shape congruent with a mathematical function called the Gaussian distribution. The mathematical expression that describes this shape is

$$G(x) = e^{-x^2} \tag{2-28}$$

as shown in the plot of Fig. 2-15.

To gain an understanding of the source of distortion due to the IF filter in a spectrum analyzer, consider the fact that because of the continuously sweeping nature of the spectrum analyzer, signals will be within the passband of the IF filter for only a finite amount of time. An example is a spectrum analyzer that scans 100 MHz at a rate that does not cause objectionable flicker of 50 scans per second. Assume the retrace time is 10% of the repetition rate, so that 18 ms are required for a scan and 2 ms for the retrace. This results in a scan rate of 5.6 MHz per ms. If the IF filter in use has a 3-dB bandwidth of 50 kHz, the swept signal is present in the passband of the filter for only 8.9 μs. Such a short pulse does not have the energy to cause all of the reactive elements in the filter to respond to the input signal, and the result is a loss of amplitude at the filter output relative to the continuous wave (CW) insertion loss.

Several mathematical derivations have been made of this loss; the relationship generally accepted is

$$a = \left(1 + 0.195\left[\frac{S}{B^2}\right]^2\right)^{-1/4} \tag{2-29}$$

where a is the loss factor, S is the scan rate, and B is the IF filter bandwidth.

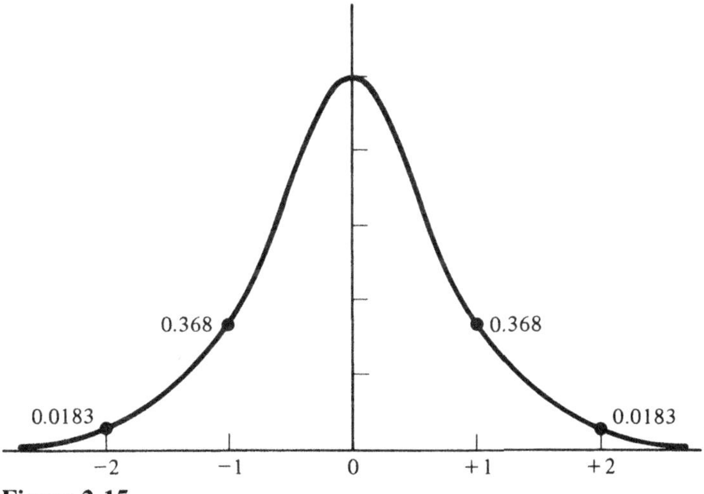

Figure 2-15
A plot of the mathematical expression that describes the shape congruent with the Gaussian distribution.

This relationship is valid for filters having a Gaussian or near-Gaussian response. Most other filter shapes, such as flat-top filters, will have even more loss.

As an example the values discussed are entered into (2-25) and the scan loss is calculated.

$$a = \left[1 + 0.195\left(\frac{5.6 \times 10^9}{2.5 \times 10^9}\right)^2\right]^{-1/4} = 0.843$$

Another phenomenon exhibited by an IF filter when the scan rate is excessive is the apparent broadening of the filter bandwidth. This is due to the energy in the reactance dissipating when the swept frequency is well outside of the normal filter passband. What takes place is a combination of reduced output and an apparent broader bandwidth, as shown in Fig. 2-16. The figure shows the greater the sweep rate, the lower the output and the broader the bandwidth. An expression of the apparent bandwidth as a function of the scan rate is

$$R = \left[B + 0.195\left(\frac{S^2}{B^3}\right)\right]^{1/2} \tag{2-30}$$

where R is the apparent bandwidth or resolution.

As the equation shows, there is always a broadening of the filter bandwidth, producing a trace on the spectrum analyzer that is greater than the bandwidth of the IF filter. This broadening can be reduced by increasing the scan time; but in a spectrum analyzer, it is desirable to have a scan rate that produces a flicker-free display. Therefore for the minimum scan rate that produces a flicker-free display, there exists an optimum bandwidth that produces the minimum resolution for the scan width. To determine this bandwidth, Eq. (2-30) is rewritten and the derivative dR/dB is taken and set to zero looking for the relative minima.

$$\frac{dR}{dB} = \frac{1}{2}\left[B + 0.195\left(\frac{S^2}{B^2}\right)\right]^{1/2}\left[1 - \frac{(0.585S^2)}{B^4}\right] = 0 \tag{2-31}$$

from which it follows that

$$1 - \frac{(0.585)S^2}{B^4} = 0$$

$$B_0 = 0.874\sqrt{S_0} \tag{2-32}$$

where B_0 is the optimum IF bandwidth for the scan rate S_0.

Most spectrum analyzer filters are close but not exactly equal to the Gaussian formula. The important criterion for the IF filter is not to match the Gaussian exactly, but to create a gentle-skirted filter so that the maximum scan rate may be employed. There are spectrum analyzer applications such as the measurement of thermal noise where the shape of the IF filter will be critical. For this reason it is desirable not to deviate excessively from the basic Gaussian filter passband.

The simplest IF filter is a cascading of simple tuned circuits. There are two basic methods of cascading IF filter tuned circuits. The first is to distribute the

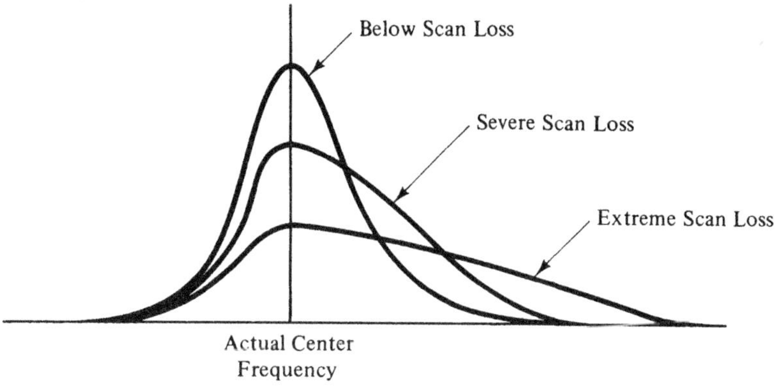

Figure 2-16
Reduced output and apparent broader bandwidth exhibited by an IF filter when the scan rate is excessive.

tuning throughout the IF amplifier, often by using impedance coupling devices between the stages of the amplifier. A second method is to couple tuned circuits together without intervening amplifiers.

There are several overwhelming reasons not to distribute the IF selectivity throughout the IF amplifier. It must not be forgotten that the IF amplifier in a spectrum analyzer is a log amplifier and does not serve the identical purpose of a radio receiver IF amplifier. If the selectivity were inserted between the stages of a limiting type of log amplifier, the selectivity would be affected by the signal level in the amplifier. As an amplifier stage entered saturation, that stage would supply only a constant term to the output equation. The effects of the tuned circuit following that amplifier stage would be lost for all signal levels above saturation.

In spite of the foregoing reasons for not introducing tuned circuits, a small number of tuned circuits, and often only one, is inserted midway through the log IF amplifier to reduce the noise at the DLV output. When a log amplifier has six stages or more, the amount of noise generated within the IF amplifier raises the noise floor of the IF amplifier well above the theoretical noise floor of the spectrum analyzer.

To reduce the noise level, a simple tuned circuit is inserted as shown in Fig. 2-17. In order not to destroy the logarithmic accuracy of the amplifier, it is imperative that the voltage ratio between input and output be exactly one. If not, the amplifier stage following the tuned circuit will appear to have less gain than the other stages and thus will distort the logarithmic relationship.

Another reason for not distributing the tuned circuits throughout the IF amplifier is the reduction of intermodulation within the IF amplifier. Placing all the IF selectivity ahead of the IF amplifier reduces the bandwidth of the input signals to the IF amplifier. This reduces the chances for intermodulation distortion and improves the dynamic range of the analyzer.

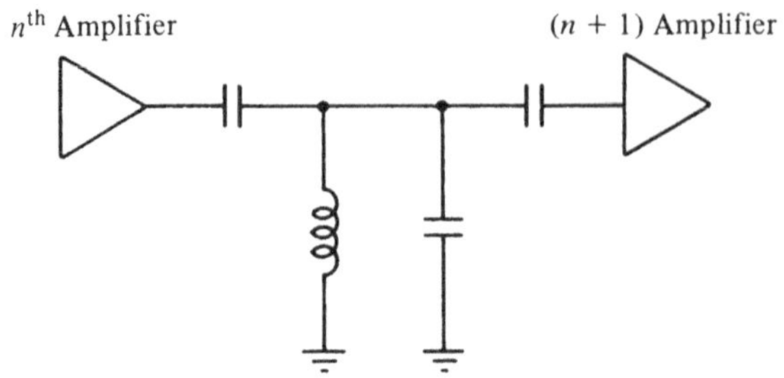

Figure 2-17
A very simple tuned circuit is required between the center stages of a successive approximation log amplifier to reduce noise. This shows a simple tuned circuit with nearly zero loss.

The tuned circuits of the IF filter are simply lumped together and placed before the IF amplifier. Cascading tuned circuits causes energy from one tuned circuit to couple to an adjacent tuned circuit and, therefore, the two circuits interact. The amount of interaction is a function of the coupling which, in a simple sense, has three categories: undercoupled, critically coupled, and overcoupled. Figure 2-18 shows some representative filter shapes. Figure 2-18(a) shows the undercoupled filter in which the amount of coupling between the tuned circuits is slight, where there is considerable loss, but a passband that appears to be Gaussian. The overcoupled filter is shown in Fig. 2-18(b). In this case, the coupling is so great that it causes the two tuned circuits to interact and produce a "two hump" passband that does not represent a Gaussian passband by any standards. Figure 2-18(c) shows the critically coupled filter with a flat passband and a minimal amount of loss.

For a spectrum analyzer application, a filter with a basic passband some-

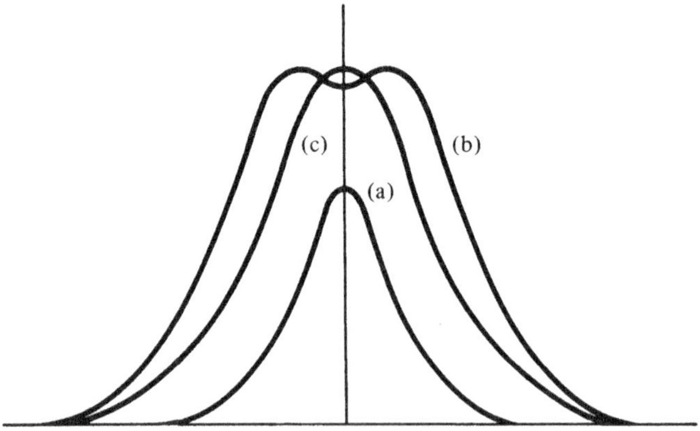

Figure 2-18
The passband obtained from three degrees of coupling in an IF filter.

where between undercoupled and critically coupled is ideal. More than two tuned circuits may be used for the spectrum analyzer filter, but since no extreme "adjacent channel" style selectivity is required, such as that required for radio communication systems, a filter with only four tuned circuits may be more than adequate.

Practical unloaded Qs that may be obtained with conventional inductors is on the order of 100 to 200. Of course, when these inductors are placed into the circuit the loaded Q will be somewhat less, perhaps one-half.

As an example, a filter used in a 21.4-MHz spectrum analyzer IF using a loaded Q of 75 would have a minimum bandwidth capability of 285 kHz.

Much of the analysis that would use a spectrum analyzer requires a bandwidth much less than 285 kHz. For narrower bandwidths down to 1 kHz without resorting to an additional frequency conversion, crystal filters are usually used.

The quartz crystal is, in essence, a tuned circuit with a very high Q and great stability. For the creation of narrow filters, the need for high Q is obvious. The frequency stability characteristic of the quartz resonator is also necessary, to prevent the center frequency of the tuned circuits from drifting apart and destroying the characteristics of the filter.

The equivalent circuit of the quartz resonator is shown in Fig. 2-19. The piezoelectric resonator is shown as a series resonant circuit consisting of L_m, C_m, and R_1.

Typical values of L_m, C_m, and R depend on the resonant frequency of the crystal and the quality of the crystal. Some typical values are shown in Table 2-3.

The capacitance C_o is due to the structure of the quartz resonator. The quartz is held between two supporting wires, and the resonator is coupled to the circuit with metallized surfaces of the quartz crystal. These surfaces constitute

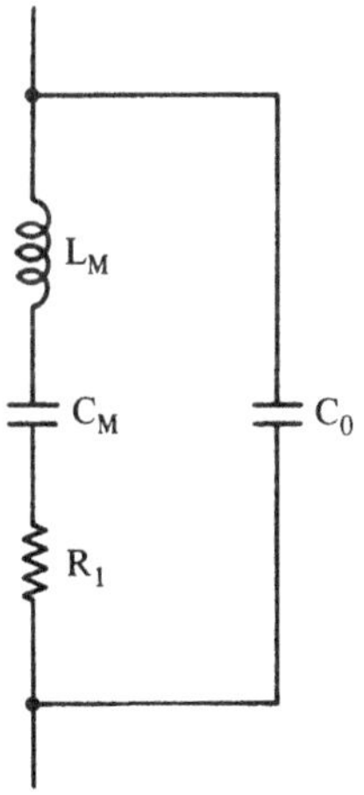

$$Q = \sqrt{\frac{L}{R^2 C}}$$

Figure 2-19
The equivalent circuit of a quartz resonator.

Table 2-3

	Parameter				
Frequency	L_m	C_m	R_1	Q	C_o
500 kHz	25 Hy	24 fF[a]	2 k	18,000	9.1 pF
2 MHz	.5 Hy	12 fF	100	54,000	3.9 pF
10 MHz	.1 Hy	2.5 fF	50	126,000	3.9 pF
30 MHz	.01 Hy	2.5 fF	20	100,000	6 pF

[a]fF = femtofarad (1×10^{-15} farads)

the plates of a capacitor and, along with capacitance due to the supporting structure, generate C_o.

The extreme high Q of the quartz crystal is due primarily to the high value of the inductance and the corresponding small capacitance. As a comparison, it would be totally impossible to create an inductance with any of the values shown in Table 2-3 to operate at the frequencies in question. Values similar to those shown in the table are achievable, but it would be nearly impossible outside the realm of superconductivity to achieve an inductance with the low resistance shown in the table.

A small capacitance would not be difficult to achieve. However, the large inductance, if it could be made from wire, would contain much more distributed capacitance than the values of C_m shown in the table. Therefore, the quartz crystal is unique in that an equivalent circuit could not be made from conventional components.

The quartz resonator may be used as a simple filter for narrow passbands. However, the passband is skewed because of the effect of the parallel capacitor C_0. Current is conducted around the quartz resonator through the capacitive reactance. The passband can be balanced by nulling out the effects of C_0 by feeding a signal of the same magnitude but out of phase through a variable capacitor, as shown in Fig. 2-20. Theoretically, this capacitor will be set to a value C_0, thus subtracting the current through the C_0 of the quartz resonator.

Single quartz resonators are separated by amplifiers to prevent coupling. In this fashion undercoupling can be achieved without the attendant loss.

The minimum bandwidth of a quartz resonator is set by the equivalent series resistance. Generally, this parameter is difficult to control, and an external resistance is used to set the bandwidth of the resonator. In addition, by increasing this resistance the quartz resonator may be used to provide more than one bandwidth.

Figure 2-21 shows a three-bandwidth filter for spectrum analyzer. In this example, two bandwidths are obtained from conventional L-C resonant circuits and two additional bandwidths from quartz resonators. Two amplifiers are used to provide not only isolation but the phase reversal required for nulling the effects of the resonator capacitance.

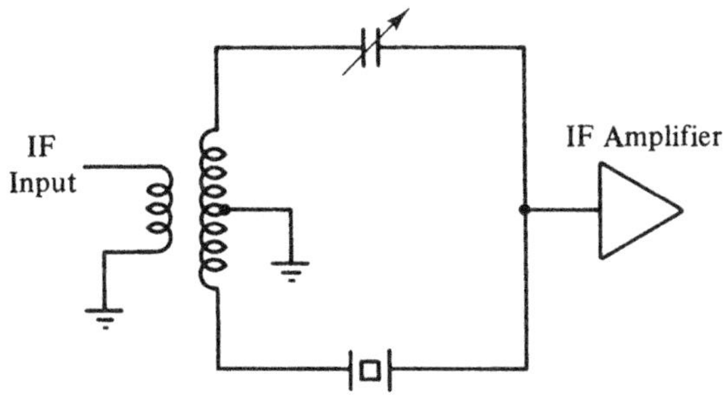

Figure 2-20
A bridge circuit for canceling the currents from the crystal holder capacitance.

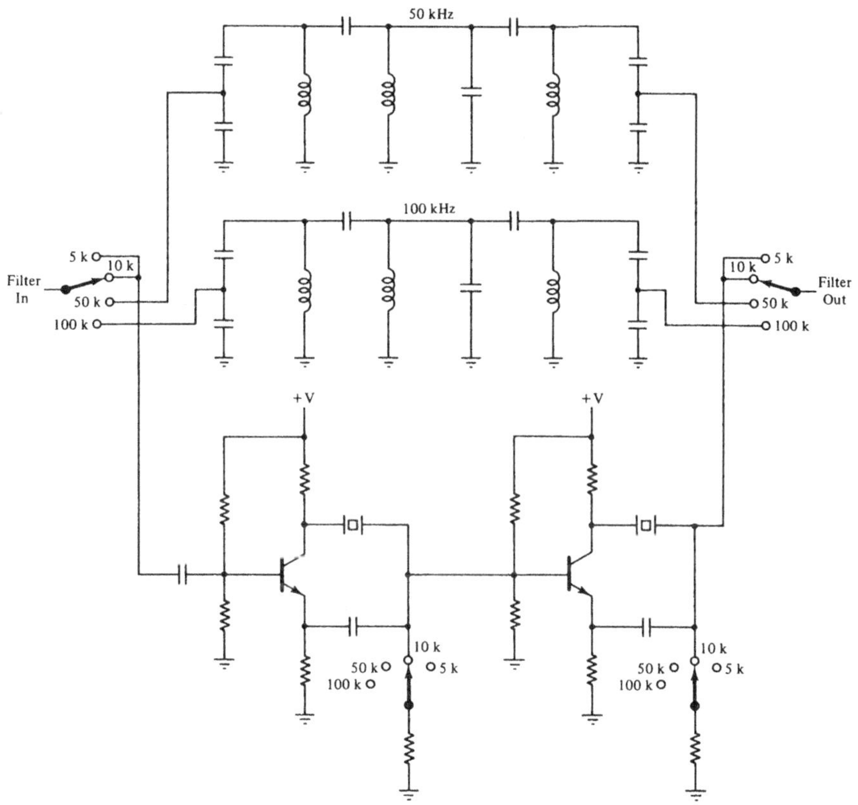

Figure 2-21
A three-bandwidth spectrum analyzer filter showing two bandwidths obtained from conventional LC filters and a third from quartz resonators.

Another form of piezoelectric resonator with a considerably wider bandwidth is the ceramic resonator. The equivalent circuit of the ceramic resonator is identical in topology to the quartz resonator except that the motional inductance is relatively less and the capacitance is proportionately greater. Typical ceramic resonators have *Q*s on the order of 750 to 1000 compared to 20,000 to as much as 1,000,000 for quartz resonators. The ceramic resonator is handled in a fashion similar to the quartz resonator.

Ceramic resonators are used to fabricate filters using a common ceramic element. These filters are available with about 0.5 to 3% bandwidths and are available in Gaussian passbands.

2.3.7 Mixers

The passive diode type mixer is practically the only type of mixer ever used in a spectrum analyzer. The more important characteristics for the mixers of the spectrum analyzer, particularly the first mixer, are wide dynamic range and constant loss as a function of frequency. It is good to have some reasonable isolation from the local oscillator to the RF port and the IF port, but high isolation is not necessary as the IF filter and the input filter will reject the majority of the leakage. Impedance match over a broad range of frequencies, especially at the RF port, is another reasonable expectation as an extreme mismatch will affect the passband of the low-pass filter at the input of the analyzer.

Figure 2-22 shows the very popular double-balanced mixer, which is an excellent choice for a spectrum analyzer. In any mixer the local oscillator input

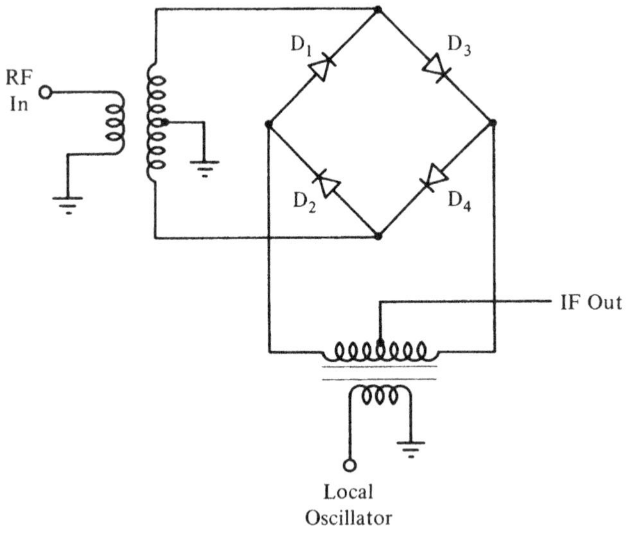

Figure 2-22
Double-balanced mixer.

should be 10 to 20 dB greater than the largest signal applied to the RF port. Thus the local oscillator signal switches the diodes from conduction to reverse biased and causes the mixer to act as a switch to the RF port. Consider the diode pair D_1 and D_2 to conduct during the positive half-cycle of the local oscillator while D_3 and D_4 conduct during the negative half-cycle. This causes the RF input to be switched to the IF port with alternating polarities. Since the voltage from the local oscillator that passes through the diodes is of an opposite polarity, the net result is a canceling of the local oscillator signal. Thus the local oscillator is balanced from the IF port and to the RF port as well.

Review Questions for Chapter 2

1. Relative to electrical signals, what is a spectrum?
2. What are the two basic methods of spectral analysis? How do these differ?
3. What are the advantages of the parallel filter spectrum analyzer?
4. What are the significant advantages of the superheterodyne spectrum analyzer?
5. What is the reason for the first IF being higher in frequency than the greatest input frequency?
6. What is an image frequency and how is it removed?
7. What limits the ability of a superheterodyne spectrum analyzer to display spectral information near zero frequency?
8. What is the first local oscillator frequency range for a spectrum analyzer with a 1020-MHz first IF and a 0–750-MHz input range? What would be the image band? What would be a good cutoff frequency for the input low-pass filter?
9. What are the advantages of a logarithmic display?
10. What power level is indicated by +23 dBm?
11. Why is it necessary to use more than one frequency conversion in a superheterodyne spectrum analyzer?
12. Why are two varactor diodes in series used to tune a voltage-controlled oscillator?
13. Which is more likely to produce a linear tuning curve, an abrupt junction diode or a hyper-abrupt junction?
14. What parameters limit the tuning range of a voltage-tuned oscillator?
15. Why are buffer amplifier stages used following an oscillator?
16. What are the advantages of a YIG oscillator over a varactor-tuned oscillator?
17. Why are frequency linearizers used?
18. What are some of the technologies used to generate IF filters?
19. What is the advantage of an IF filter with a Gaussian shape?
20. What is scan loss?
21. What is optimum bandwidth?
22. Draw the equivalent circuit of a quartz resonator.
23. When are quartz resonators used for IF filters?

3

Frequency Control, Phase Lock, and Microprocessor-Controlled Spectrum Analyzers

3.1 Frequency Display

The spectrum analyzer circuits and systems outlined in the previous chapter covered the basic spectrum analyzer but not the additional features and enhancements that are found on modern spectrum analyzers.

Most modern spectrum analyzers have a digital display of frequency rather than a dial. Often the reference level of the spectrum analyzer is displayed digitally, which requires the settings of the RF and IF attenuators in the calculation. In many spectrum analyzers, the optimum scanning velocity is selected relative to the frequency span and the IF filter in use. Modern spectrum analyzers often have only a single knob that controls the center frequency and span while automatically selecting the optimum scanning velocity, resolution bandwidth, video bandwidth, and IF and RF attenuators. These devices are the subject of this chapter.

Practically any spectrum analyzer manufactured uses a form of digital display. Early spectrum analyzers used various arrangements of mechanical dials that usually were linked to a 10-turn potentiometer. Because it is necessary to have a linear relationship between the tuning voltage and the frequency of the first local oscillator to insure an accurate display of wide frequency spans, the center frequency of the analyzer may be set with a DC voltage generated from an accurate potentiometer. Care was taken to linearize the VCO tuning voltage to insure a good linear relationship. With the advent of inexpensive digital voltmeter chips, it was a simple matter of displaying the voltage provided from the potentiometer, scaling it, and providing an offset so that the voltage from the potentiometer would display frequency.

Figure 3-1 shows a tuning voltage generator for a spectrum analyzer local oscillator. A sawtooth generator provides the basic sweep voltage. It is necessary that the average value of this voltage be zero, which means the positive peak and the negative peak of the sawtooth must be exactly the same. This is so that when the sawtooth is attenuated, the amplitude is reduced to around 0 V. Otherwise, when the attenuation is increased, the offset voltage will be likewise attenuated and will affect the center frequency.

For the convenience of discussion, the parameters of the example spectrum analyzer will be used.

The sweep voltage of Fig. 3-1 is ± 2.5 V or 5 V peak to peak. This voltage is attenuated with the frequency span control and the output is fed to a unity gain, noninverting amplifier. This amplifier presents a high impedance to the frequency span attenuator and prevents gain errors due to the loading of the amplifier. The output of this amplifier feeds an inverting amplifier with a gain of 2, which provides an output voltage of 10 V peak to peak. This output feeds the linearizer, which provides the full 0–500 MHz sweep for the example spectrum analyzer. The actual VCO frequency is 700–1200 MHz, which corresponds to 0–500 MHz.

In addition to the sweep voltage, a fixed voltage is summed in this amplifier. This voltage is derived from a 10-turn potentiometer and, like the sweep voltage, has a range from -2.5 to $+2.5$ V and also provides a frequency variation of 0–500 MHz. Therefore, the center frequency is set by the fixed voltage, and the frequency varies above and below the center frequency.

The center frequency may be read from a simple mechanical dial driven from the 10-turn potentiometer shaft; but a more elegant solution, as shown in the figure, is to use a digital voltmeter. The voltmeter should read 0 to 500, corresponding to the center frequency in megahertz. The center frequency potentiometer provides a 5-V change, but from -2.5 to $+2.5$ V. This is corrected by simply referencing the voltmeter to 2.5 V by connecting the negative input of the voltmeter to a 2.5-V source. Thus the 0–5-V input to the meter corresponds to 0–500 MHz.

The voltmeter technique is very successful when used with a YIG oscillator because of the YIG oscillator's excellent linearity. In the previous example, the 1-MHz resolution provided by a three-digit voltmeter would provide a fre-

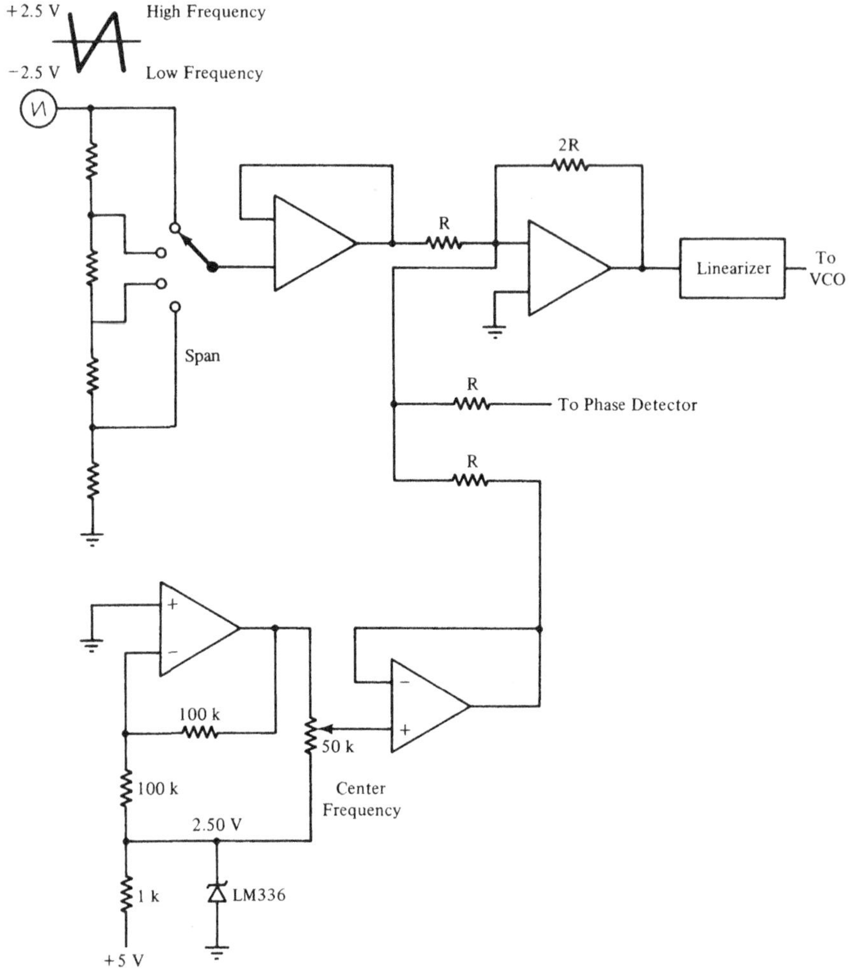

Figure 3-1
The sweep voltage and linearizer circuits for the first local oscillator of a spectrum analyzer.

quency readout of 0.2%, which would be better than the linearity of a varactor-tuned VCO with a linearizer circuit. A well-designed YIG oscillator could obtain a frequency accuracy of 0.1%.

A more elegant method would be to actually count the local oscillator frequency. This would require overcoming some significant hurdles. First, since the first local oscillator is constantly sweeping, the frequency would have to be counted while the frequency is changing. If a short count gate is used and if the count gate is carefully synchronized with the sweep voltage so that the count occurs at the center of the display, this technique can provide a stable and accurate display.

Figure 3-2 shows a frequency counter method of displaying the center frequency. In this example, a frequency resolution of 0.1 MHz is desired; this is achieved with a gate time of 640 μs. Normally, for a frequency resolution of 100

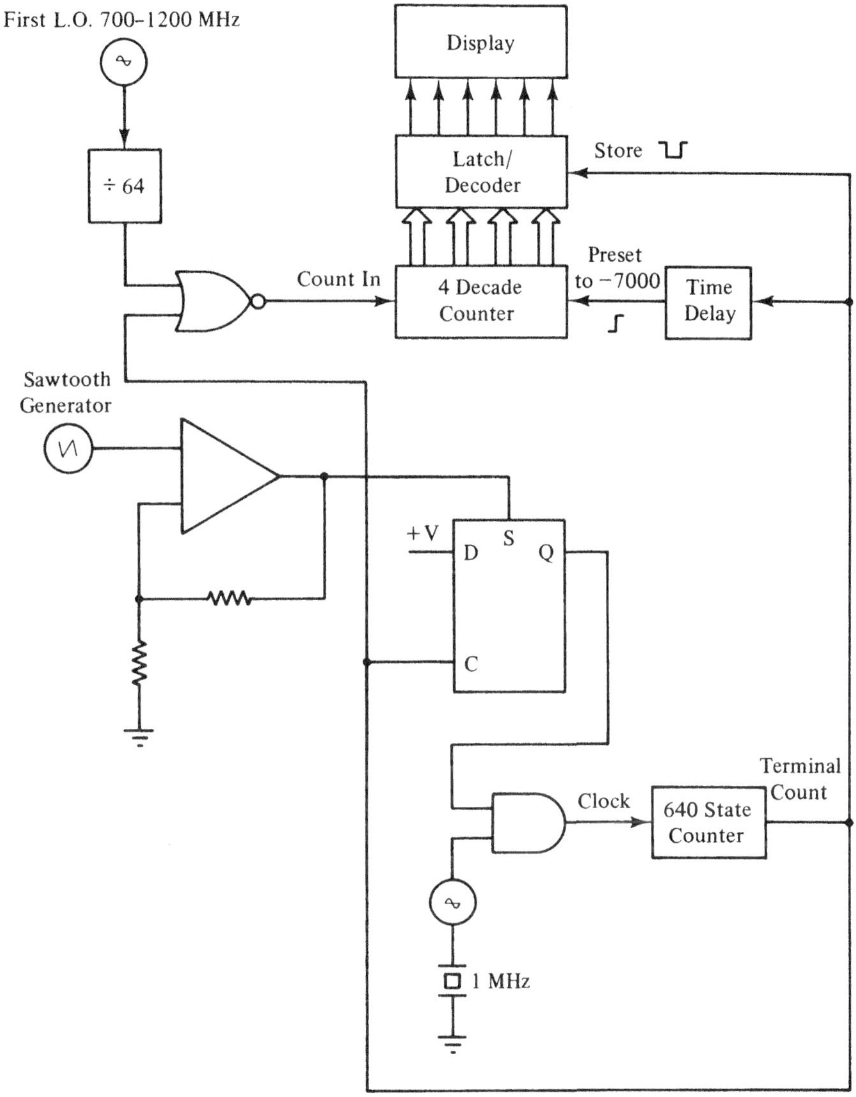

Figure 3-2
A detailed block diagram of a frequency counter for use in counting the center frequency of a spectrum analyzer.

kHz, a count gate of 10 μs would be required. A fixed prescaler of 64 is used in this example, requiring a 640-μs count gate to achieve the required 100-kHz resolution.

The counter is enabled as the sweep voltage generator crosses zero, and thus the actual counting period is slightly off-center. It is usually not necesaary to use a sweep rate any greater than that which provides a flicker-free display, or about 50 Hz. This represents a scan time of about 18 ms and a retrace time approximately one tenth the trace time—2 ms. The count time, 640 μs, represents 1/28th of the trace, which is hardly noticeable.

The zero crossing of the sweep voltage sets the D-type flip-flop, which causes the modulo-640 reference counter to begin counting. This counter is initially at a state of 1010000000 binary, which is 640 decimal. The terminal count output is at a logic one, which indicates that 640 is the terminal count. The first 1-MHz clock edge after the zero crossing of the sweep voltage causes the counter to increment to zero, and thus the terminal count output goes low. The counter continues until the terminal count is reached again, when the terminal count output goes to logic one. The zero-to-one edge of the terminal count clocks the D-type flip-flop to the zero state, which disables the reference counter and stops the counter in the 640 state. The first 1-MHz clock after the sweep zero crossing causes the terminal count of the reference counter to go to logic zero, and the 640th clock causes the terminal count output to return to the logic one state. Thus the terminal count output is logic zero for exactly 640 μs.

The terminal count output is used to gate the prescaled count from the first local oscillator into the display counter. At the end of the counting period, the state of the display counter is latched into the display latch and the counter is set to -7000. It is necessary for a small time delay to be introduced into the terminal count pulse so that the display counter has settled before the output is latched into the display latch. The display counter is initially set to -7000 counts, which is the same as the full count minus 6999. This implies that 7000 counts are required to return the counter to zero. Because the 640-μs count gate allows more than 7000 counts into the display counter, the display counter will display the amount accumulated after reaching a count of zero. Therefore, the display will indicate the number of counts minus 7000.

After the reference counter has reached a count of 640, which represents a count gate of exactly 640 μs, the display counter is stopped and the result is displayed.

Setting the display counter to -7000 performs the operation of subtracting 700 MHz from the counted frequency.

The accuracy of the center frequency display is a function of not only the voltmeter, in the voltmeter method, or the frequency counter, in the frequency counter method, but the frequency accuracy of the second local oscillator and the IFs.

The actual input frequency of a two-conversion spectrum analyzer is

$$F_{in} = f_1 - f_2 - f_{IF} \tag{3-1}$$

where f_1 is the frequency of the first local oscillator, f_2 is the frequency of the second local oscillator, and f_{IF} is the frequency of the second IF.

Counting the first local oscillator frequency determines only one of the terms of Eq. (3-1), leaving the second local oscillator frequency and the last IF unknown. For a spectrum analyzer with more than two conversions, all the local oscillator frequencies as well as the last IF would be involved. To have an accurate center-frequency display by counting only the first local oscillator, the remaining local oscillators as well as the last IF must be accurate and stable.

Typically, the second and later local oscillators are crystal stabilized, and the last IF is usually set by a crystal filter that is also stable and accurate.

Counting the local oscillator requires that the local oscillator drive a digital prescaler to bring the oscillator frequency down to a range where the frequency can be handled by traditional logic. Having a sample of the local oscillator frequency in the form of a division of the local oscillator frequency allows several other useful variations of the basic spectrum analyzer. One, phase-locking the first local oscillator to provide stability, will be discussed later in this chapter. Another application of the divided local oscillator frequency is for frequency linearization.

The linearizing circuit described in Chapter 2 was the classic open-loop system, which usually required careful adjustment of resistors that interact. A superior method is to use a feedback system as shown in Fig. 3-3.

In this system, the output of the prescaler drives a monostable multivibrator that supplies a constant output pulse width. The resulting waveform is filtered to allow only the average value of the waveform to be present at the filter output. The average voltage of the resulting waveform is

$$V_{av} = tf/N \tag{3-2}$$

where V_{av} is the average voltage, t is the time of the multivibrator, f is the local oscillator frequency, and N is the division of the prescaler.

This average voltage is compared with a fixed voltage that would be a summation of the tuning or center-frequency voltage and frequency span sawtooth waveform, as shown in Fig. 3-3.

Because the relationship between voltage and frequency of Eq. (3-2) is linear, the frequency will track the comparison voltage perfectly.

As an example, assume the spectrum analyzer used throughout this text is designed to use this technique. It is beneficial to have the highest duty cycle possible correspond to the highest desired frequency of the local oscillator. In this example the highest local oscillator frequency is 1200 MHz, and a division of 128 is chosen to take advantage of inexpensive prescalers as well as to provide

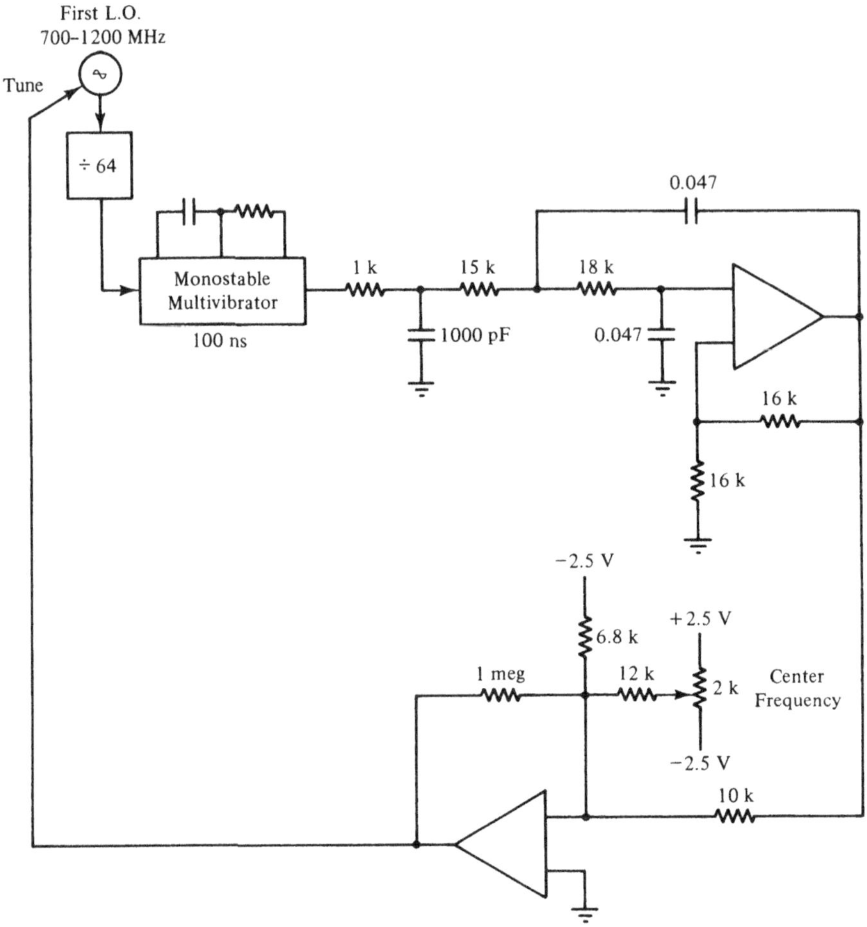

Figure 3-3
A feedback type of frequency linearizer using a monostable multivibrator.

a comfortable range of output frequencies for the frequency counter. At the highest local oscillator frequency, the prescaler output frequency is 9.375 MHz, which has a period of 106.67 ns. A monostable period of 100 ns would provide a duty cycle of 93.75% at the highest VCO frequency.

At the lowest VCO frequency, the prescaler output frequency is 5.46875 MHz, which has a period of 182.86 ns. The duty cycle at this frequency would be 54.69%.

Thus, for a monostable multivibrator output of 10 V, the filtered output would vary from 2.73 to 4.69 V for a total variation of 1.96 V.

The amount of filtering required of the pulse waveform is great. To gain an insight into the necessary filtering, the average sensitivity of the local oscillator VCO is

$$S = F/V \tag{3-3}$$

where S is the tuning sensitivity, F is the total frequency span of the VCO, and V is the variation of tuning voltage to achieve this frequency range. Equation (3-3) relates to the average tuning sensitivity; generally, the sensitivity is greater at the lower frequency end of the VCO.

Any ripple from the pulse waveform at the output of the monostable multivibrator that escapes filtering and manages to be applied to the VCO will generate sidebands. To prevent this modulation from causing a distorted display, the level of generated sidebands should be reduced to a point that will not be visible, or to a level below the dynamic range of the analyzer.

The level of sidebands generated by angle modulation of a carrier is expressed by an expansion involving Bessel functions. However, for small modulation indices, the sidebands are expressed by a simple algebraic relationship.

$$\begin{aligned} e(t) &\cong A_c \cos(\omega_c t + \beta \sin \omega_m t) \\ &= A_c \cos \omega_c t - \frac{A_c\beta}{2} \cos (\omega_c - \omega_m)t \\ &+ \frac{A_c\beta}{2} \cos(\omega_c + \omega_m)t \end{aligned} \tag{3-4}$$

where

$$\beta \sin \omega_m = \Delta\omega$$

and A_c is the amplitude of the carrier, ω_c is the frequency of the carrier, ω_m is the modulation frequency, β is the modulation index, and $\Delta\omega$ is the peak frequency deviation.

Equation 3-4 is the actual time-dependent function of the generated sideband. Since only the ratio of the amplitudes of the carrier to the generated sidebands is important for this evaluation, the ratio is evaluated.

$$\mathrm{R} = \left| \frac{-A_c\beta/2}{A_c} \right| = \frac{\beta}{2} = \frac{\Delta\omega}{2 \sin \omega_m} \tag{3-5}$$

This ratio is the instantaneous ratio that depends on the instantaneous phase of the modulating waveform. To calculate the RMS ratio and to convert from radians to frequency the following is derived:

$$R = \frac{2\pi}{\sqrt{2}} \Delta f = \sqrt{2}\, \pi\, \Delta f \tag{3-6}$$

Returning to the example analyzer, the gain constant at the ouput of the monostable multivibrator is the tuning range, 500 MHz, divided by 1.96 V, the difference between the maximum and the minimum frequency voltages, which results in a figure of 255 MHz per volt.

The maximum amount of frequency modulation allowed on the first local oscillator is calculated from Eq. (3-6) for 80-dB reduction.

$$R = 10^4 = \sqrt{2}\pi\,\Delta f \qquad \Delta f = 1.1\ \text{KHz} \tag{3-7}$$

Using the tuning constant of 255 MHz per volt results in a maximum ripple voltage at the output of the linearizer of

$$\frac{1.1\ \text{KHz}}{255\ \text{MHz/V}} = 4.3\ \mu\text{V} \tag{3-8}$$

The relative amount of energy present due to the AC components of the variable duty-cycle waveform at the monostable multivibrator output is a function of the duty cycle. The highest energy content occurs when the duty cycle is 50% and the energy is contained at the fundamental frequency. From the Fourier series of a square wave, which is a 50% duty-cycle waveform,

$$C_1 = 2V_{\text{peak}}/\pi \tag{3-9}$$

where V_{peak} is the peak voltage of the square wave and C_1 is the Fourier coefficient for the fundamental.

Using the values for the example spectrum analyzer, with a peak voltage from the monostable multivibrator of 5 V, the gain constant or tuning sensitivity of the VCO is 255 MHz/V and the RMS value of the fundamental frequency component is 3.18 V. To reduce the amplitude of the ripple due to the fundamental to less than 4.3 μV requires a reduction of 117 dB.

Happily, the difference in frequency between the scan voltage, which does not need to be greater than that necessary to produce a flicker-free display, and the output frequency from the prescaler is great. Typically a 50-Hz scan frequency is the most that will ever be needed, which is 109 thousand times less than the output of the prescaler. Since this represents more than 5 decades, a filter with a theoretical 23 dB per decade will produce the necessary attenuation.

In practice, however, a bandwidth greater than 50 Hz will be used for VCO tuning voltage to prevent lagging the VCO tuning voltage behind the sawtooth waveform; several filters, each with more than 23 dB per decade, will be used and great care will be taken in shielding and grounding to prevent sideband generation.

3.2 Phase-Locked Frequency Tuning

Perhaps the most often-used addition to the basic spectrum analyzer is phase-locked tuning. The example spectrum analyzer outlined in the previous chapter used a 700–1200-MHz first local oscillator. To achieve a narrow frequency span it is necessary to decrease the sweeping voltage to the first local oscillator and thus reduce the amount of frequency sweep. This is simple in theory; but the first local oscillator has two frequency-sweep mechanisms of its own, called short-term and long-term frequency instability.

Long-term instability would cause the spectrum to slowly drift across the display. The short-term instability would appear as a very unstable display with ragged edges and so badly distorted that it would be difficult, if not impossible, to decipher the spectrum. The narrower the dispersion, the more the frequency instability limits the ability of the analyzer to perform.

The technique used to combat frequency instability is to phase lock the first local oscillator to a stable source, usually a crystal oscillator, and sweep the second local oscillator. This can involve considerable circuitry and careful design.

Frequency stabilization is not a new technique; it was employed in spectrum analyzers before the advent of high-speed programmable dividers and modern frequency-synthesis techniques. Figure 3-4 shows a simple phase-lock method for stabilizing the frequency of the example spectrum analyzer. A crystal oscillator operating at a frequency of 1.000 MHz is fed to a step-recovery diode. This diode is a specialized form of varactor diode that has the characteristic of recovering from a conduction state very rapidly and thus generating a sudden change of current. This characteristic gives rise to another name for the diode: the "snap" diode, because of its characteristic to snap off. This very rapid turn-off generates energy at a large number of harmonics of the driving voltage, and a range of these harmonics are filtered and called a frequency "comb" because of the appearance of the spectrum.

Figure 3-4 shows a comb generator using the 1-MHz crystal oscillator, step-recovery diode, a low-pass filter, and a high-pass filter. The output of this comb generator is used to provide the low-level, RF input to a passive diode

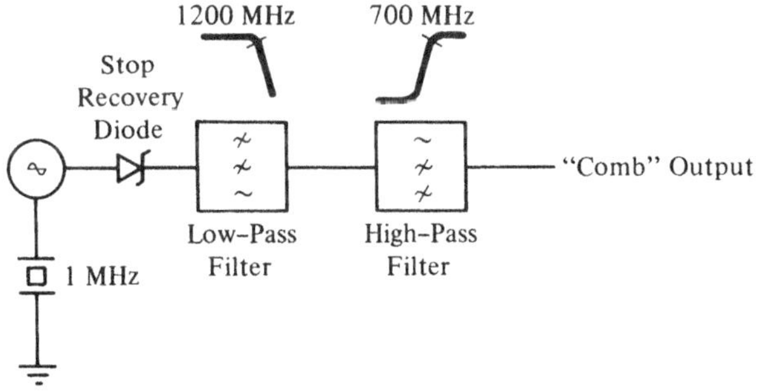

Figure 3-4
A block diagram of a comb generator for providing a large number of well-known harmonics of a crystal source.

mixer. Recall from the previous chapter that one of the two inputs to a diode-type mixer must have a considerably lower level than the other, the larger being called the local oscillator and the smaller of the two, the RF. The local oscillator input to this mixer is the same local oscillator used in the spectrum analyzer.

The IF output from the mixer is low-pass filtered so that the output bandwidth is limited to less than 500 kHz. Therefore, the output of the mixer is the difference frequency between the local oscillator and the closest frequency component in the comb. Because a frequency component of the comb less than 500 kHz is always present, the output of the filter will pass the difference frequency of only the nearest harmonic.

When the local oscillator frequency is equal to the frequency of one of the harmonics of the comb, the output of the mixer is a steady DC voltage and the mixer operates as a phase detector.

This output frequency is further filtered and fed to the local oscillator to create a phase-locked loop using the mixer as a phase detector. A simple concept indeed, but there are many difficulties and problems yet to be solved.

The characteristics of a phase-locked loop are primarily set by the loop filter. These characteristics include the ability of the loop to achieve lock from an unlocked condition, the way it approaches the lock condition, and the ability of the loop to remain locked. The ability of the loop to remove phase noise is also a function of the loop filter.

There are two basic methods of generating a loop filter. One is a passive filter in which no gain is introduced to the loop. Most spectrum analyzer applications would require an active loop filter where additional gain may be obtained, as shown in Fig. 3-5.

One parameter of the phase-locked loop that dictates other characteristics is the natural loop frequency. Essentially, if the phase-locked loop were unstable and were set into oscillation, the natural loop frequency would be the frequency at which the loop would oscillate. The natural loop frequency is

$$\omega_n = \sqrt{\frac{K_0 K_d}{\tau_1}} \tag{3-10}$$

where ω_n is the natural loop frequency, K_0 is the VCO constant in radians/second/volt, K_d is the phase detector constant in volts/radian, and τ_1 is the time constant R_1C. The natural loop frequency itself is not all that important, but it is a parameter that is involved in the setting of other loop characteristics.

The path followed by the phase-locked loop in settling to the desired frequency is set by a factor called the damping of the loop. A loop that is overdamped takes a long time to achieve lock but does it without any overshoot or oscillations. On the other hand, a loop that is underdamped achieves lock by oscillating around the desired frequency, repeatedly passing the desired frequency before settling down. The ideal compromise is called critical damping, represented by a damping factor of one, where the frequency is achieved in the

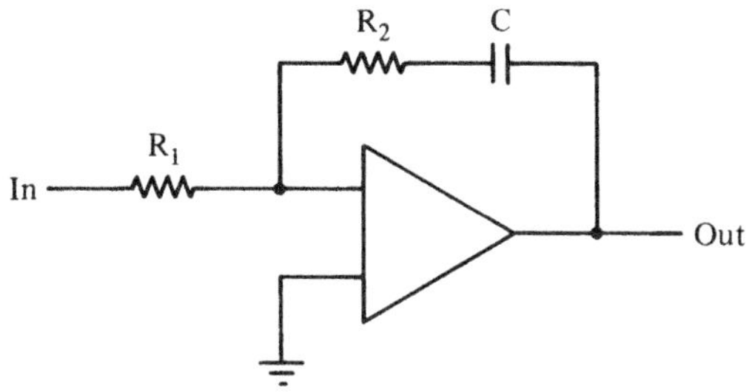

Figure 3-5
A simple loop filter with infinite DC gain for a phase-locked loop.

minimum time without oscillation or overshoot. The damping of the phase-locked loop is given by

$$\zeta = \frac{\tau_2}{2}\sqrt{\frac{K_0 K_d}{\tau_1}} = \frac{\tau_2\,\omega_n}{2} \tag{3-11}$$

where ζ is the damping factor and $\tau_2 = R_2C$.

The pull-in frequency is the amount of frequency a phase-locked loop can slew to achieve lock and is given by

$$\Delta\omega_p = 2\sqrt{\zeta\omega_m K_v} \tag{3-12}$$

where $\Delta\omega_p$ is the pull-in range and K_v is the loop gain at DC, which is

$$K_v = K_0 K_d G(0) \tag{3-13}$$

where $G(0)$ is the gain of the active loop filter at DC.

It would be possible to create a phase-locked loop without a loop amplifier or active loop filter. However, it is usually necessary to increase the DC loop gain to insure capture.

The loop filter that closes the loop must have a cutoff frequency well below 1 MHz, in this example; otherwise, sidebands due to the 1-MHz reference frequency will be present.

Although the frequencies generated by the comb generator contain components well into the VHF spectrum, the basic repetition rate of the comb is, in fact, 1 MHz and this spurious sideband will appear in the phase-locked spectrum.

When designing a phase-locked loop for a spectrum analyzer, the capture range should be greater than one-half the frequency of the comb so that the loop is guaranteed to lock on the nearest harmonic.

In the phase-locked loop used to stabilize the spectrum analyzer local oscillator, the phase detector constant is indeed a constant. The VCO, however, is not. It was discussed previously that the typical VCO (this excludes the YIG oscillator) does not have an unchanging tuning rate and for this reason a linearizer is present. But why not lump the VCO and linearizer together and create a quasi-VCO with a constant tuning rate? This would appear to solve the problem and allow a simple connection of the phase detector output to the summing amplifier, as shown in Fig. 3-1. However, the linearizer has some serious drawbacks, which render this nearly impossible. First, for many frequency-stabilization systems, the reference frequency is on the order of 1 MHz or higher, where it would be advantageous to have a loop bandwidth of 50 kHz or higher. Most linearizers do not have a bandwidth this great, as they are constructed from operational amplifiers. In addition, the linearizer is not a linear circuit but has a transfer function constructed of line segments. Thus, if the phase-locked loop attempts to lock at a frequency that happens to be at a breakpoint, the linearizer will destroy rather than enhance the linearity.

Some change in the VCO constant is acceptable while allowing the phase-locked loop to remain stable. A reasonable alternative is to add a second varactor diode that will be used only for the phase-locked loop. This allows the frequency response of the loop filter to be adjusted to suit the requirements of the phase-locked loop while avoiding the normal tuning circuits. The high-frequency components of the phase-locked loop are routed to the additional varactor, and the low-frequency components are routed to the summing amplifier.

Using Eq. 3-10, 3-11, 3-12, and 3-13, a phase-locked frequency-stabilizing system will be designed for the example spectrum analyzer.

The individual frequency components of the 1-MHz comb are on the order of -10 dBm, which provides an output from the balanced mixer, when used as a phase detector, of ± 10 mV for a -90- and $+90$-degree phase angle. This results in a phase detector constant of 3.18 millivolts per radian.

The phase detector output is filtered and fed to the first local oscillator after the linearizer circuit, as previously explained. The VCO constant is about 30 V for a 500-MHz frequency change. This results in a constant of 1.05×10^8 radians per second per volt. The natural loop frequency is set to be about 1 kHz or 6280 radians per second. In addition, the damping factor will be set to one to provide a critically damped loop. The DC gain of the active loop filter is set to 1000, which results in a capture range of

$$\Delta\omega_p = 2\sqrt{\zeta\omega_n K_v} = 2\sqrt{6.28 \times 10^3 \times 3.34 \times 10^8}$$

$$= 2.89 \text{ MHz}$$

It is evident from the value calculated for the capture range that the loop will capture the nearest harmonic.

Now that it has been determined that the loop will capture and that the natural loop frequency has been chosen, the filter parameters will be calculated.

The first of the two time constants is calculated.

$$\tau_1 = \frac{K_0 K_d}{\omega_n^2} = \frac{3.34 \times 10^5}{3.94 \times 10^7} = 8.5 \times 10^{-3}\text{sec}$$

The second time constant is

$$\tau_2 = \frac{2}{\omega_n} = \frac{2}{6.28 \times 10^3} = 3.18 \times 10^{-4}$$

Using a capacitor value of 1 μF and calculating for R_1 and R_2, the active loop filter is derived as shown in Fig. 3-5. From this figure it can be seen the values involved are within the realm of reality, and a loop filter may be constructed along these values.

Once the first local oscillator has been phase locked to a harmonic of the crystal oscillator, meaning that the oscillator frequency is N(1 MHz), where N is an integer, the second local oscillator can be swept in frequency, but not to exceed a total of 1 MHz. Therefore, the frequency span of the spectrum analyzer must be a maximum of 1 MHz before the phase lock is enabled for the example spectrum analyzer. The long and short-term frequency stability of the first local oscillator must not be such that the analyzer is useless at 1-MHz frequency span, just before the phase lock is enabled. In a practical sense, this is realistic.

The frequency stability of the second local oscillator is considerably greater than the first local oscillator. This is because the maximum tuning range of the second local oscillator is less than the first local oscillator, and it is also at a lower center frequency. Much of the frequency instability comes from the varactor diodes in the VCO, and a relatively small tuning range has a proportionately lower frequency instability.

Although the described phase-locked method of frequency stabilization has been used in spectrum analyzers for many years, it has been difficult to apply and to thoroughly solve all of the problems attendant with the technique.

One serious problem is that the frequency of the first local oscillator can only be a multiple of the frequency of the reference crystal. In the example spectrum analyzer, when the first local oscillator is phase locked, the frequency can exist only in multiples of 1 MHz. Before the phase lock is enabled, the first local oscillator frequency is set by analog voltages; and when the phase lock is enabled the frequency of the first local oscillator will jump as much as 500 kHz in either direction—up or down. This implies the spectrum analyzer trace will jump in an unknown direction when the frequency span is reduced to a point where the phase-locked system is enabled.

There are several methods of solving this problem. One method allows the frequency of the crystal to be moved slightly so that the frequency component of the comb is equal to the center frequency of the first local oscillator.

The phase-locked loop system as shown in Fig. 3-6 is programmed by the value of N as set into the programmable divider. This value is determined by counting the VCO frequency, perhaps by an on-the-fly method as described earlier, and loading that number into the programmable divider. Therefore, the phase-locked loop will synthesize the frequency as it was counted before the phase-locked loop was enabled.

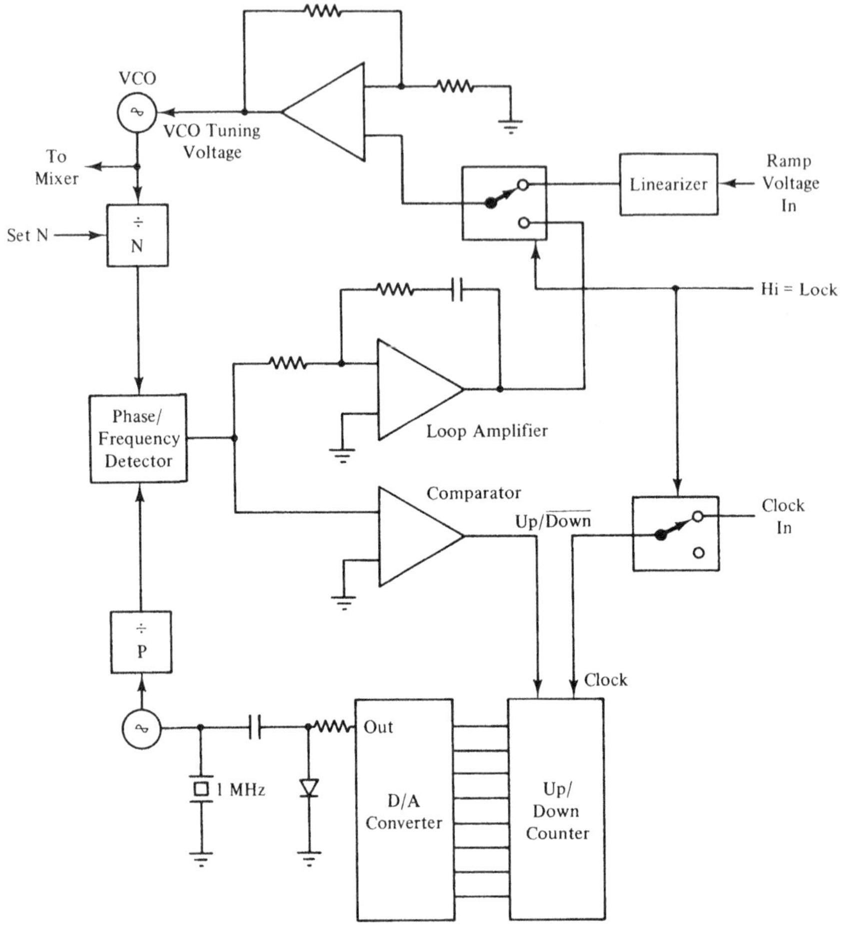

Figure 3-6
A phase-locked loop system using a variable reference frequency to prevent the local oscillator from jumping in frequency when the phase lock is enabled.

Initially, the reference is locked to the local oscillator. The up/down counter will count up or down, depending on the state of the phase detector. It will thus apply increasing or decreasing values to the D/A converter that controls the reverse bias on a varactor diode and hence "pull" the frequency of the crystal oscillator. The switch, S1, controls the frequency of the VCO from the linearizer; and the frequency of the reference oscillator is varied, to attempt phase lock. The up/down counter will probably not be able to achieve a good quality phase lock. The purpose of attempting to phase lock the crystal oscillator is to have NF_{ref}/P near the center of the display by varying the value of F_{ref}. Once the reference frequency is near phase lock to the frequency of the VCO, the switch S1 is changed in state and the control of the VCO is from the phase-locked loop. Since the reference frequency was varied so that the phase-locked condition was near the center of the frequency span, the display should move only slightly to achieve a solid phase lock.

The reference frequency is usually generated with a crystal oscillator. In the example spectrum analyzer, the amount the crystal must be "pulled" from the nominal frequency is one part in 1400 at the lowest frequency, which is beyond the comfortable limit to pull a quartz crystal.

A ceramic resonator could be used as the frequency-controlling element in the reference oscillator. This device has a *Q* considerably lower than a quartz resonator but high enough to significantly reduce the short-term and long-term frequency drift of the local oscillator.

A second solution to the problem is to divide 1-MHz crystal frequency by a factor of two and generate a comb with component frequencies separated by 500 kHz. Therefore, the most the reference frequency must be pulled is one part in 2800 from the nominal for the example spectrum analyzer, which is achievable. In this case, the phase-locked frequencies will be in steps of 500 kHz, which requires the local oscillator to have a reasonable short-term and long-term frequency stability at a 500-kHz dispersion. This is, of course, more difficult than the 1-MHz example given earlier, but not out of reach of practical circuits.

The universal difficulty in the design and construction of a spectrum analyzer is the generation of spurious responses, and it is not different with any frequency-stabilizing system.

The crystal oscillator that generates the drive for the step-recovery diode, and ultimately provides the frequency reference, must provide a relatively high-level signal to drive the diode. This is because the efficiency of the step-recovery diode comb generator is rather low. Remember that a 1-MHz signal must provide literally hundreds of signals at hundreds of megahertz, which requires that the input energy be spread out over a wide range of frequencies.

Whenever a large signal must be generated, there is the attendant problem of containment. Extreme care must be taken to assure that the 1-MHz oscillator and any harmonics falling in the input frequency range of the analyzer are not allowed to cause spurious responses.

This is not an insignificant amount of shielding. If 0.5 W is required to adequately drive the step recovery diode, and this is not usual, and the spectrum analyzer noise floor is -100 dBm, which is also not usual, 127 dB of isolation between the oscillator and the spectrum analyzer input is required. Careful shielding and filtering of leads can achieve this level of isolation; spectrum analyzers have used this method of frequency stabilization for many years. As test equipment becomes more complex, smaller, and portable, the extra shielding and the power required for the step-recovery diode becomes more of a problem.

There are alternate methods of frequency stabilization that involve digital frequency-synthesizer techniques. The development of digital frequency dividers extending well into the VHF and UHF regions allow more effective frequency stabilization of spectrum analyzers.

The comb generator and phase-locked loop represent the frequency stabilization method for what is actually an analog spectrum analyzer. What if the first local oscillator were phase locked at all times? Would the frequency stability be superb for all frequency spans?

The answer, of course, is yes. But how is this achieved?

The ideal method would be to synthesize, by phase locking, all local oscillators.

To gain an understanding into the frequency steps of the synthesizer required, consider the narrowest frequency span desired of the analyzer.

Because the first local oscillator of the spectrum analyzer will assume discrete steps, the display is quantized, which is to say the display is created from discrete data points. If the display is to have sufficient resolution, 8, 9, or 10 bits are required, which would provide 256, 512, or 1024 data points. The 256-point display is usable but appears quantized. The 512 data points still appears quantized but is much less objectionable, while 1024 data points is very smooth and does not appear digitized.

To determine the minimum frequency step of the synthesized first local oscillator, the minimum desired dispersion is divided by the total number of steps desired or

$$F_s = \Delta f / 2^N \tag{3-14}$$

where F_s is the frequency step, Δf is the frequency span, and N is the number of bits of the horizontal resolution.

To gain an insight into how this will affect the synthesizer design, assume the example synthesizer will have a minimum frequency span of 10 kHz with 9-bit resolution. Therefore, the frequency synthesizer step is

$$10{,}000/512 = 19.5 \text{ Hz} \tag{3-15}$$

A synthesizer with a 19.5-Hz frequency step at a frequency of 700–1200 MHz is very difficult to design. This is not to imply that such a design is not possible but that it involves a considerable amount of circuitry. To alleviate the design requirements, the first local oscillator will be varied in frequency for frequency spans greater than 500 kHz and the second local oscillator frequency will be varied for frequency spans less than 500 kHz.

Using this technique, the frequency synthesizer step is

$$500{,}000/512 = 976.5625 \text{ Hz} \tag{3-16}$$

The first local oscillator is synthesized using a phase-locked loop with a programmable divider rather than locking to a harmonic of a crystal as previously described. A block diagram of this method is shown in Fig. 3-7. The first

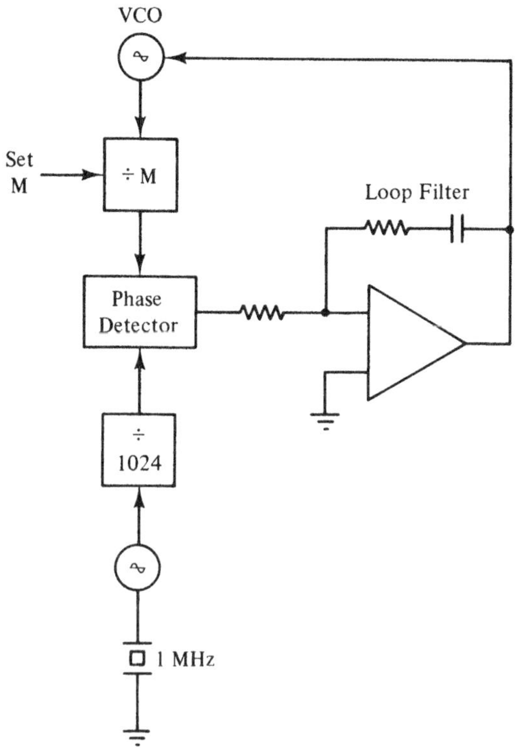

Figure 3-7
A simple single loop phase-locked system for stabilizing the local oscillator of a spectrum analyzer. This method has difficulties that are nearly impossible to overcome with practical circuits.

local oscillator is swept in frequency by simply changing the value of *M* and causing the oscillator frequency to change. The reference frequency is about 1 kHz and *M* is very large, about 700,000–1,200,000, which will restrict the performance of this loop. Because of the low reference frequency, it will be very difficult to achieve wide dispersions without changing either the reference frequency, the loop filter bandwidth, or both.

In summary, a single-loop phase-locked loop frequency-stabilization system has insurmountable problems and is not suited for this application.

Figure 3-8 shows a different method of synthesizing the first local oscillator of a spectrum analyzer. Although shown for the example analyzer with a 700–1200-MHz first local oscillator, the technique is applicable to spectrum analyzers with considerably higher local oscillator frequencies.

Several important criteria must be met when designing a phase-locked frequency synthesizer for spectrum analyzer use. First, all phase-locked loop reference frequencies must be as high as practical. This is necessary to insure that

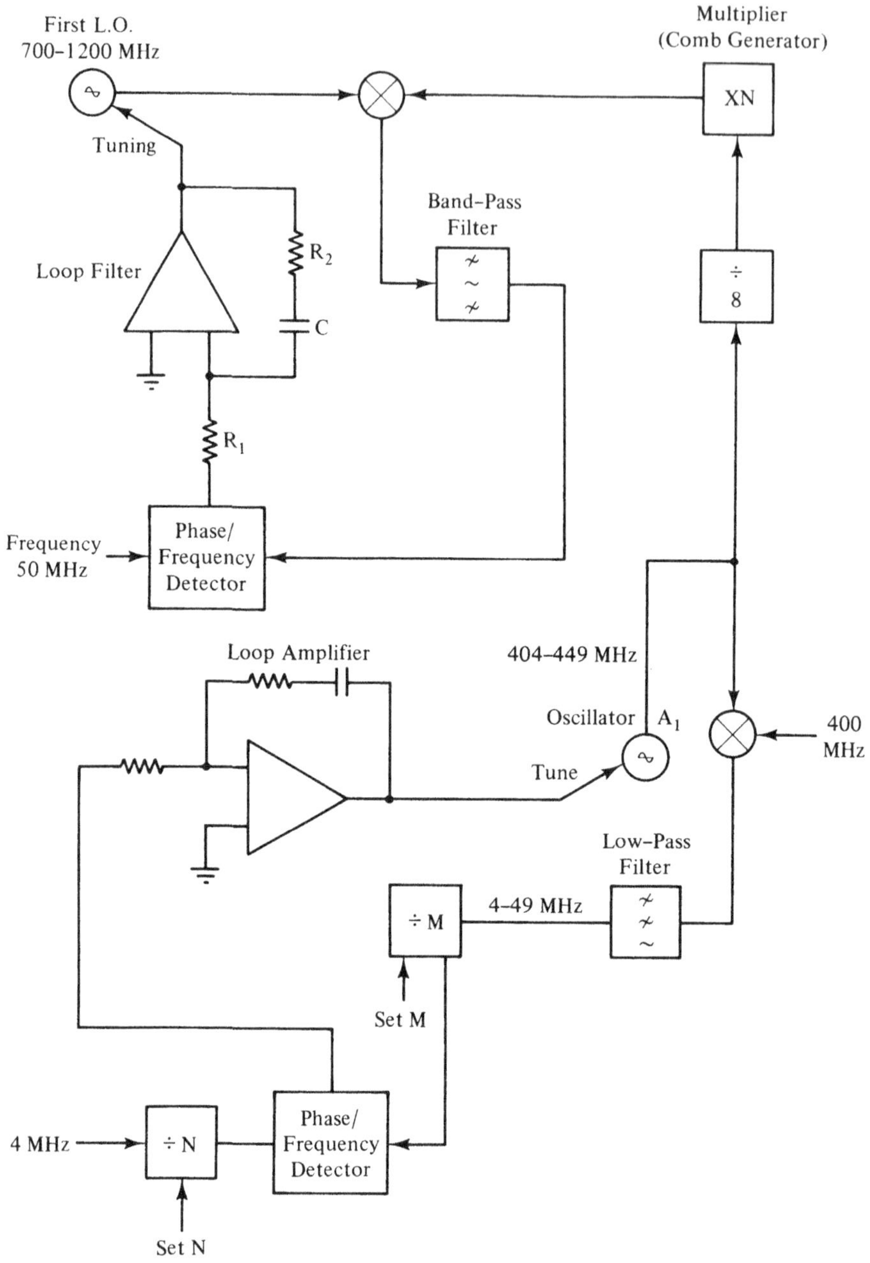

Figure 3-8
A complete phase-locked system for a spectrum analyzer. The added complexity from Fig. 3-7 is necessary to overcome the significant difficulties of the simpler system.

the phase-locked loop bandwidth is sufficiently high to make a significant reduction in the phase noise of the local oscillator and also to insure that frequency changes are rapid, so as not to hinder the sweeping of the analyzer. A sufficiently high reference frequency permits a wide-bandwidth loop filter while achieving sufficient reduction of reference sidebands.

A second criterion is that the variation of loop gain must not be so great that there are noticeable differences in loop behavior between frequencies.

Finally, the frequencies involved must be compatible with available technology. As an example, mixing is possible well into gigahertz region, whereas a phase detector at this frequency is difficult.

The method of synthesizing the first local oscillator of the example spectrum analyzer uses one phase-locked loop other than the phase-locked first local oscillator. The oscillator A_1 is mixed with an accurate offset frequency of 400 MHz, which is generated from a crystal-controlled source. The difference frequency is low-pass filtered and divided by a factor of *M*, which is a variable. This is fed to a phase detector along with a reference frequency of 4 MHz, also from a crystal source, divided by integers between the values of 10 and 23. This results in a reference frequency of 173.9–400 kHz, depending on the value of *M* and *N*. This reference frequency is sufficiently high to satisfy the requirements outlined previously. The output of the phase/frequency detector is fed to a loop filter and to the VCO, A_1, to close the loop.

The frequency of the VCO, A_1, is

$$F_1 = 4M/N + 400 \text{ MHz} \tag{3-17}$$

where F_1 is the frequency of the VCO, A_1, and M and N are the integers of Fig. 3-8.

The output frequency of the VCO, A_1, is divided by 8 and fed to a harmonic generator that provides a comb using a step-recovery diode. Similar to the phase-locked stabilization system described previously, a frequency comb is fed to the RF port of mixer while the local oscillator is fed to the LO port of the mixer. Unlike the simple phase-lock system previously described, the mixer is not used as a phase detector but as a mixer passing a range of frequencies, which is also in keeping with the criteria presented above.

Because the RF port of the mixer is a comb of frequencies, a number of frequencies of the local oscillator provide a nominal 50-MHz output and allow the loop to lock. The local oscillator must be tuned using an analog method so that the difference frequency is within the passband of the filter.

The analog tuning is arranged such that the value of *N*, when selecting the *N*th harmonic, is the same as that used for the divide-by-*N* between the 4.00-MHz reference frequency and the phase detector. Therefore, the value of the *N*th harmonic of the comb is

$$F = M/2 + 50N \tag{3-18}$$

where F is the frequency of the local oscillator in megahertz.

Notice that an increment in the value of M produces a 500-kHz change in the frequency of F, while an increment in the value of N causes a 50-MHz change in the frequency of F. For a continuous change of frequency without gaps, M must change by 100 to fill in the gaps between the 50-MHz steps provided by a change of N.

The selected harmonic, which has a frequency defined by Eq. (3-18), is heterodyned with the spectrum analyzer local oscillator such that the selected harmonic is greater in frequency than the local oscillator, and an IF nominally 50 MHz is filtered. This IF is compared to a 50-MHz reference in a phase/frequency detector. The output of the phase/frequency detector feeds a loop filter and is returned to the spectrum analyzer to close the loop. The equation for the frequency of the first local oscillator of the example spectrum analyzer is

$$F_{LO} = M/2 + 50N - 50 \tag{3-19}$$

where F_{LO} is the local oscillator frequency in megahertz.

There is some latitude in the selection of the values M and N; but to satisfy the criteria outlined previously, M will span from 24 to 123, which requires N to span from 10 to 23.

As an example, to stabilize a local oscillator frequency of 500 MHz, which would represent "zero" frequency in the example spectrum analyzer, requires the value of N to be 10 and of M to be 100. To stabilize frequencies above 500 MHz, the value of M is increased to the maximum of 123 while N remains at 10. This results in 500-kHz increments to 511.5 MHz. To synthesize 512 MHz, N is increased to 11 and M is reduced to 24, M's minimum value.

The range of frequency of the VCO, A_1, is determined by substituting the minimum and maximum values of M and N into Eq. (3-17). The frequency F_1 is highest when M is the greatest and N is the least, which occurs when $M = 123$ and $N = 10$ and results in a frequency of 449.2 MHz. The lowest frequency for F_1 is when M is the least and N is the greatest, which occurs for $M = 24$ and $N = 23$; this represents a frequency of 404.17 MHz. This results in a maximum-to-minimum frequency ratio of 1.1, which is a relatively small tuning ratio for a VCO. This small tuning ratio coupled with a reference frequency of 174–400 kHz results in a low phase-noise spectrum for the VCO, A_1.

The phase noise is multiplied by

$$K = 20 \log Q \tag{3-20}$$

where K is the multiplication of the phase noise Q is the frequency multiplier. As an example, the greatest multiplication occurs when $N = 23$. Since the VCO A_1 is first divided by 8 then multiplied by 23, the total multiplication is 2.88. If the phase noise of the VCO A_1 is -90 dBc at 1 kHz removed from the carrier, after division by 8 and multiplication the phase noise is 9.2 dB greater at the same offset frequency, or -80.8 dBc at 1 kHz removed.

Rather than sweeping the second local oscillator, the frequency-stabilization system presented may be modified to include a fine-tune capability to the 50-MHz offset of Eq. (3-19). This can be done very simply by sweeping the 50-MHz reference. because the reference is swept by only 500 kHz and at a center frequency of 50 MHz, linearity and stability are easily achieved.

The inclusion of a microprocessor has drastically changed the way many test systems have functioned. The microprocessor in the spectrum analyzer, not to be confused with all-digital FFT analyzer, has made the instrument an even more powerful tool.

Perhaps the most significant improvement the microprocessor has made in the spectrum analyzer is to tie together the frequency span, the scan rate, the IF filters, the input attenuator, the IF filter, and the video filter so that the operator can obtain the most accurate picture of a spectrum. Before the microprocessor-controlled spectrum analyzer, operator errors prevented accurate spectrum displays on a regular basis.

3.3 Microwave Spectrum Analyzers

The example spectrum analyzer was provided with an input low-pass filter, which removed the image and permitted a spurious-free spectrum display. In the example analyzer, the image frequency range was from 1400 to 1900 MHz. If the low-pass filter were eliminated, two input frequency ranges would exist simultaneously: 0–500 MHz and 1400–1900 MHz. If a bandpass filter with a passband of 1400–1900 MHz were inserted, the spectrum analyzer would provide this additional frequency range. If the input filter were switched from the 500-MHz low-pass filter to a 1400–1900 MHz and 1400 MHz added to the spectrum analyzer dial, the result would be a two-band analyzer. There is a significant problem in that the range from 500 to 1400 MHz lacks coverage.

Most frequency mixers are capable of converting a frequency by not only the fundamental frequency of the local oscillator but, to varying degrees, by the harmonics of the local oscillator. Generally, this is not a desirable characteristic, and mixers are designed to eliminate harmonic mixing. As an example, a very useful characteristic of balanced mixers is an inherent rejection of mixing by even multiples of the local oscillator.

The use of a mixer that does not reject mixing by harmonics allows the range of the spectrum analyzer to be extended by allowing frequency ranges of the form

$$F_{\text{in}} = NF_{\text{LO}} \pm F_{\text{IF}} \tag{3-21}$$

where F_{in} is the input frequency of the analyzer, F_{LO} is the local oscillator frequency, F_{IF} is the first IF frequency, and N is any integer.

The level of the local oscillator signal of the spectrum analyzer is required to be considerably greater than the level of any input signal level. This is so that the diode conduction is controlled by the local oscillator signal only and not by the input signal. For a very large local oscillator signal, the mixer diode(s) would be in either an "on" or "off" state and would be equivalent to a switch. If the local oscillator signal were a perfect sine wave, the duty cycle of the local oscillator would be exactly 50%. This is equivalent to multiplying the input signal by a square wave that has only odd harmonics.

Usually the local oscillator is not a perfect sine wave, and the diodes do not instantaneously change from nonconducting to conducting, thus permitting mixing by other than odd harmonics.

Returning to the example analyzer, if the input were mixed with the third harmonic of the 700–1200-MHz local oscillator, corresponding to $N = 3$, a frequency range of 1400–2900 MHz could be accommodated by using the difference frequency, and a range of 2800–4300 MHz by using the sum. Notice, the frequency range now covers from 1400 to 4300 MHz without gaps, as well as the original 0 to 500 MHz. The range from 500 to 1400 MHz is still not covered.

Using the second harmonic of the local oscillator, or $N = 2$ of Eq. (3-19), would provide an input range of 700–1700 MHz using the difference and 2100–3100 MHz using the sum frequency.

The local oscillator would feed through every range where the oscillator reached 700 MHz. This has been referred to previously as the "zero" frequency. When these other ranges are used, the local oscillator feedthrough does not occur at zero but at multiples of the first IF, which in this case are 1400 MHz, 2100 MHz, 2800 MHz, etc. The spurious "zero" frequency can be supressed by restricting the bands of the harmonic mixing spectrum analyzer to not include a 700-MHz local oscillator frequency for harmonic mixing.

Combining the inputs allowed by mixing with both the sum and differences of the second and third harmonics of the local oscillator, the frequency range of the example spectrum analyzer may be extended as shown in Table 3-1.

The local oscillator frequency range for the first band is 700–1200 MHz. The second band is from 750 to 1200 MHz; the third band, from 733.333 to 1200 MHz; and the fourth band, from 725 to 1200 MHz. The result is three overlapping frequency ranges from 800 to 4300 MHz with no spurious zero-frequency responses.

Table 3-1

Range 1	0–500 MHz	1XLO - IF
Range 2	800–1700 MHz	2XLO - IF
Range 3	1500–2900 MHz	3XLO - IF
Range 4	2200–4300 MHz	4XLO - IF

Notice that in Table 3-1 the provided bands were based only on a harmonic of the local oscillator minus the IF. Bands based on the sum of the local oscillator harmonic and the IF are also possible. These bands would be useful if the spectrum of interest lay in two of the bands outlined in Table 3-1. Then a sum frequency range could be used.

To display the spectrum obtained by using harmonics of the local oscillator, certain corrections must be made to the display.

Clearly, the center-frequency dial must be corrected. The original spectrum analyzer covered from 0 to 500 MHz. Band 2 covers from 700 to 1700 MHz, which requires that the original dial readout be multiplied by two and 700 MHz added. In addition, the frequency scan would be twice the rate of the original 0–500-MHz range. This is corrected by simply dividing the scan voltage by two. In addition, the mixer loss would be greater for harmonic mixing and the amplitude of the displayed signal would be corrected. This is handled in a simple fashion. For a logarimthic display, to correct for a constant loss the position of the display is simply shifted, using a constant DC level, by an amount of additional loss acquired by the mixer due to the harmonic mixing.

As an example, if the loss of the mixer is 7 dB greater using the third harmonic relative to the fundamental, the display is simply raised by the equivalent of 7 dB. This has the effect of raising the noise floor, which is correct because the noise figure of the spectrum analyzer is higher for the harmonic mixing and raises the signals by 6 dB, thus compensating for the additional loss.

Many early microwave spectrum analyzers did not have bandpass filters to provide for the harmonic mixing bands. This resulted in a large number of spurious signals present in the spectrum display. The required filters were microwave filters, which were quite expensive. A large number were required, as well as methods of switching—also expensive at microwave frequencies. Therefore it was up to the operator to either provide filters or sort out the large number of spurious signals and interpret the display.

Table 3-1 has a gap in the frequency coverage from 500 to 800 MHz. The usual method of filling this gap was to provide a second IF frequency for the missing band. As an example, if an auxiliary IF of 1000 MHz were provided and heterodyned with the second harmonic of the local oscillator, a frequency range of 400 to 900 MHz could be covered using the second harmonic of the 700- to 950-MHz range of local oscillator. In this example, to prevent a spurious response, the local oscillator must not pass 1000 MHz.

A continuously tuned spectrum analyzer could be created from the bands outlined in Table 3.1 if the local oscillator could be tuned from one frequency range to another while the input filters were switched. While in theory this may be done, the logistics of rapidly switching the input filters, where a broad range of frequencies are covered, is difficult.

An improved harmonic mixing microwave spectrum analyzer uses a YIG bandpass filter ahead of the mixer. Like the YIG oscillator, the YIG filter is current tuned and is made to track the input frequency of the spectrum analyzer. The YIG filter can be made to cover a broad range of frequencies while maintaining a good linearity between the control current and the center frequency and maintaining a high Q.

The tracking YIG filter, which is often called a tracking preselector, can maintain a bandwidth of a few percent of the selected center frequency while maintaining a current-to-frequency relationship within a few tenths of a percent.

By using the tracking preselector, a broad-band microwave spectrum analyzer may be designed using electronically switched bands without the necessity of switching input filters. In addition, because the bandwidth of the YIG preselector is narrow, a relatively low IF may be used without excessive image response.

3.4 Microprocessor Control of the Spectrum Analyzer

There are many advantages to controlling some of the settings of a spectrum analyzer to enhance the operation of the unit. Perhaps the first "automatic" feature to appear in a spectrum analyzer was the automatic setting of the IF bandwidth and the scan rate as a function of the selected frequency span. This had been done in earlier spectrum analyzers by simply mechanically coupling the filter switch to the span switch so that the filter selected for the span setting would allow a fixed scan rate that was sufficiently fast to provide a flicker-free display.

The advantage of the microprocessor is the ability to select any frequency span; the microprocessor selects the narrowest IF filter that allows the scan rate to provide a flicker-free display.

In the spectrum analyzer there is usually a fixed number of IF filters and frequency span settings. It would be possible to set practically any span, but odd frequency spans would make the analyzer difficult to use. Typically, a spectrum analyzer would have the familiar 5-2-1 sequence for frequency span and a 10-3-1 sequence for the IF filters. Other sequences are possible but these are the most popular. The IF filter bandwidth is usually set to be a small percentage of the entire display, typically 1% or less. The scan rate is then adjusted to be as great as possible, to provide a flicker-free display.

For the nonstorage spectrum analyzer (storage in this sense is digital storage rather than a storage cathode ray tube), the scan repetition rate must be sufficiently fast to prevent an annoying flicker. The repetition rate is the reciprocal of the sum of the scan time and the retrace time. Typically, the retrace time is less than 10% of the total scan time.

Shown below is a table of the frequency span and IF filter for an analyzer using the IF bandwidths described above. A scan time of 10 ms for trace would be sufficiently slow to prevent scan loss for any combination shown.

Frequency Span	IF Filter
1000 MHz	1 MHz
500 MHz	1 MHz
200 MHz	300 kHz
100 MHz	300 kHz
50 MHz	100 kHz
20 MHz	100 kHz
10 MHz	30 kHz
5 MHz	30 kHz
2 MHz	10 kHz
1 MHz	10 kHz
500 kHz	10 kHz
200 kHz	3 kHz
100 kHz	3 kHz

Some of the less visible tasks handled by the microprocessor are the manipulations of the internal switching of the analyzer. In the example of the microwave analyzer, where the frequency and amplitude display had to be manipulated to correct for the effects of harmonic mixing, the microprocessor would "invisibly" handle these tasks. Dialing a desired center frequency would result in the correct display while the processor selected the desired harmonic, corrected the frequency display, set the amplitude correction, etc.

For spectrum analyzers using a digital display, mathematical operations such as subtracting one display from another, calculating a linear display from a log display, time averaging, etc., are handled by the microprocessor. This will be discussed in the next section.

3.5 Digital Display Storage

The effects of excessive frequency-scan rate were outlined in Chapter 2. There are applications when a very slow frequency-scan rate is necessary, such as to produce a line spectrum or when fine resolution is required. These applications require a method of storing the spectrum trace for viewing, as the update rate is much lower than that which produces a flicker-free display.

Early spectrum analyzers used either storage cathode ray tubes or very long-persistence phosphors on a conventional cathode ray tube screen. Although there are many storage and long-persistence cathode ray tubes in regular use, the newer design spectrum analyzers are using a digital storage technique.

Generally, the digital storage for a spectrum analyzer uses techniques similar to a digital storage oscilloscope. Unlike the digital storage oscilloscope, however, the spectrum analyzer does not require a significant writing speed or bandwidth. Also, there may not be trigger circuits, dual trace, vertical attenuators, etc. The digital storage for a spectrum analyzer may operate from the internally generated sweep voltage and derives the vertical deflection from detected log video or the linear output from the IF amplifier.

As shown in Fig. 3-9, the digital storage requires that the video signal be digitized and the data stored in a memory in sequential memory locations. These locations may be written at a slow rate, depending on the sweep speed of the spectrum analyzer, and read out and displayed at a faster rate.

The quality of the display depends on the number of bits used for the data conversion. In the discussion of the frequency-synthesized spectrum analyzer, the point was made that an eight-bit resolution looks digitized, a nine-bit resolution still appears digitized but is much cleaner, and a 10-bit resolution is as good as practically any analog display. Therefore, the detected log video, or linear output, from the IF amplifier is digitized to 10 bits.

Practically any method of A/D conversion is suitable for converting the detected IF output for storage. If the aspect ratio of the display is 1 to 1, which would be suitable for a modern spectrum analyzer, there would be a 10-bit resolution on both the vertical and horizontal axis. This implies that 1024 A/D conversions would be required per frequency sweep. As previously discussed, a 50-Hz sweep rate would provide a flicker-free display, which translates to an 18-ms trace with a 2-ms retrace. At this rate, a complete A/D conversion would have to be made within 17.6 μs. An A/D converter with this speed is not difficult to design; even low-cost monolithic converters are capable of this level of performance.

The address of the memory is a function of the horizontal or X axis of the spectrum analyzer display, while the value of the vertical or Y axis is stored in the memory location in question. Therefore, the memory is stored sequentially—that is, from location 9 to the highest address of the memory.

The memory is loaded with the date for each sweep of the spectrum analyzer. The data may be stored from a single sweep or from repetitive sweeps. The data is read from the memory on a continuous basis at a constant rate. The readout rate is fast enough to provide a display without noticeable flicker, or flicker-free.

If a digital storage were retrofitted to a conventional "analog" spectrum analyzer, the horizontal sawtooth waveform would be digitized and used as the memory address. In a fully synthesized analyzer—that is, where the spectrum analyzer is always phase locked and where the frequency is always under digital control—the analyzer is frequency swept by incrementing a digital number, which is used to program the synthesizer. This digital number may also be used to address the memory in the digital storage.

The memory is constantly accessed to retrieve the data for the display. Also, the memory is accessed to write the latest data. Therefore, the memory is shared by the display, which accesses the memory for the display update while the latest data is constantly being written into the memory.

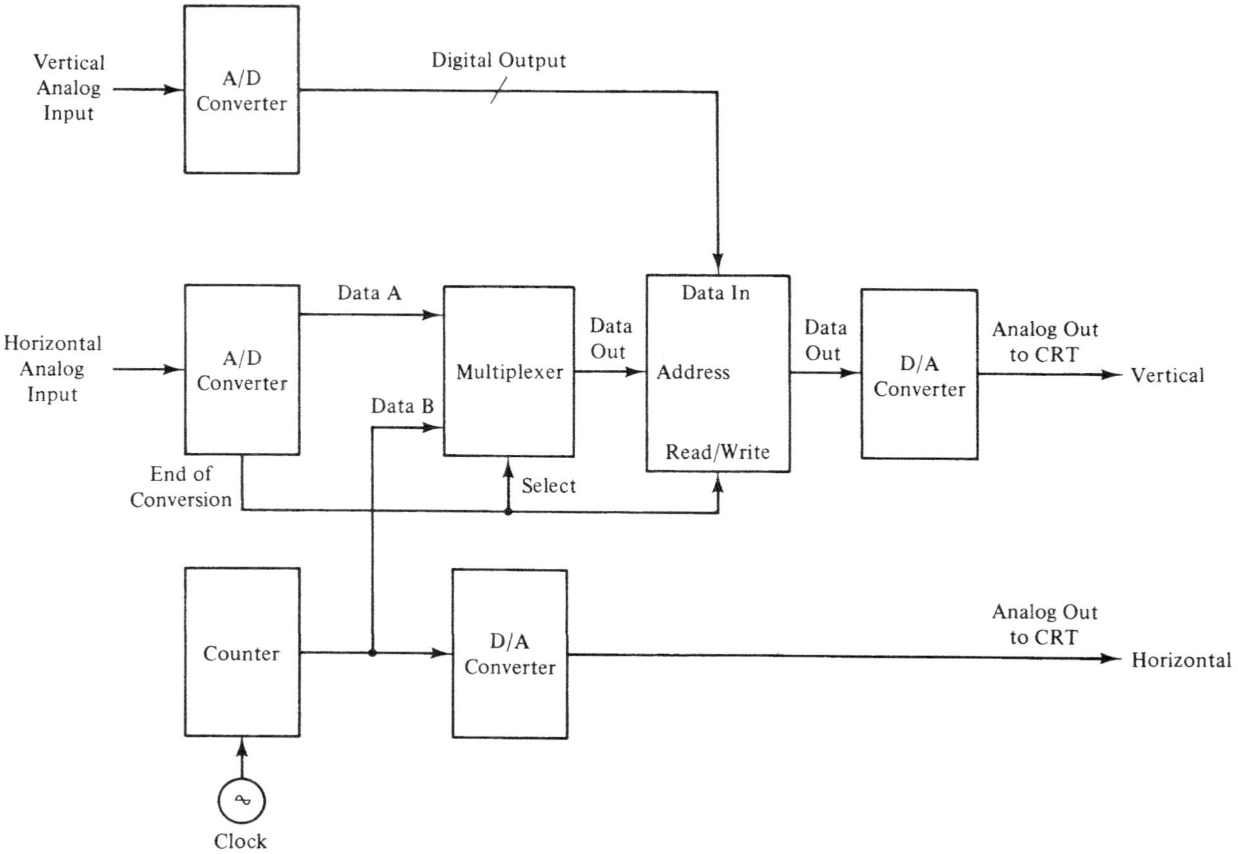

Figure 3-9
A digital storage system for storing spectrum analyzer traces.

A dual-port RAM would be a suitable device for the memory used in a digital display. However, the relatively slow speeds required of the memory for the digital display allows a conventional RAM to be used with multiplexing to share the read and write functions.

Referring to Figure 3-8, a data multiplexer is used to switch the memory address from read to write. The data input and output are shared by allowing the data from the A/D converter to assume the high impedance state while the data is read the display latch. When data is to be stored in the memory, the read function is temporarily halted. This temporary halt in the display of data is for a very short time period and does not have a significant effect on the display.

The horizontal drive for the cathode ray tube is derived from a D/A converter. When the display is halted because of a write cycle, the horizontal drive is also temporarily halted to allow the write cycle.

Interesting data manipulation can take place once the data has been written into the memory. One simple application is the ability to store two traces in the memory and compare the two on the oscilloscope screen.

To do this, the memory is split into two halves. This would produce only one-half the resolution when two independent traces are stored. As previously explained, 10 bits of resolution is as good as analog and nine bits is not bad. If it is necessary to retain full resolution for the two traces, then additional memory must be provided.

Also, it would be possible to subtract or add the two stored waveforms. This has a very important application for correcting a reference-level variation. Assume that a spectrum is being analyzed through a test fixture. The fixture has a certain frequency response, and this is stored in one of the memories. The device to be analyzed is placed in the test fixture and the frequency-response trace is added to it. Therefore, the spectrum of the device in the fixture may be evaluated in spite of the lack of a flat frequency response of the fixture.

Also, data can be read from the memory into a computer or a printer for further processing.

Review Questions for Chapter 3

1. What are some of the methods of displaying the center frequency of a spectrum analyzer? What are the relative merits of each method?
2. What are some of the significant difficulties involved when counting the first local oscillator to generate a frequency display?
3. Determine the minimum count gate time required to display the center frequency of a 1-GHz spectrum analyzer to within 0.1%.
4. If the maximum sweep rate is 100 Hz, with an 8-ms sweep and a 2-ms retrace what percentage of the total display would represent the counting period? Compare this to the display resolution.

5. If a fixed modulus prescaler is used to divide the local oscillator frequency of the analyzer described in problem 3 by a factor of 4, what would the required count gate period be? As in problem 4, what percentage of the trace would this represent? Compare this to the required accuracy. Is this consistent with the required frequency display resolution?
6. For a spectrum analyzer with a local oscillator frequency from 1150 to 2150 MHz and a first IF of 1150 MHz, what mathematical operation must be taken with the counted frequency before it is displayed?
7. If a pulse-width discriminator type of frequency linearizer were to be used with the spectrum analyzer of problem 6 where the first local oscillator frequency is divided by a fixed modulus of 128 before the linearizer, what would be a suitable pulse width for the discriminator?
8. If the pulse amplitude from the pulse-width discriminator were 10 volts, how much filtering would be required to reduce the sidebands generated by 90 dB?
9. When using a comb generator for phase locking the first local oscillator, what are some of the precautions required to prevent the generation of spurious signals?
10. What is the capture range of a phase-locked loop with a damping factor of 1, a natural loop frequency of 100 kHz, and loop gain of 60 dB?
11. What are some of the disadvantages of phase locking to harmonics of a crystal oscillator to stabilize a local oscillator? How can these be overcome?
12. If a local oscillator is to be fully synthesized to sweep from 100 MHz per division to 50 kHz per division with 10 bits of horizontal resolution, what would be the required frequency steps? Is this practical?
13. What is harmonic mixing and how may it increase the frequency range of a spectrum analyzer?
14. Why are corrections in the vertical and horizontal displays required when harmonic mixing is used?
15. What device may be used to eliminate spurious responses when harmonic mixing is used?

4

Spectrum Analyzer Applications

Perhaps the first question to come to mind after reading the title of this chapter is "Applications? Isn't the spectrum analyzer used only for viewing spectra?" No, the spectrum analyzer may be used for much more than just viewing the spectrum of a signal under test.

This chapter will discuss the techniques for viewing spectra such as methods of protecting the spectrum analyzer from errors and damage, checking for internally generated spurious responses, and so on. In addition, several other nonspectrum applications of the spectrum analyzer will be discussed.

4.1 Measuring Spectra

To measure the spectrum of a signal, one would be naive to believe it is simply a matter of plugging the unknown signal into the spectrum analyzer and viewing the spectrum. Selections of the proper IF bandwidth, video bandwidth, scan rate, and RF attenuator are necessary for an accurate and reliable spectrum display. However, a spectrum analyzer is an expensive and fragile tool and a cavalier attitude about using the instrument has led to a large number of spectrum analyzers being damaged.

The most important precaution an operator can take before connecting an unknown signal to a spectrum analyzer is to determine the nature of the signal to be measured.

The RF input to a spectrum analyzer connects to an attenuator and then through a low-pass filter to the input mixer. Most input attenuators can handle a watt or two, and the input low-pass filter could probably handle much more power. The input mixer, on the other hand, will most likely be damaged, if not totally destroyed, when presented with a power of a watt or more.

Therefore, to provide the most protection to the input mixer, the input attenuator should be placed in the position of highest attenuation before the signal is applied.

If the input attenuator can handle a watt or two and can provide an attenuation of 50 or 60 dB, reducing the power of 1 W to 10 μW, well below the burnout point of the mixer, is the analyzer protected? Well, not quite. One serious problem when measuring some RF systems is the presence of voltages other than RF. As an example, it is not unusual in cable television amplifiers to supply the power to the amplifier by transmitting 60-Hz power through the same coaxial cable that provides an input or output signal. Therefore, some cable television signals contain not only RF in the VHF and UHF range but also a large 60-Hz voltage. More than one input attenuator has been destroyed by the application of a millivolt of RF and 24 V of 60 Hz.

Another danger to the front end of a spectrum analyzer are the effects of pulse power. Pulse-modulated carriers may have high peak powers and a low duty cycle such that the average power may not endanger the input attenuator. The destruction of the input mixer is instantaneous, and it is this element of the spectrum analyzer that is vulnerable to pulse power.

As an example, consider a pulse-modulated carrier that has a duty cycle of 0.1%. Thus, a 1000-W, +60-dBm, peak pulse power has an average power of 1 W, which is +30 dBm. The input attenuator could probably handle the average power but a mixer that can withstand a power level of +20 dBm without damage would require 40 dB of attenuation to prevent damage to the mixer. Long before damage occurred to the mixer, perhaps 30 dB or more below the damage level, the mixer would produce a distortion of the pulsed waveform, which should also be avoided.

Pulse power is deceiving. A device that produces thousands of watts of continuous power is large, probably with cooling fans or water, usually hums, growls, and really makes it clear that this is serious power to be handled carefully. A pulse transmitter where the peak power may be thousands of watts but the duty cycle is very low so the average power is a few watts may be held with one hand and, therefore, appears innocuous.

The power of a pulse-modulated carrier is spread over a range of frequencies depending on the duty cycle of the pulse and the repetition rate. For a very narrow pulse and the repetition rate. For a very narrow pulse such as 0.1 μs, the power is spread over a range of 20 MHz. Depending on the bandwidth of the IF filter, the displayed amplitude of the pulse spectrum could be 40 dB, 50 dB, or more, below the actual pulse power level. The response to a pulsed carrier is called the impulse response of the IF filter and will be discussed later in this chapter. The important point to be made here is that the actual peak power of the pulsed carrier to the spectrum analyzer is possibly much greater than the displayed peak. The operator, assuming the displayed amplitude is well within the safe range of the analyzer, may be damaging the unit without realizing it.

It is important to know as much about the pulse signal to be investigated as possible—primarily the peak pulse power. It is also helpful to know the pulse width as an indication of how much the IF filter is distorting the displayed amplitude. This will be discussed further in this chapter.

4.2 Measuring Wide-Band Spectra

Wide-band signals are those in which the total bandwidth of the signal investigated is significantly greater than the bandwidth of the filter being used. As an example, consider a CW signal, which is about as narrow as a signal can be. In this case, the signal is not wide band regardless of the IF filter used in the spectrum analyzer, since the bandwidth of the signal in question is zero. Consider, now, the same CW signal AM modulated with a 1-kHz audio sine wave. The modulated signal has a carrier and two sidebands. As long as a filter significantly less than 1-kHz bandwidth is used, the spectrum display will show the carrier and sidebands. If a filter significantly greater than 1 kHz is used, the sidebands will not be resolved but the 1-kHz modulation will appear on the envelope of the spectrum analyzer display. There is an area of bandwidth between "significantly less than" and "significantly greater than" in which the displayed spectrum is a combination of the actual spectral lines and the modulation waveform. This area should be avoided or, when avoidance is impossible, the displayed spectrum should be carefully interpreted.

Assume the amplitude modulation applied to the carrier is not a simple 1-kHz sine wave but a very complex waveform with energy in the region of a few hertz to 1 kHz. In this case, no filter, regardless of how narrow, will resolve the sidebands, and some of the modulation will appear on the envelope. An example of a wide-band signal that is difficult to analyze is a television visual carrier. In this case, the lower frequency limit of the modulation is 30 Hz, the frame rate, while the upper limit is about 4.2 MHz. If a 30-Hz filter were used, indeed 30-Hz sidebands would be resolved. However, the displayed spectrum would include 280,000 sidebands. For an unchanging video scene such as a test pattern, the amplitude of each sideband at 30-Hz intervals would remain constant over time. Such a spectrum would take a long time to generate, as it would require a narrow IF filter and consequently a long scan time. The actual amplitude of the individual 30-Hz sidebands is not important, but it is a general indication of the level of energy at frequencies removed from the carrier by hundreds of kilohertz to several megahertz. If an IF bandwidth wider than 30 Hz but more narrow than 15 kHz were used, the analyzer would display the 15-kHz sidebands due to the scanning line rate but not the 30-Hz sidebands. This spectrum would be just as valuable as the narrower spectrum and would take much less time to generate. Only about 600 spectral lines would be present in the display. The spectral lines would contain modulation due to the energy of the modulating signal within the passband of the IF filter. If a wider bandwidth were used, such as 100 kHz, the spectrum display would resolve no spectral lines since there are no repetitive waveforms above 15 kHz. (If a stationary test pattern is used, it is possible to generate sidebands above 15 kHz. For example, if a checkerboard pattern is used with six alternating white and black blocks, a strong spectral line at three times the horizontal rate will be present. Normal photographic scenes do not have strong repetitive patterns.) This spectrum using the 100-kHz filter would provide information concerning the total bandwidth occupied, since the total bandwidth of the visual carrier is on the order of 4 MHz or so. In spite of the fact that there are no discrete spectral lines, the spectrum of a video-modulated carrier conveys important information.

It was made clear that when wide-band signals are measured some of the modulation would appear on the spectrum display, since it is not resolved as a spectral line. Therefore, it is important to have *a priori* knowledge of the response of the IF filter to various waveforms. In previous chapters, a discussion of filter bandwidth centered on the response of the IF filter to a sweeping signal, used to calculate the resolution bandwidth of the spectrum analyzer. It is necessary to investigate the IF filter again to determine the response to a modulated signal. In the investigation, two types of modulations will be considered: impulse type modulation and noise modulation.

Impulse modulation refers to a low repetition rate signal with a low duty cycle. A pulsed radar signal is an example of impulse modulation. Another example is the interference signals generated by the brushes of electric motors and automobile ignitions. These two examples are often referred to as radio noise and have given rise to the term impulse noise. There are similarities between impulse noise and random thermal-style noise. The major difference is that impulse noise has a definite repetition rate and thus is not true noise, while true random noise has absolutely no repetition rate.

Relative to spectrum analysis, an impulse signal is a modulated RF carrier in which the total spectrum of the signal is significantly greater thant the bandwidth of the IF filter, but the repetition rate is less than the IF bandwidth. Therefore, the modulation due to the pulse repetition frequency will be present in the output of the log amplifier and will cause vertical deflection of the display. This produces the so-called envelope or dense display as shown in Fig. 4-1.

There are several important characteristics of the envelope display shown in Fig. 4-1 that should be understood. First, notice that the spectrum is symmetrical around the modulated carrier, which is characteristic of amplitude modulation. Second, notice that the envelope has points where the amplitude is zero. These zero points are a function of the pulse width alone and occur at a frequency N/t Hz from the unmodulated carrier, where N is an integer from 1 to infinity and t is the period of the pulse repetition frequency. This will be discussed later in this chapter.

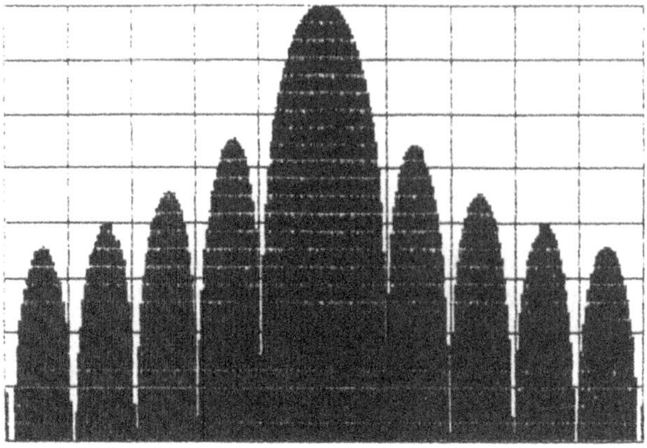

Figure 4-1
An example of the "dense" or "envelope" display generated when the repetition rate of the spectrum displayed is less than the IF filter bandwidth.

In general, the shorter the pulse, the wider the frequency range that contains the modulated carrier energy.

The amplitude of the pulse modulation that appears at the output of the log amplifier and is eventually displayed on the spectrum analyzer is a function of the impulse bandwidth of the IF filter. For an IF filter of finite bandwidth, there is a finite minimum rise time of pulse-modulated carriers passed through the filter. If the rise time is not fast enough to allow the pulse to rise to its full amplitude, there will be an attenuation of the pulse amplitude.

By definition, an impulse-modulated carrier has a spectrum well beyond the measurement bandwidth, or in the case of a spectrum analyzer, the IF bandwidth. By using the simple relationship that a spectrum is as broad as the reciprocal of the rise and fall times of a pulse-modulated waveform, it is clear that the rise time of the pulse-modulated signal is much shorter than the rise time of the analyzer bandwidth.

In a broad-band signal such as impulse or random noise, in which it is impossible or difficult to resolve sidebands, the energy distribution of the signal is continuous rather than discrete. When the spectrum analyzer displays an impulse-modulated signal, the amplitude of the display is a function of the bandwidth of the IF filter, as the spectrum analyzer IF filter can pass only a portion of the total energy. Therefore, the energy distribution of an impulse spectrum is given as volts per hertz where hertz is the impulse bandwidth of the IF filter.

Previous discussions of IF bandwidths centered on the 3-dB bandwidth of the IF filter as an indicator of the resolution of the filter for resolving the sidebands of a spectrum. The impulse bandwidth of an IF filter is different than the 3-dB bandwidth and may be calculated from the 3-dB bandwidth in the following manner.

The impulse bandwidth of a filter is a theoretical rectangular passband that has an area equal to the spectrum analyzer's IF filter, as shown conceptually in Fig. 4-2. The amplitude of an impulse passing through a filter is proportional to the filter bandwidth. Therefore, increasing the impulse bandwidth of a filter by a factor of two will increase the amplitude of the impulse from the filter also by a factor of two. This implies the peak power from the filter is proportional to the square of the filter bandwidth. Assuming a constant distribution of energy in a pulse-modulated carrier, the rectangular filter will pass an amount of power equal to

$$P_d = P(f)(BW_i)^2 \qquad (4\text{-}1)$$

where $P(f)$ is the power density in watts; BW_i is the impulse bandwidth in hertz, which is equivalent to the width of the rectangular filter; and P_d is the displayed power level.

Assuming that power displayed by the spectrum analyzer is at constant resistance that is the input resistance of the analyzer, the displayed power may be rewritten in terms of displayed voltage introducing the parameter Z, which is the input impedance, so that

$$P_d = \frac{V_d^2}{Z} = \frac{V(f)^2}{Z}(BW_i)^2$$

$$V_d = V(f)(BW_i) \qquad (4\text{-}2)$$

where $V(f)$ is the voltage distribution and V_d is the displayed voltage.

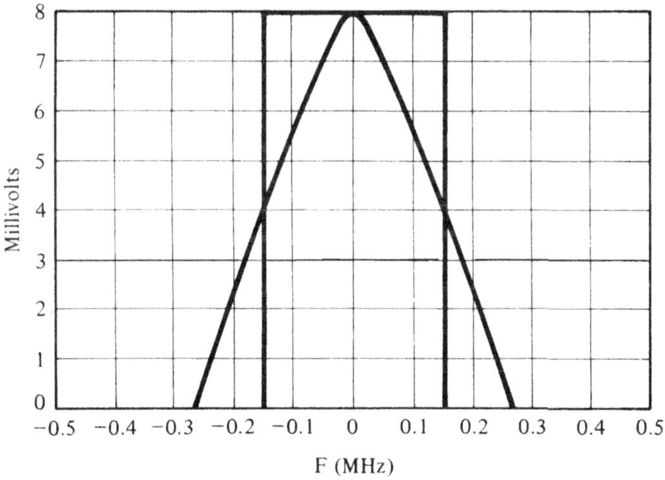

Figure 4-2
An IF filter passband on a linear/voltage scale showing the rectangular equivalent bandwidth.

In Fig. 4-2 a typical Gaussian filter passband is shown on which is superimposed a rectangular bandwidth that has the same area enclosed under the passband. An impulse signal passing through the Gaussian filter will have a response amplitude proportional to the bandwidth of the shown rectangular filter. This is not to imply that a sharp-skirted filter with a passband similar to the rectangular filter superimposed on the Gaussian filter will pass an impulse signal the same as the Gaussian filter. Notice the passbands shown in Fig. 4-2 are in terms of voltage.

When dealing with totally random noise, such as thermal noise, spectral lines are never resolved. Because a true noise signal lacks all coherency, the displayed power is directly proportional to the analyzer bandwidth. Compare this with impulse noise where the displayed voltage is directly proportional to the filter bandwidth. In this case, the response of the spectrum analyzer is a function of the noise bandwidth of the IF filter. Figure 4-3 shows the relationship of a typical Gaussian IF filter and the equivalent noise bandwidth is the same as the area of the Gaussian filter. Notice the similarity to Fig. 4-2. Also notice the important difference. Figure 4-2 has voltage as its ordinate while Fig. 4-3 has power as the ordinate. It is important to note the Gaussian shape is the same for either the voltage plot or the power plot. Since power is proportional to voltage squared, squaring the Gaussian function is a matter of adjusting the constant k by a factor of two.

Calculating the equivalent bandwidth of either filter is not difficult. A Gaussian filter has a passband that fits the form

$$Ae^{-kx^2} \tag{4-3}$$

To make this equation fit the specific case of an IF filter, the independent variable x is

$$x = (f_0 - f) \tag{4-4}$$

where f_0 is the filter center frequency and f is the independent variable. For an IF filter, the function is the loss through the filter; thus (4-3) is rewritten as

$$L = e^{-k(f_0 - f)^2} \tag{4-5}$$

where L is the loss in an ideal filter.

To calculate the constant k, set the loss L to 3 dB and the frequency to the 3-dB frequency and evaluate Eq. (4-5) for k.

$$L = 0.707 = e^{-k(f_0 - f_{3\mathrm{dB}})^2} \tag{4-6}$$

However, $(f_0 - f_{3\mathrm{dB}})$ is one-half the 3-dB bandwidth of the filter and, thus, the equation may be rewritten as

$$0.707 = e^{-k(\mathrm{BW}/2)^2} \tag{4-7}$$

where BW is the 3-dB bandwidth.

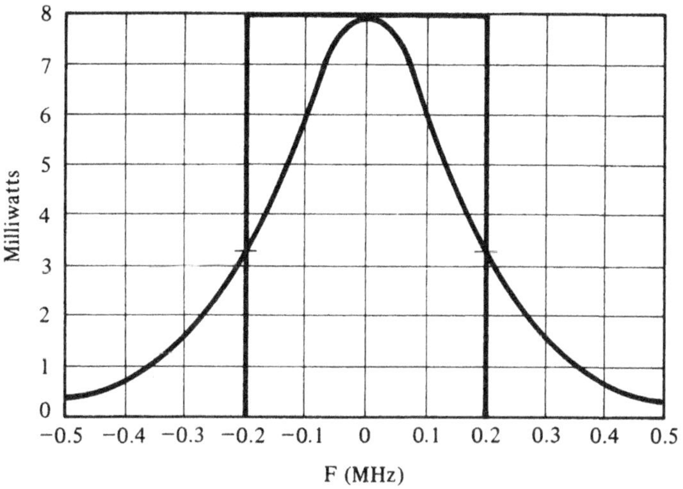

Figure 4-3
An IF filter passband on a square-law demodulator; display shows a rectangular passband with equal area.

Taking the natural log of both sides of this equation and solving for k, the following is obtained.

$$-0.347 = -k(\mathrm{BW}/2)^2$$

$$k = 1.39/(\mathrm{BW})^2 \tag{4-8}$$

The area under the curve of the Gaussian filter is equal to the integral

$$\int_{-\infty}^{\infty} e^{-k(f_0-f)^2}\, df \tag{4-9}$$

Fortunately, this is one of the definite integrals found in practically any mathematics handbook. The result is

$$\int_{-\infty}^{\infty} e^{-k(f_0-f)^2}\, df = \sqrt{\frac{\pi}{k}} = \mathrm{BW}\sqrt{\frac{\pi}{1.39}}$$

$$= (1.5)\mathrm{BW} \tag{4-10}$$

The rectangular passband that has the same area as a Gaussian filter is 1.5 times the bandwidth of the Gaussian filter.

Therefore, when using a true Gaussian filter, the impulse bandwidth is 1.5 times the 3-dB bandwidth of the filter. However, most spectrum analyzers have filters that deviate from the true Gaussian, and it will be necessary to measure and determine the impulse bandwidth of the analyzer's filters.

To measure the impulse bandwidth of a filter, feed a CW signal into the spectrum analyzer and use the linear display mode. Select the filter to be measured and adjust the frequency-span control so the displayed filter shape fills the display. Adjust the RF and IF attenuators so that the top of the display is at the very top of the screen. Now, count the number of full graticule rectangles and estimate the partial rectangles, to determine the area encompassed by the filter passband.

Determine the bandwidth of a rectangular filter with the same height as the IF filter that would encompass the same area as shown in Fig. 4-2.

To calculate the noise bandwidth of a Gaussian filter, a calculation similar to that used to determine the impulse bandwidth is employed. The equation used to describe the filter is exactly as before, since it is not a different filter. However, the value of k must be recalculated because when the 3-dB frequency is substituted into the equation, the equation is set to equal 0.5 rather than 0.707 because the ordinate is now power and 3 dB down relative to power is one-half the 0-dB level. Therefore

$$e^{-k(f_0-f_{3\mathrm{dB}})^2} = 0.5$$

$$-k(f_0 - f_{3\mathrm{dB}})^2 = -k\left(\frac{\mathrm{BW}}{2}\right)^2 = 0.693$$

$$k = \frac{4 \times 0.693}{\mathrm{BW}^2} = \frac{2.77}{\mathrm{BW}^2} \tag{4-11}$$

Substituting this value of k into Eq. (4-9) and evaluating the integral, the equivalent bandwidth is calculated.

$$\int_{-\infty}^{\infty} e^{-k(f-f_0)^2}\, df = \sqrt{\frac{\pi}{k}}$$

$$= \mathrm{BW}\sqrt{\frac{\pi}{2.77}} = (1.06)\mathrm{BW} \tag{4-12}$$

Therefore the noise bandwidth of a Gaussian filter is essentially the same as the 3-dB bandwidth. Again, since most spectrum analyzers have filter shapes that deviate from the Gaussian, the noise bandwidth must be measured.

The noise bandwidth of an IF filter may be measured by displaying the filter passband using a square-law display, which is proportional to power, and determining the rectangular area that would be equal to the area of the filter. Many spectrum analyzers do not have square-law displays, and calculating the noise bandwidth using this technique would be difficult.

Often, the spectrum analyzer instruction manual provides the noise bandwidth for each IF filter, and measuring the bandwidth would be unnecessary. Lacking a square-law display and the actual noise bandwidth figure, the noise bandwidth may be estimated by taking the 3-dB bandwidth and multiplying by 1.1.

Calculating the impulse and noise bandwidth of the IF filter of a spectrum analyzer was for the purpose of evaluating how those filters would affect impulse and noise signals. In addition to these filters, the IF log amplifier and the display or video amplifiers will also have an effect on the display.

The spectrum analyzer uses a logarithmic IF amplifier, as described in previous chapters. Since the log amp provides an output directly proportional to the logarithm of the input signal, the log output will follow the log of the modulating waveform, which results in a distorted display of the modulation. The average of the log amplifier output is the average of the logarithm of the imput, which is neither the RMS value of the input nor the average.

In the case of impulse noise, the amplitude of the displayed spectrum is a function not only of the impulse bandwidth of the IF filter but of the impulse bandwidth of the log IF amplifier and the vertical deflection amplifiers in the display section of the analyzer.

The log IF amplifier also is a peak responding detector, which is the desired mode of operation for the measurement of impulse noise but not for pure noise. Correction factors must be employed for the effects of the log detector and, if necessary, the impulse bandwidth of the video amplifiers.

Generally, the bandwidth of the video amplifiers of the spectrum analyzer display is significantly greater than the impulse bandwidth of the widest IF filter, and thus is not a factor when making impulse noise measurements. This should be checked, however.

To check the impulse bandwidth of the log and video amplifiers, apply a pulse-modulated signal of known impulse bandwidth. Set the IF filter to the widest setting, and note the displayed amplitude. Reduce the IF bandwidth to the filter narrower than the widest, and note the reduction in displayed amplitude. The amplitude of the display should be reduced by an amount equal to the ratio of the impulse bandwidths of the filters. If the reduction is less than the ratio, the actual maximum impulse bandwidth of the analyzer is limited by the video amplifiers and the display of the spectrum analyzer. If this is a problem, check to insure all video filters have been turned off.

In the case of true noise, a "fuzzy" output will result with the peak of the "fuzz" corresponding to the peak of the noise input. The average or center of the "fuzz" is, as before, the average of the log of the noise signal. Since the preferred amplitude measurement for noise measurements is RMS, a correction factor must be used.

Averaging the center of the "fuzz" is not difficult, and one simple technique is to use the video filter to provide a thin reference line. Most spectrum analyzers are provided with a video filter that will average the amplitude of the "fuzz" and provide a smooth line to measure the level of noise. The resulting average of the log of the input is still not the desired RMS level. However, a correction factor, which takes into account the fact that a peak detector is used in addition to log responding, may be used to convert this measured level to the equivalent RMS value. Notice the video filter may never be used for impulse noise measurement as this will severely reduce the impulse bandwidth of the analyzer.

The actual correction value depends on the type of broadband signal involved. For random noise, about 2.5 dB is added to the average value. The actual value is a function of the spectrum analyzer.

For impulse noise, the desired display is the peak of the input and no correction factor is required.

The RMS value of an impulse-modulated RF carrier after passing through a filter such as the IF filter of an analyzer is

$$V_{RMS} = Vt_2(BW_i) \quad (4\text{-}13)$$

where V_{RMS} is the RMS value of a pulsed carrier, V is the amplitude of the carrier, t_2 is the pulse width, and BW_i is the impulse bandwidth of the spectrum analyzer.

When measurements are made using the dense spectrum, the actual modulation waveform appears within the envelope of the spectrum. The number of lines within the envelope depends on the scan rate of the analyzer. If the scan rate is such that only a few pulses are scanned each sweep, the dense spectrum will have visible lines within the envelope.

Some spectrum analyzers have a video trigger feature that will cause the trace to synchronize with the modulation and produce what appears to be a spectrum of narrow lines. This may be mistaken for a spectrum of individual lines. If the synchronization is disabled, the individual lines will begin to move horizontally across the display, which indicates that these lines are not true spectral lines.

If the sweep time of the spectrum analyzer is too fast, only a few of the pulses will appear on the display screen. As an example, if a pulsed carrier with a pulse repetition rate of 100 PPS were investigated with a sweep rate of 50 sweeps per second, only two pulses would occur during a sweep and thus would provide two vertical lines per sweep. Of course, after a second, 100 pulses would have come and gone. If the persistence of the display were very long, eventually the desired envelope would appear. Also, if the spectrum analyzer has a peak hold feature, the envelope would eventually appear. However, if a slow sweep were used such as one sweep per 10 seconds, the spectrum would appear after one sweep. The actual time required to achieve the desired envelope display is about the same for either a fast or a slow sweep, because it is a matter of energy. Each pulse contains a specific amount of energy and each point in the spectrum display represents one of those packets of energy. Whether all the display points are obtained in a single sweep or whether they are obtained over a period several sweeps, the result is the same.

The pulse-modulated carrier has spectral components, spaced at intervals equal to the pulse repetition rate, which are centered around the carrier frequency. Usually the actual spectral components are not of importance, only the envelope. Important characteristics of the pulse-modulated carrier can be determined from the envelope spectrum.

From the Fourier transform discussion presented in Chapter 1, recall the spectrum of a rectangular pulse that followed the $(\sin x)/x$ form. When a complex waveform amplitude modulates a carrier, which means a complex waveform is multiplied by a sine function, the resulting spectrum is a translation of the spectrum of the complex waveform to the carrier frequency. Thus, the rectangular pulse when modulating a carrier results in a $(\sin x)/x$ form of spectrum centered aound a carrier frequency of ω_0.

The relative amplitudes of the sidebands around the carrier frequency are dependent on the duty cycle of the modulation. The envelope of the spectrum rises and falls and becomes zero at specific offset frequencies from the carrier.

The zeros of the envelope occur at frequencies of

$$F_0 \pm N/t \tag{4-14}$$

where F_0 is the carrier frequency, N is an integer, and t is the pulse width.

It is simple, therefore, to determine the duty cycle of a pulse-modulated carrier. It was for the purpose of microwave-pulse carrier-modulated waveforms that spectrum analysis was created.

Many other measurements of pulsed carriers may be made using a spectrum analyzer. One of the more important measurements is the determination of frequency modulation superimposed on pulse-amplitude modulation.

When a carrier is pulse modulated, a spectrum that is symmetric around the carrier frequency results. When frequency or phase modulation exists simultaneously with the pulse modulation, the resulting spectrum becomes asymmetrical around the carrier frequency.

Figure 4-1 shows a pulse-modulated carrier with a steady carrier frequency. Figure 4-4 shows the same pulse modulation with simultaneous frequency modulation present.

The dynamic range of a spectrum analyzer was discussed in an earlier chapter. Basically, the dynamic range of the analyzer was the difference in signal level between the noise level of the analyzer and two signals that would produce a spurious response of the analyzer that is visible above the noise level. The generation of spurious responses is still a consideration when pulse spectra are measured, but the dynamic range for most pulse measurements is a function of the overload level of the input mixer.

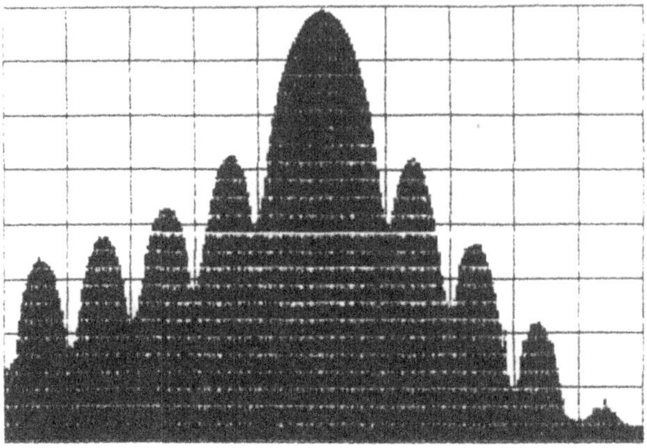

Figure 4-4
A pulse-modulated carrier with simultaneous frequency modulation produces a skewed spectrum. Neither amplitude nor frequency modulation alone can produce an assymmetrical spectrum as the one shown.

The pulse level present on the spectrum analyzer display represents an amplitude that is less than the actual pulse amplitude because the pulse has passed through the IF filter. Recall from Eq. (4-13), the displayed output is related to the actual RMS input signal voltage by the factor t_2BW_i. As an example, assume a 100-ns pulse is viewed using a 100-kHz (3-dB) filter that has an impulse bandwidth of approximately 150 kHz. The resulting spectrum display is 36 dB below the actual input pulse peak level.

The absolute maximum input level that may be presented to the spectrum analyzer is the maximum level that will not destroy or damage the input mixer. For accurate level measurements, a level below that which causes severe distortion in the mixer would be required. One often-specified level is that which causes the gain of the input mixer to be reduced by 1 dB. This point is usually less than the burnout point and provides the highest input signal that the spectrum analyzer may accommodate. The 1-dB compression point represents a point where saturation begins and the ouput of the mixer deviates from the ideal input/output transfer function by 1 dB.

The 1-dB compression point is usually much higher than the maximum CW input level that would generate visible spurious responses. This is because the pulse signals displayed by the analyzer are attenuated by the impulse bandwidth of the IF filter. This means spurious pulse signals will be attenuated by the IF filter by the same amount as any other pulsed signal. The 1-dB compression point of the input mixer that would undoubtedly produce a spurious response above the noise level for a CW input may not produce a visible pulse spurious.

To calculate the impulse dynamic range of an analyzer, the previous example of a 0.1-μs pulse with a 100-kHz IF bandwidth will be used. A typical 1-dB compression point for a spectrum analyzer is on the order of −5 dBm. As previously explained, the displayed pulse through a 150-kHz impulse bandwidth filter is 36 dB down from the actual peak that would permit a maximum displayed pulse level of −41 dBm. This results from an input pulse amplitude of −5 dBm, a level equal to the 1-dB compression point minus the 36 dB lost in the response of the IF filter.

The noise level of the spectrum analyzer is the same for pulse measurement as for any other measurement; it is a function of the IF filter bandwidth. A typical noise floor for a spectrum analyzer would be on the order of −90 dBm for a 100-kHz 3-dB bandwidth. In this example, the maximum displayed amplitude would be −41 dBm with a noise floor at −90 dBm, which produces a dynamic range of 49 dB.

How does the IF bandwidth affect the dynamic range of the spectrum analyzer? Is there an optimum bandwidth that would maximize the dynamic range of the analyzer? If the IF filters used in the analyzer were of a similar shape such that the relationship between the impulse bandwidth and the 3-dB bandwidth were the same for all the filters, increasing the bandwidth of the IF filter would cause an equal increase in displayed spectra as well as in the noise level. For true noise spectra, the displayed spectra would increase by the same amount as the noise floor. For impulse spectra, on the other hand, the displayed spectra would increase by 6 dB each time the bandwidth was increased by a factor of two, while the noise floor would only increase by 3 dB. Therefore, for a spectrum analyzer employing IF filters with a similar shape, an increase in IF bandwidth will increase the dynamic range of the measurement of impulse spectra, but it will have no effect on the dynamic range of true noise spectra.

It was explained early in this chapter that measuring pulse spectra must be done with great care. To present an example, consider a pulse waveform with a 100-ns pulse at a 1-kHz repetition rate, as would be found on a radar transmitter. Assume the ratio of on-to-off level should be 80 dB, which is not an unusual requirement. Remember, using the example analyzer with a −5 dBm, 1-dB compression point, and a noise floor of −90 dBm with a 100 kHz IF filter, the displayed amplitude is 36 dB below the actual amplitude. Consider the signal to be measured as two signals—one appears while the other is gone. Therefore, the pulsed signal appears for 100 ns and is turned off. Then the carrier appears with a pulse width of 999.9 μs. Therefore, the carrier represents a pulsed waveform itself. However, because the pulse width is 999.9 μs, the reduction in amplitude through an IF filter of 100-kHz, 3-dB bandwidth is practically nil. Therefore, the display would contain, essentially, two pulse spectra, one for the pulse and a second for the carrier. The displayed amplitude of the "on" pulse is 36 dB below the actual peak power due to its 100-ns pulse width. The carrier signal has a pulse width of 999.9 μs with a period of 1 ms and is displayed at its actual level.

The carrier-to-pulse ratio is the difference in level between the peak level of the pulse spectrum and the level of the carrier spectrum plus 36 dB. This is necessary, as the pulse peak amplitude is displayed 36 dB below the real amplitude of the display.

The maximum on/off ratio that may be measured using this example analyzer is 85 dB. This is the 49-dB pulse dynamic range plus the 36-dB advantage of the carrier or equivalent long pulse. This will allow very little margin for the measurement of an 80-dB on-to-off ratio.

If it were necessary to measure the ratio between two short pulses, the 36-dB advantage would be lost and the dynamic range would revert to 49 dB.

It is pulsed measurements of this type that lead spectrum analyzer operators to create conditions that may damage the instrument. In their zeal to measure the level of the carrier in a pulsed system, spectrum analyzer operators reduce the input attenuator so that the carrier is well out of the noise and the pulse amplitude is near the top of the display, providing a clear picture to make the measurement. What goes ignored is that the actual pulse peak power is considerably higher than the displayed value—high enough, in fact, to damage the analyzer. Although the displayed pulse is below the point of damage and the carrier feedthrough is clearly above the noise level of the analyzer, the actual peak pulse power is near the damage level and may cause irreversible damage.

4.3 Measuring Amplitude and Frequency Modulation

In the previous section, the spectra of pulse modulated carriers were investigated. In this section, the spectra of amplitude and frequency modulation with sine functions will be investigated.

It is a well-known fact that the sidebands generated from the amplitude modulation of a carrier with sine-wave modulation produces two sidebands above and below carrier by a frequency difference equal to the modulation frequency. The amplitude of the sidebands, relative to the amplitude of the carrier, is

$$V_s = V_c \frac{I_m}{2} \tag{4-15}$$

where V_s is the sideband voltage, V_c is the carrier voltage, and I_m is the modulation index or 100 times the percentage of modulation.

When investigating higher modulation percentages, the relative amplitude of the sidebands is close to 6 dB down from the carrier. As an example, the sidebands due to a 90% amplitude-modulated carrier are 6.49 dB down from the carrier while a 100% modulated carrier has sidebands that are 6.0 dB down. The difference between 100% and 90% modulation is only about 0.5 dB. Therefore, it is desirable to investigate the level of amplitude modulation using a linear mode of the spectrum analyzer.

In addition, rather than measuring the amplitude of the sidebands it is more effective to use zero span and observe the demodulated carrier in the time domain.

Using the linear mode of display, the demodulated sine-wave modulation, of course, appears as a sine wave. The linear gain is set so that the unmodulated carrier is in the center of the display screen and the modulation deflects above and below the unmodulated carrier. One hundred percent modulation results in an amplitude that goes from half-screen upward to full-screen and down to zero.

For the determination of very high modulation indices, the log display is easier to use. When investigating the power of the sidebands generated by amplitude modulation, the log scale is a detriment. However, when investigating very high modulation indices the log scale is a help.

When a carrier is 100% amplitude modulated, the carrier is increased in amplitude to twice the unmodulated carrier, or an increase of 6 dB. The negative amplitude of the modulation decreases to near zero, or a decrease of an infinite number of decibels. This permits an accurate assessment of high-level amplitude modulation. As an example, 99% amplitude modulation results in an increase of essentially 6 dB. The negative peak is a decrease of 40 dB. A modulation level of 99.9% is still an increase of 6 dB, while the negative reduction is 60 dB. As it can be seen, the use of the log scale and measurement of the negative peaks results in an easy method of measuring high-level amplitude modulation.

Observing the negative peak of amplitude modulation and assuming it is the same as the positive peak carries some risk. If the positive and negative peaks differ, the average, or the carrier level, is different than the unmodulated value. This is called carrier shift. In many systems where very high percentages of amplitude modulation are required, small amounts of carrier shift are not important and the spectrum analyzer method of modulation measurement is suitable. What is important, however, is that the negative peaks do not become zero for any period of time. Maximum amplitude modulation requires that the negative peaks approach zero; but to be zero for any period of time causes a severe increase of the occupied spectrum of the amplitude-modulated signal. The spectrum analyzer is capable of displaying this type of distortion.

Frequency modulation is also easily measured using the spectrum analyzer. Three categories of frequency modulation are used in this discussion: narrow band, wide band, and ultra wide band. These catagories are not official nomenclature, but are divisions that separate the amount of frequency modulation into workable measurement techniques.

Frequency modulation, unlike amplitude modulation, produces an infinite number of sidebands when a carrier is modulated by a simple sine wave. These sidebands decrease in amplitude farther from the carrier and, for small modulation indices, the sidebands fall off so rapidly from the carrier frequency that there is, essentially, only one set of sidebands.

The amplitude of the sidebands may be determined from a set of mathematical functions called the Bessel functions.

When amplitude modulation is supplied to a carrier, additional power is added to the carrier that becomes the source of energy for the sidebands. The carrier power remains constant and the added power is supplied to the sidebands.

A frequency-modulated carrier does not require additional power to affect modulation. The power contained in the sidebands generated when a carrier is frequency modulated is taken from the carrier. Unlike amplitude modulation, in which the carrier remains at the same level regardless of the percentage of modulation, the level of the carrier in a frequency-modulated signal is a variable. There are, in fact, certain modulation indices that reduce the power in the carrier to zero.

There is an entire set of Bessel functions of differing orders. The amplitude of the carrier or a sideband of a frequency-modulated carrier is proportional to an order of the Bessel function. The order of the Bessel function is equivalent to the order of the sideband to which it relates. The carrier is order zero, the first sideband from the carrier is order 1, the second order 2, and so on. The frequency-modulated carrier has a symmetrical spectrum, and the amplitude of any sideband is the same as its counterpart on the other side of the carrier.

The amplitude of a sideband of a frequency-modulated carrier is

$$V_n = KJ_n(I) \tag{4-16}$$

where the sideband voltage of an Nth order sideband is V_n, K is a constant of proportionality, I is the modulation index, and J_n is the Bessel function of order n.

What is important about Eq. (4-16) is that the value of J_n has zeros at specific modulation indices, which results in the reduction to zero of various sidebands, including the carrier as the "zero order" sideband. These reductions are easily visible on a spectrum analyzer display and can be used to measure modulation indices.

All Bessel functions, with the exception of the zero-order function, have a zero at a modulation index of zero. The zero-order Bessel function has a value of one at a modulation index of zero. This means, simply, that with no modulation there is only a carrier and no sidebands. The first zero is of the zero-order Bessel function, and this occurs at a modulation index of 2.4. Thus at a modulation index of 2.4 there is no carrier but only sidebands. Therefore, for modulation indices of less than 2.4, the Bessel function zero is not an indicator of modulation index.

The ratio of J_0 to J_1, J_2, and J_3 will provide an accurate indication of modulation index for small indices.

For modulation indices greater than 2.4 and less than 10 or so, the nulls of specific sidebands and the carrier may be used to determine the modulation index. Theoretically, it should be possible to take the amplitudes of the sidebands and the carrier and determine the modulation index directly. However, it should be noted that the Bessel functions have negative values that will not be resolved as negative on the spectrum analyzer. Therefore, it will not be possible to measure the true amplitude (including the sign) of the sidebands. Even if it were possible to resolve negative sidebands, for the larger modulation indices where there are many sidebands, it would be difficult to accurately find the modulation index.

The method of Bessel function nulls uses only those sidebands where the amplitude is zero. This effectively negates the need to determinc the sign of the sideband, as a zero-amplitude sideband does not require knowledge of the sign.

The significant disadvantage of this method is that not every modulation index has a zero-amplitude sideband or carrier. This method usually requires a means to vary the modulation level so that several carrier or sideband nulls may be obtained and the desired modulation can be set or measured by interpolation.

As an example, the first null is of the carrier and occurs at a modulation index of 2.4. The second null is of J_1 and occurs at a modulation index of 3.8. The third null occurs at a modulation of 5.2 of J_2. The fourth null is the carrier, again, and occurs at a modulation index of 5.5.

Additional points may be located from some relationships such as, at a modulation index of 1.4, the carrier and the first sideband are of equal amplitude. The second sideband and the carrier are of equal amplitude at a modulation index of 1.8. The third sideband and the carrier are of equal amplitude at a modulation index of 2.2, and so on.

From the above relationships and additional points, the modulation indices shown in Table 4-1 are identified.

Table 4-1

Modulation index	Relationship
1.4	$J_0 = J_1$
1.8	$J_0 = J_2$
2.2	$J_0 = J_3$
2.4	$J_0 = 0$
2.6	$J_1 = J_2$
3.1	$J_1 = J_3$
3.8	$J_0 = J_3$
3.8	$J_1 = 0$
4.6	$J_0 = J_1$
5.2	$J_2 = 0$
6.1	$J_1 = J_2$
6.4	$J_3 = 0$

There are many nulls and intersecting points of the Bessel functions that may be used to find calibration points. One caution when using a table such as Table 4-1 should be mentioned. Notice that some of the key indicators such as $J_1 = J_2$, as an example, occur twice in the table, at 2.6 and 6.1. If it is not certain which modulation index is being measured, a secondary indicator must be used. In this case, at a modulation index of 6.1, J_4 and J_5 will be at approximately the same amplitude and greater than J_1 and J_2. At a modulation index of 1.4, J_4 and J_5 barely exist.

Figure 4-5 shows the spectrum display for a modulation index of 2.4 where the carrier is absent, and Figure 4-6 shows the spectrum display for a modulation index of 3.8 where the first sidebands are zero.

This technique is useful to a modulation index of about 10. For greater modulation indices the number of sidebands increases and the number of calibration points becomes increasingly complex. This technique is also only valid for sine-wave modulation.

There is a very important error source when using the Bessel function nulls and intersect points to measure modulation index. Since a carrier frequency modulated by a sine wave produces sidebands at multiples of the modulation frequency, it is not distinguishable from harmonic distortion of the modulating waveform. As an example, consider a clipped sine wave that begins to approach a square wave and introduces a strong third harmonic. Assume that a modulation index of 1 relative to the fundamental modulation frequency is measured. The third sideband would be expected to be 32 dB down from the carrier if the modulation were clean. The third harmonic of a square wave is nominally down 9.5

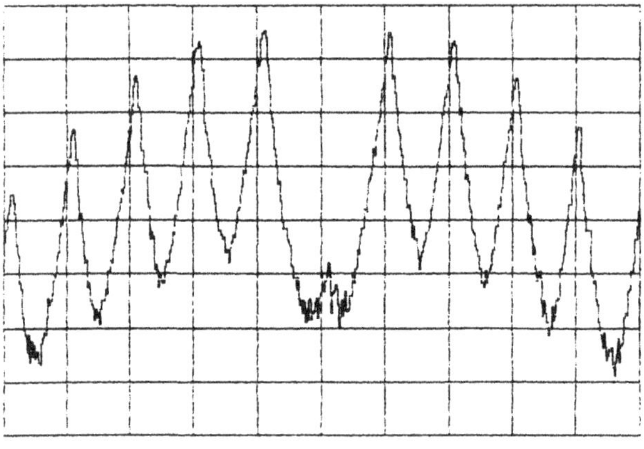

Figure 4-5
The spectrum of a frequency-modulated carrier with a modulation index of 2.4 showing the absence of energy at the carrier frequency.

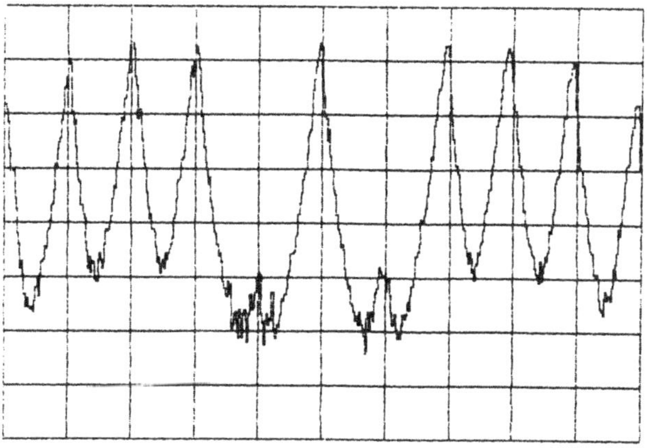

Figure 4-6
The spectrum of a frequency-modulated carrier with a modulation index of 3.8 showing only a small amount of energy at the first set of sidebands.

dB from the fundamental. In addition, it is three times the modulation frequency and causes the third harmonic to have a modulation index of 0.11.

This third harmonic has sidebands of its own and will have a magnitude similar to J_3. By vector addition, the amplitude of the third sideband will be different than expected. Generally, the effects of harmonic distortion of the modulating waveform are slight and will not cause excessive errors. But when the modulation index is high and the threat of harmonic distortion is significant, considerable errors may be produced.

The spectrum analyzer may be used to measure the modulation indices of very wide-band frequency modulation. Generally, narrow-band and wide-band frequency modulation are found in communications systems. Ultra-wide-band frequency modulation is found in radar systems, magnetic tape recording, electronic warfare systems, etc. Many of these systems have modulation rates that are quite low and would produce sidebands very close in frequency that would be difficult to resolve. Even if the analyzer were capable of resolving the sidebands, the number of sidebands would be huge due to the very large modulation index; it would be difficult if not impossible to sort the carrier from the sidebands.

Fortunately, the spectrum analyzer can easily display the modulation index and frequency.

The ultra-wide-band frequency-modulated signal is displayed using a frequency span about twice the expected modulation-frequency deviation. Depending on the scan rate, the ultra-wide-band frequency-modulated carrier will move across the spectrum analyzer display as shown in Fig. 4-7. By using the peak

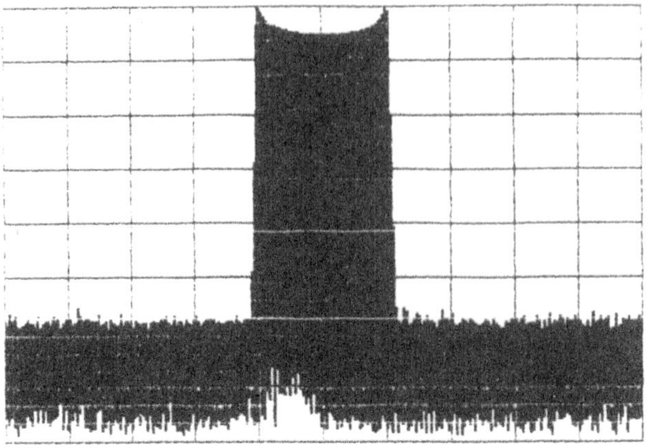

Figure 4-7
The frequency spectrum obtained with an ultra-wide-band frequency modulation.

hold feature of the analyzer, if it is available, the actual peak deviation of the modulation is displayed. It is necessary to measure the modulation frequency to determine the modulation index.

In many cases, the modulation frequency is either known or may be determined by observing the modulating waveform using a conventional oscilloscope. However, the spectrum analyzer may be used to view the modulation of the device under test. This technique is applicable to other levels of modulation.

The technique employed is called slope detection and takes advantage of the frequency-to-amplitude conversion characteristics of the analyzer's IF filters.

Consider the Gaussian filter shape as shown in Fig. 4-2. For a signal on the skirts of the filter, a change in frequency results in a change in amplitude. The filter transforms the frequency modulation of a signal placed on the slope of this filter by the transfer function of the filter slope. This slope is calculated easily by determining the magnitude of the slope in terms of decibels per hertz. This is measured empirically by observing the filter passband on the spectrum analyzer. It is necessary to understand that the slope is not a constant and that the same portion of the filter slope that is characterized must be the same portion of the slope that is used for measuring.

To do this, measure the slope of a filter at a known number of decibels from the peak of the filter passband. Place the spectrum analyzer in the zero-span position and adjust the center frequency of the analyzer to the peak. At this point there should be little, if any, demodulation of the frequency modulation. Tune the analyzer off center—either up or down depending on which portion of the filter slope was characterized—so that the amplitude of the display drops by the same amount as the characterized portion of the filter. As an example, if the filter was characterized at 20 dB down from the peak, tune the input signal to peak and lower the center frequency of the analyzer to place the signal 20 dB from the peak. If the modulation can be removed, tune the analyzer so that the carrier is 20 dB from the peak. If the modulation is present, tune the center frequency so that the center of the modulation is 20 dB down from the peak.

4.4 Spurious Responses

The dynamic range of a spectrum analyzer was defined as the differences in signal level between two signals that produced an intermodulation equal to the noise level of the analyzer. In the normal operation of a spectrum analyzer, excessive input levels may be present, well below the level of burnout, which may generate visible spurious responses.

There are simple techniques to check for the existence of spurious signals. In the spectrum analyzer, two types of spurious responses may be visible. First are second-order responses, which are second harmonics, and third-order responses, which are third-order intermodulation. What is characteristic of these spurious responses is an attenuation of the input signals resulting in an apparent greater attenuation of the spurious response. As an example, a second harmonic generated within the spectrum analyzer will be reduced 2 dB for every 1 dB of attenuation of the input signals. Third-order intermodulation, which requires two or more input signals or a complex signal that contains two or more spectral lines, will be reduced 3 dB for every 1 dB of input attenuation.

It is a good practice to reduce the input attenuation occasionally when making measurements with the spectrum analyzer, reduce the input attenuator by one step, and check the displayed spectra. Any spectral component that is reduced by more than the input attenuator is generated within the analyzer. Those spectral components that will be reduced by more than the input attenuator step are spurious signals, and the input attenuator should be reduced another step to insure that the display does not contain other spurious responses. When the display is free of spurious responses from the spectrum analyzer, a reduction of the input attenuator by 10 dB, as an example, will cause the entire display to be reduced by 10 dB.

When a spectrum analyzer is used to measure the output of a cascaded system containing several devices and spurious output are encountered, the source of harmonics and intermodulation, assuming the spectrum analyzer is not the cause, may be from any one of the elements in the cascaded system. The technique just described may be used to find the element in the system that is responsible for the generation of the spurious responses.

An attenuator, preferably with 1-dB steps, is inserted at various locations throughout the system being measured, and a variable attenuation is inserted. If the attenuator is ahead of the element generating the spurious response, the addition of the attenuation will have a greater effect on the spurious response.

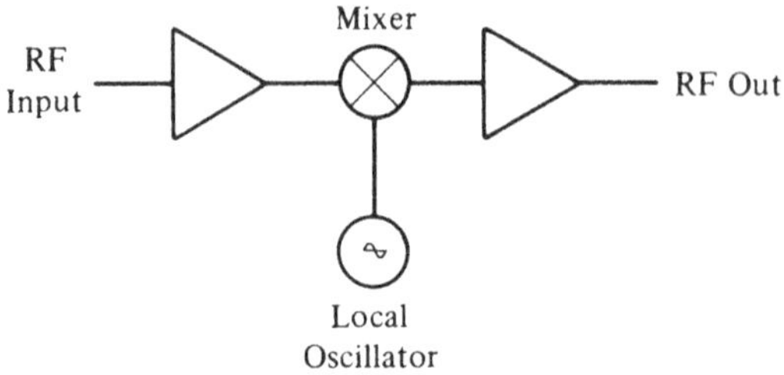

Figure 4-8
An example of a system where the origin of spurious responses can be found with the use of an adjustable attenuator.

As an example, Fig. 4-8 shows a cascaded system consisting of an amplifier, a mixer, and a second amplifier.

Placing the attenuator ahead of the entire system shows that a 1-dB decrease in signal level causes a 3-dB decrease in third order intermodulation. Moving the attenuator between the input of the mixer and the first amplifier shows a similar behavior. This eliminates the input amplifier as the culprit. Moving the attenuator again to the output of the first mixer and the second amplifier results in a situation in which the increase of 1 dB of attenuation does not affect the spurious responses. Therefore, the spurious signals are being generated in the mixer.

Review Questions for Chapter 4

1. What general precautions should be taken when using a spectrum analyzer to prevent damage to the input mixer?
2. What specific precautions should be taken when measuring pulse spectra?
3. What is an impulse modulated signal?
4. How is an envelope display generated? How does this differ from a line display?
5. What is the relationship between the pulse width of a modulated carrier and the spectrum?
6. A filter has a bandwidth that is proportional to a cosine^2 function. The 3-dB bandwidth of this filter is 100 kHz; what is the impulse bandwidth?
7. The difference between the 3-dB, impulse, and noise bandwidths, in many spectrum analyzers is very small. For problems 7, 8, and 9, assume the noise and impulse bandwidths are the same. An impulse signal with a density of 100 μV/MHz is applied to a spectrum analyzer and viewed with a 300-kHz impulse bandwidth IF filter. What would be the amplitude of the display, in dBm?
8. If a true-random noise signal produced the same amplitude as the impulse-modulated signal in problem 7, with an IF filter that had a noise bandwidth of 300 kHz, what would the noise power density be in dBm/MHz?

9. If the IF bandwidth was changed from 300 kHz to 100 kHz for both noise and impulse bandwidth, what would be the resulting amplitudes for the noise and impulse-modulated signals?
10. A spectrum analyzer has a 1-dB compression point of -7 dBm and a noise floor of -75 dBm when using an IF filter with an impulse bandwidth of 1 MHz. If a pulse-modulated signal with a voltage density of 1mV/MHz were applied to the analyzer, what would be the available dynamic range?
11. If it were desired to measure the on/off ratio of the signal described in problem 10, what would be the maximum ratio that could be measured?
12. Relative to the unmodulated carrier amplitude how much above the carrier amplitude, in decibels, would the peak of a 75% modulated carrier rise? How far below?
13. Relative to the carrier amplitude, how far above and below would the carrier level would a 75% modulated signal rise and fall?
14. To calibrate a broadcast transmitter-exciter modulation meter at the stereo pilot tone frequency of 19 kHz, a spectrum analyzer is used with Bessel nulls. What nulls would be useful and what peak deviation calibration points would be available?
15. If the attenuator at the input of the spectrum analyzer were reduced 10 dB and some of the displayed signals reduced by 10 dB, others by 20, and others by 30, which signals are spurious signals? Where are they generated? What types of spurious signals do they represent?
16. If reducing the input attenuator to a spectrum analyzer by 10 dB causes the displayed signal to be reduced by 15 dB, what is this an indication of?

5

Advanced Spectrum Analyzer Applications

This chapter will present additional spectrum analyzer applications using more sophisticated techniques and additional auxiliary devices.

5.1 Transmitter Measurements

5.1.1 Spurious Outputs

Measuring the spectral purity of radio transmitters is a specific application of a simple spectrum measurement. The techniques of making transmitter measurements involve the prevention of damage to the analyzer from the transmitter power and preventing spurious responses due to incidental radiation from the transmitter case. This radiation, should it ingress through the spectrum analyzer, would cause erroneous measurements.

When measuring the spectrum of a radio transmitter, it is necessary that the transmitter be terminated with a load that matches the impedance of the unit under test. Usually the termination is 50 Ω, which may be obtained from one of two sources. First, the transmitter may be terminated with a power attenuator that will present a good 50-Ω load while providing an attenuated output for the spectrum analyzer. A second method involves connecting the transmitter to a 50-Ω power termination, often referred to as a "dummy load," or "dummy antenna." The power supplied to the spectrum analyzer may be obtained by inserting a directional coupler between the transmitter and the dummy load.

Power attenuators provide between 20 and 30 dB attenuation, which reduces the power of a radio transmitter to a level where normal laboratory attenuators may be used to provide further attenuation. As an example, a 1000-W transmitter connected to a 30-dB power attenuator would reduce the transmitter power to 1 W, which could be further attenuated with a typical laboratory attenuator or connected directly to the spectrum analyzer.

For the safety and proper operation of the radio transmitter, it is necessary that the transmitter be terminated with an impedance relatively close to the design value. Generally, high-power radio transmitters have safety circuits that will shut down the radio transmitter when the load is different from the design value. A mismatched load will produce standing waves that could cause damage to the transmitter. The power attenuator with an impedance equal to the design value and which offers 20- or 30-dB attenuation will provide a termination sufficiently close to the design value, regardless of whether the output of the attenuator is connected to the spectrum analyzer or is open. Therefore, it is perfectly safe to disconnect the spectrum analyzer from the output of the attenuator.

When a dummy load and a directional coupler are used, a 30-dB coupler will provide a termination similar to that provided by the 30-dB power attenuator. Likewise, it is safe to disconnect the spectrum analyzer from the coupled port on the directional coupler.

When measuring a radio transmitter, it is very important to determine the amount of signal leakage from the transmitter to the spectrum analyzer.

The spectrum analyzer is capable of displaying signals as weak as −115 dBm. A 1000-W radio transmitter has a power of +60 dBm. This requires an attenuation of 175 dB to prevent any signal power from the radio transmitter from reaching the spectrum analyzer from a path other than the normal signal flow. When using a spectrum analyzer, it is not normally necessary to determine the amount of signal leakage into the spectrum analyzer. However, when a very large amplitude signal is being measured, it is important to determine the amount of leakage from the transmitter to the spectrum analyzer. The transmitter is terminated with its design impedance using either the dummy load or the power attenuator. The spectrum analyzer is terminated with a resistive termination, and the input attenuator is set to the amount of greatest attenuation.

The spectrum analyzer display should show no signals when the transmitter is activated. In the case of a single-sideband transmitter, be sure that modulation is applied to the transmitter so that the transmitter is producing an output power.

Vary the attenuator from the amount of greatest attenuation to the setting of least attenuation while checking for spurious responses. Be sure to check any potential spurious responses by removing the radio transmitter power to be certain the spurious response is due to the transmitter and not from some other source.

The discovery of a leakage does not make transmitter measurements impossible. It is necessary to know at what frequency and at what level the spurious response due to leakage occurs. Most likely, the leakage will not cause an error of measurement, but this fact will not be known unless the location and level of the spurious leakages are determined.

Generally, if the spurious leakage is more than 10 dB below the desired measurement level, the error due to the leakage is less than 0.5 dB and may be ignored.

Many transmitter measurements are required by law and are for harmonics and other nonharmonic spurious outputs. Another required measurement is occupied bandwidth, which is the frequency bandwidth that encompasses 99% of the transmitted energy.

In many cases, the harmonics of the transmitter are required to be lower than the level of the internally generated spurious responses within the spectrum analyzer. If this is the case, it is necessary to reduce the fundamental of the transmitter output with a notch filter or high-pass filter.

For some low-power transmitters, the level of harmonic generation required by law may be within the harmonic dynamic range of the analyzer, and a filter is not required. As always, it is a prudent habit to check the spectrum analyzer display for the internal generation of spurious responses before a measurement is accepted as correct.

Figure 5-1 shows the connections for the measurement of the harmonic level of a radio transmitter using a high-pass filter. The cutoff frequency of the high-pass filter must be greater than the transmitter output frequency, and the filter should have minimal loss at the second harmonic. The levels of the harmonics are measured with the high-pass filter in place.

The high-pass filter will affect the level of each spurious signal by a differ-

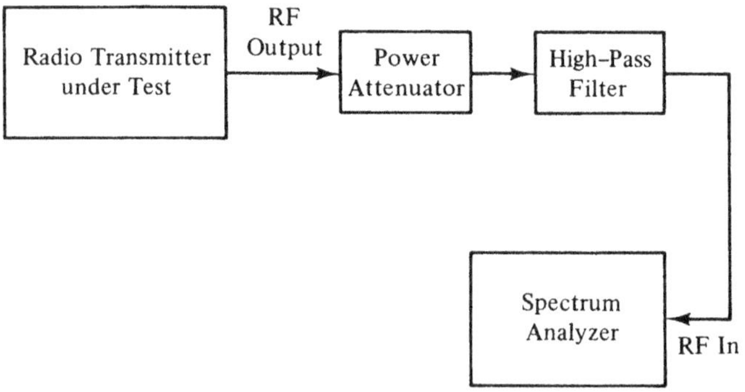

Figure 5-1
For the measurement of the harmonics of a radio transmitter, a high-pass filter reduces the level of the carrier to prevent generation of harmonics within the spectrum analyzer.

ent amount. It is necessary to know the shape of the high-pass filter to make an accurate measurement.

Spurious levels are often specified by law relative to the carrier level or the peak transmitter power, which requires the measurement of the transmitter power. The transmitter power may be measured using a wattmeter rather than the spectrum analyzer, as long as the potential errors of this method are understood. RF power meters take two forms. First is the in-line meter, which uses a directional coupler and a diode detector. A second type is a bolometer type of meter that requires an external directional coupler, or it may terminate the transmitter through suitable attenuation.

The in-line wattmeter using the diode detector responds to the average *voltage* of the RF signal. It is important to understand that the term voltage is used here. The wattmeter may be calibrated in "watts," but the measurement is voltage.

On the other hand, the bolometer type of RF power measurement is a true RMS power measurement.

The level of transmitter spurious outputs is relative to the transmitter carrier power or, in some cases, peak power output, but neither power meter is capable of measuring peak power. Unless the modulation is removed, the power meter tends to have errors when measuring the carrier level of amplitude-modulated transmitters.

The high-pass filter method of making transmitter spurious-level measurements is suited to harmonic outputs but has a potentially serious flaw for other spurious outputs. The high-pass filter must effectively block the fundamental output of the transmitter while passing the harmonics. The region below the frequency of the second harmonic but above the transmitter output frequency is a region where the high-pass filter makes a transition from rejection to minimal attenuation. The closer the frequency of interest is to the carrier frequency, the more difficult it is to make an accurate assessment. An alternate method is to use a notch filter and to suppress only the carrier frequency and allow the remaining spectrum to be measured without attenuation.

Figure 5-2 shows an arrangement for the measurement of transmitter spurious outputs using a notch filter. It is important to assure that once the notch is tuned to the transmitter output frequency, the transmitter is not allowed to operate at another frequency without the notch being retuned. If the notch is relied on to provide attenuation of the transmitter power that is below the damage level of the analyzer, this unexpected change in transmitter frequency could cause damage to the analyzer. It would be prudent to attenuate the transmitter output to a level below the damage level of the analyzer and rely on the notch only to increase the measurement dynamic range.

To obtain a deep attenuation of the carrier and to allow measurement of spurious outputs close to the carrier, it is necessary for the notch filter to have a

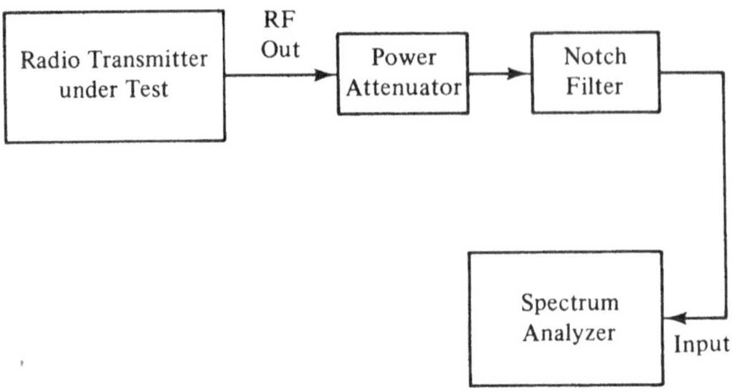

Figure 5-2
In this setup for transmitter measurements, a notch filter is used to reduce the level of the carrier and provide increased dynamic range for spurious outputs.

high Q. In the VHF region, tunable cavities are used; at HF and lower frequency regions, conventional L-C circuits using high-Q inductors and low-loss capacitors are used. Typically, a 3-dB bandwidth of a few percent is possible, which will allow the measurement of spurious outputs to within 10% or so of the operating frequency.

5.1.2 Occupied Bandwidth

Many regulatory requirements insist that a certain percentage of the energy of a radio transmission be contained within a specified bandwidth. The spectrum analyzer provides an indication of the power at a specific frequency. When measuring the occupied bandwidth, it is not necessary to determine the absolute energy transmitted but to determine the energy distribution, to be sure the required percentage of transmitted energy is contained within the necessary bandwidth.

For the case of a transmitter in which the modulation produces discrete sidebands, it is necessary to sum the energy of the carrier and the sidebands and determine the percentage of energy within the required bandwidth.

As an example, consider the frequency-modulated transmitter shown in Fig. 5-3. In this example, a carrier is frequency modulated with a 1-kHz sine wave. Since the absolute energy is not important, take the largest spectral component and assign to it an arbitrary power level. In this example, the greatest spectral component is the carrier, and it is assigned a power level of m watts.

The first sideband is 6 dB below the carrier and has a power level of $m/4$ watts. However, there are two sidebands, each with a power level of $m/4$ watts for a total power of $m/2$ watts. The second sideband is 15 dB down from the carrier, which is a power level of $m/32$ watts. Again, since there are two side-

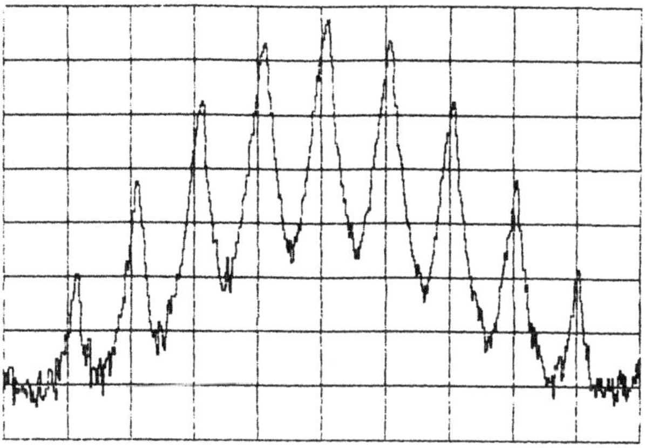

Figure 5-3
An example of a frequency-modulated carrier for determining the occupied bandwidth.

bands, the total power from the two sidebands is $m/16$ watts. The third pair of sidebands are 30 dB down from the carrier, and thus the power contributed by these sidebands is $m/500$ watts. Since all the remaining sidebands are 40 dB or greater below the carrier, the power contributed by these sidebands is less than 0.02% per sideband pair and may be omitted from the calculation.

The total power from the carrier and the first three sidebands is $m + m/2 + m/16 + m/500$ watts $= 1.5645m$ watts. Normalizing all the energy contributions yields 63.92% from the carrier, 31.96% from the first pair of sidebands, 3.99% from the second pair of sidebands, and 0.128% from the third pair of sidebands.

From the above, it is evident that 99% of the energy of the frequency modulated carrier used as an example is contained within the carrier and the first and second sidebands. Since the modulation frequency is 1 kHz, the second sideband is removed from the carrier by 2 kHz; thus, 99% of the energy is contained within 4 kHz. The occupied bandwidth is 4 kHz.

When measuring the occupied bandwidth of a pulse-modulated carrier, a similar technique is used; but rather than discrete sidebands, the value of the modulation envelope is used.

It is important that sufficient points are taken to insure an accurate result. Figure 5-4 shows an envelope spectral display of a pulse-modulated waveform. In this case, the pulse width is 1 μs, so that the nulls of the envelope occur at intervals of 1 MHz. If the pulse-modulated signal does not have any frequency modulation, the spectrum is symmetrical. In addition, the lobes are of the same shape and width, with the exception of the center lobe, which is the same shape but twice as wide as the other lobes.

To find the actual energy contained in each lobe, the power density of that lobe would be integrated over the frequency width of the lobe.

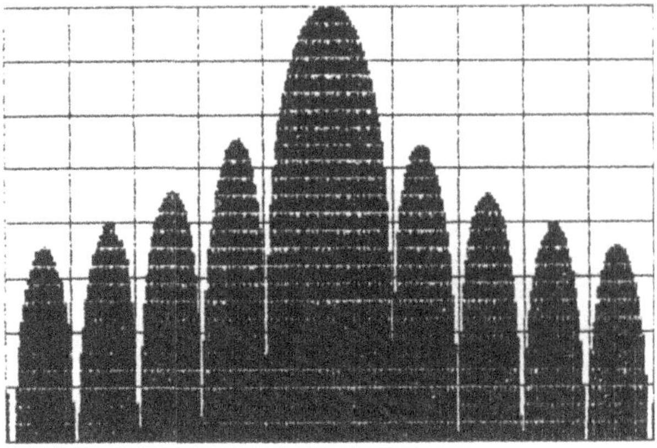

Figure 5-4
An example of a pulse-modulated carrier for the determination of occupied bandwidth.

Since the waveform shown in the figure is a pulse-modulated broad-band waveform, the voltage of each lobe is proportional to the voltage density of each lobe. Since each lobe has the same shape and width, with the exception of the main lobe, the energy contained in each lobe relative to any other lobe is equal to the square of the ratio of their peaks.

As an example, if one lobe is 10 dB below another, the energy contained in the lower lobe is one tenth of the greater. The main lobe, however, has twice the energy as any other lobe because it is twice the width.

Consider the example of Fig. 5-4. The main lobe is given an equivalent energy of $2m$. The first set of lobes are 25 dB down from the main lobe and thus would have an energy content of $m/316$. Since there are two lobes just as there are pairs of sidebands, the first upper and lower lobes as a pair add an energy of $m/158$. The next set of upper and lower lobes are 35 dB down and add an energy of $m/1580$. the contribution of the third and higher lobes is rather insignificant relative to the main and first lobes, and the effects of those lobes may be ignored.

The total energy content is $2m + 0.00633m$ which, to within 99%, puts the energy only in the main lobe. In other words, to within 99.9%, the energy is contained in the main lobe and the first two side lobes.

If the spectrum is asymmetrical due to simultaneous frequency modulation, often called pulling, each side of the spectrum must be considered separately. The addition of frequency modulation due to pulling increases the occupied bandwidth.

5.1.3 Frequency Stability

Spectrum analyzers with storage capability, particularly those with digital storage, may be used to measure the frequency drift of a radio transmitter. Of

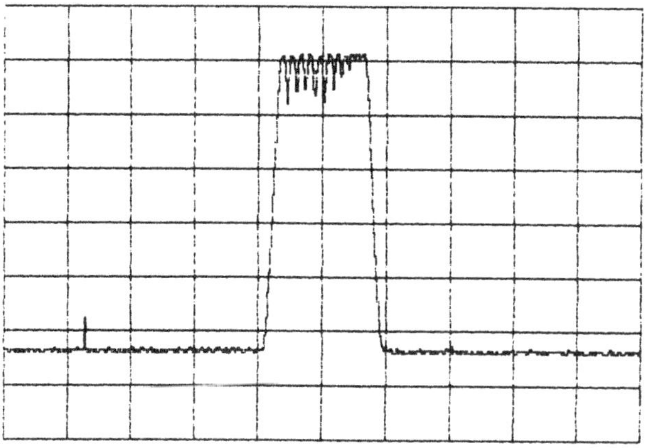

Figure 5-5
An example of the measurement of long-term frequency drift using the peak–hold feature of the spectrum analyzer.

course, since this technique may be used to measure the frequency drift of any oscillator, it is well-suited for transmitters.

Many environmental stimuli may cause frequency drift. Temperature, power supply voltage variation, and aging are some of the more prevalent ones. Of course, aging is a very long-time phenomenon and is best handled by measurements using a frequency counter. Temperature and power supply voltage-induced frequency drift is immediate and may be measured using the spectrum analyzer.

Using the storage capacity of the spectrum analyzer or the peak hold feature, the maximum and minimum frequency excursions of the measured frequency are visible, as shown in Fig. 5-5. It is very important, however, that the spectrum analyzer does not suffer from frequency instability, as the resulting data would include the frequency drift of not only the device under test but the spectrum analyzer.

5.2 In-Circuit Troubleshooting Techniques

The spectrum analyzer may be used as a powerful troubleshooting tool. The spectrum analyzer techniques described until now have involved viewing the spectrum of subsystems, usually with connectors and a well-defined impedance such as 50 Ω. The spectrum analyzer is not thought of as a troubleshooting tool, such as the oscilloscope. To locate difficulties in electronic circuits, it is normal to use the oscilloscope with a probe and make various measurements within an operating circuit and thus determine where signals are being lost, or where distortion is generated, and so on. This oscilloscope is capable of measuring signals regardless of the impedance of the circuit under test. When the oscilloscope is used with a 10X probe the oscilloscope does not load the circuit under test, as a 50-Ω spectrum analyzer is likely to do. In addition, the existence of DC voltage levels does not damage the oscilloscope.

There are two devices that may be used with the spectrum analyzer to allow the instrument to be used more like an oscilloscope. The first device is an active high-impedance probe. This device provides a unity voltage-gain amplifier that provides a 50-Ω signal output that will interface with the spectrum analyzer. In addition, the active probe provides AC coupling so that DC levels will not cause damage to the analyzer, should they be encountered. The input impedance of this device depends on the manufacturer, but is typically in the 10–50 kΩ range with a frequency range extending from near-DC to about 100 MHz. It is difficult to use a high-impedance probe for frequencies greater than about 100 MHz as the shunt capacitance of the probe will cause loading of the higher frequency circuits, with resultant errors.

A second device is available from instrument makers but is usually constructed by the analyzer owner or operator. This device is an inductive pick-up loop or "sniffer" as it is often called. This device is shown in Fig. 5-6 and is an electrostatically shielded loop.

This device may be made from any type of coaxial cable with any dimensions desired. Generally, a loop more than 1 inch in diameter is undesirable. If higher frequencies are involved, such as those above 500 MHz, the diameter of the loop should be on the order of ⅜ inch and may have fewer turns. Since the loop is so easy to construct, it would be a simple matter to have several loops available for different frequency ranges.

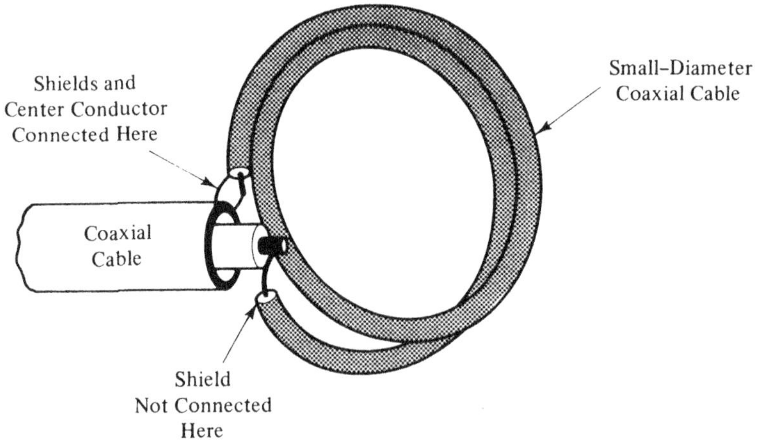

Figure 5-6
Construction details of an electrostatically shielded sampling loop for use with a spectrum analyzer.

The loop is constructed by winding three, two, or even a single turn of coaxial cable and connecting the shield of the loop to the shield of the connecting cable. It is important to not connect both ends of the coaxial cable of the loop to the shield of the connecting cable. This would cause a shorted turn and significantly decrease the sensitivity of the loop. The use of coaxial cable for the loop allows the shield of the cable to act as an electrostatic shield to prevent the pick-up of energy from electric fields.

The use of more turns allows the loop to be more sensitive, but the increased inductance causes the loop to have reduced sensitivity at higher frequencies. Fewer turns will result in a loop that has lower sensitivity overall but a broader frequency range.

The pick-up loop is used to trace signal flow in RF circuits, particularly where open inductors are involved. By placing the pick-up loop on the axis of a coil, voltage is induced in the pick-up loop. If the coil is held not too close to the circuit being investigated, these circuits may be tuned for maximum response. The pick-up loop does not allow for a calibrated measurement, only relative indications. It is quite useful for tracking signal flow to determine the loss of system gain, starting and tuning crystal oscillators, finding the source of spurious signals, and adjusting tuned circuits.

Another important application of the pick-up loop is locating the source of RF energy leakage from shielded enclosures. By passing the loop over the seams of a shielded enclosure, the "hot spots" of the seams can be located. The size of the loop will depend on the frequencies, as before. Interconnecting cables may be investigated by placing the pick-up loop near a suspected wire, as shown in Fig. 5-7.

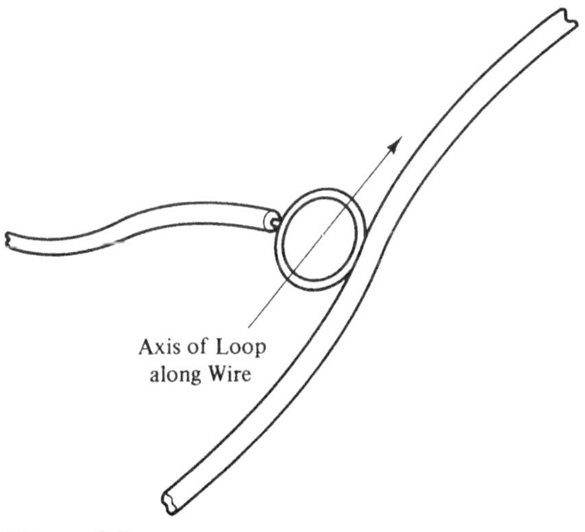

Figure 5-7
An example of the proper placement of a pick-up loop relative to a wire.

5.3 Radio Frequency Interference Measurements

The spectrum analyzer may be used for the measurement of the level of potentially interfering radiation. The spectrum analyzer is used as a broad-band radio receiver, in conjunction with various antennas, for measuring the level of radiated emissions from electronic equipment.

There are two basic types of radio interference, conducted and radiated. Often the two mix, with conducted interference becoming radiated.

Radiated interference is energy that is radiated directly from the cabinet, enclosures, or the interconnecting cables of the unit under test. Conducted interference is that which is coupled onto the interconnecting cables and is conducted into other equipment.

EMI, electromagnetic interference, is one-half of a design goal called EMC or electromagnetic compatibility. The other half of EMC is electromagnetic susceptibility. To prevent electronic equipment from mutually interfering, units should not only be prevented from emanating RF energy, but also should be immune from the effects of radiated and conducted interference.

Electromagnetic susceptibility is measured by placing the equipment under test in a known electromagnetic field and assessing the effects. In addition, the effects of conducted interference are evaluated by deliberately introducing energy of various frequencies to the interconnecting cables. Susceptibility tests and evaluations use signal sources and antennas and do not use the spectrum analyzer.

Electromagnetic interference is measured by the use of a spectrum analyzer and suitable antennas for radiated noise. For conducted noise, the spectrum analyzer is coupled to the lines under test using coupling devices.

Electromagnetic interference is divided into two basic categories, broad-band interference and narrow-band interference.

Narrow-band interference is, generally, a situation in which the true amplitude of the interfering signal may be accurately measured without the use of the impulse bandwidth of the IF filter. Broad-band interference requires the techniques discussed under pulsed-carrier measurements, in which it is necessary to define the energy relative to a distribution. To accurately measure the energy level of the broad-band signal, the impulse bandwidth of the IF filter must be known and all the precautions and corrections necessary for pulse measurements must be followed.

There are many acceptable methods of measuring electromagnetic interference. The methods describe how the equipment is arranged and operated and an attempt is made to duplicate the actual operating environment. Often, a conductive table is used in a shielded room, so the effects of interference from outside sources, such as broadcast stations, will be minimized. The length and dress of the interconnecting cables is also specified. It is not possible in this text to describe any one technique completely, or even to touch on all the possible published standards. In this chapter, as an example of the applications of the spectrum analyzer, one technique will be used as an example. This specification is from the Radio Technical Commission for Aeronautics, RTCA, and is usually the initiating document from which the FAA issues "Technical Standard Orders" (TSOs). Other EMI/EMC specifications and procedures are military, FCC, Electronics Industry Association, American National Standards Institute, IEEE, and many foreign requirements.

To measure the amount of conducted interference on a signal or power line, a device called a line impedance stabilization network is used. This device is shown in Fig. 5-8. The purpose of this device is to provide a defined termination impedance for the line under test. The actual termination impedance of the unit as it is installed within an aircraft is unknown. The actual impedance to RF currents depends on the location on the power or signal line of the device under test. To set a standard impedance, the line impedance stabilization network, LISN, will be used for all measurements. This device is a simple network that provides an inductance, and hence a high impedance, to RF current so that the spectrum analyzer provides the terminating impedance for the RF current. In the case of RTCA interference requirements, that terminating impedance is 50 Ω. The 5k resistor shown in the diagram of the LISN is for the purpose of discharging the capacitor so that, if the analyzer were connected after the power supply was energized, the capacitor would be charged to the power supply voltage and would not charge through the spectrum analyzer, possibly causing damage.

To measure the level of conducted interference on a power supply or other interconnecting line, the equipment under test is operated under normal modes of operation and the spectrum analyzer is used to measure the interference levels on the interconnecting lines.

Typically, several forms of interference will be present. There are broadband signals, such as the noise from a switching power supply. This will be the actual switching frequency, plus various harmonics that can extend well into the RF spectrum depending on the switching frequency of the unit. Computers

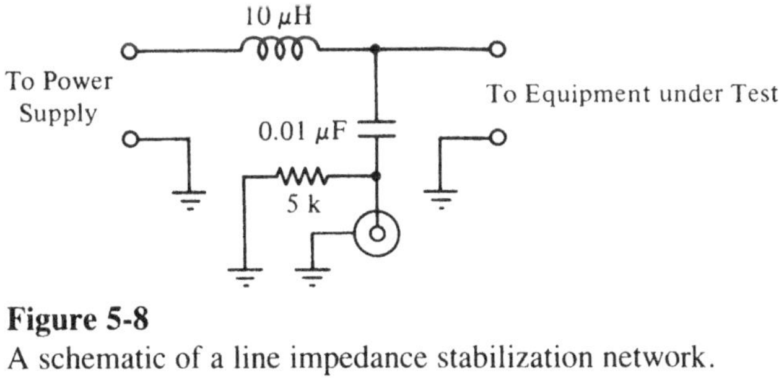

Figure 5-8
A schematic of a line impedance stabilization network.

and digital logic can cause other broad-band interference. Narrow-band interference can be caused by oscillators and other sources where there is a constant frequency.

The narrow-band signals are measured and specified as a voltage level, usually dBμV, which is decibels above one microvolt. To convert dBm, the usual unit of measurement used in spectrum analysis, to dBμV, add 107 dB. As an example, a -60-dBm signal is $+47$ dBμV.

The broad-band signals are measured and converted to the equivalent impulse spectral density. The measured power is converted to dBμV and the result divided by the impulse bandwidth, in megahertz, of the IF filter producing dBμV/MHz. All the normal precautions for impulse noise measurement must be followed in the broad-band measurement.

An alternative method of measuring conducted interference is to use a current probe. This device is a toroid transformer where the line under test is the primary of the transformer and the spectrum analyzer is connected to the secondary. Transformers of this type, with a very small number of turns for a primary and a much larger number of turns for the secondary, essentially convert current to voltage. Therefore, the transfer function of the current probe is resistance. The voltage in the secondary is

$$V_s = I_p R_t \tag{5-1}$$

where V_s is the voltage induced in the secondary, I_p is the current in the primary, and R_t is the transfer resistance.

The radiated interference is measured using test antennas. These antennas are used with a calibration factor that converts the voltage induced into the 50 Ω of the spectrum analyzer to the actual field intensity in volts per meter. This antenna factor is different for each measuring frequency.

Most test procedures require several different types of antennas to be used to cover the full frequency range of the measurements. For the low frequencies, a short vertical antenna is used in conjunction with a base-mounted tuning network. It would be totally impractical to use a full-sized dipole antenna at these lower frequencies. For the higher frequencies, beginning with 30 MHz, it is possible to use dipole antennas cut for the frequency of measurement. Above 1000 MHz, the dipole antenna becomes difficult to adjust to the operating frequency, and a horn antenna is used for the remaining frequency range.

Review Questions for Chapter 5

1. What are some of the accepted methods of reducing the power from a radio transmitter to a suitable level for use with a spectrum analyzer?
2. What precautions and checks should be made to a spectrum analyzer when measuring the output of a high-power radio transmitter?

3. How are harmonic level measurements made when the requirement for the level of harmonics is beyond the dynamic range of the spectrum analyzer?
4. What precautions should be taken when the carrier level of a transmitter is determined using a rectifier type of wattmeter?
5. A transmitter is amplitude modulated with a distorted 1-kHz sine function such that the 1-kHz sidebands are down 8 dB from the carrier; the 2-kHz sidebands, −12 dB; 3-kHz sidebands, −18 dB; the 4-kHz sidebands, −20 dB; and the higher order sidebands more than 40 dB. What is the occupied bandwidth using 99% as the energy content?
6. What causes an asymmetrical spectrum?
7. How would a spectrum analyzer be used to measure frequency stability?
8. What is an inductive pick-up loop and how would it be used?
9. In the inductive pick-up loop, why is the shield of the loop not connected to ground at both ends?
10. What is a line impedance stabilization network?

6

The Tracking Generator and Scalar Network Analysis

6.1 Tracking Generator Basics

The spectrum analyzer is a particularly useful tool for observing low-level signals at high frequencies. In conjunction with a signal generator, it is useful for tuning bandpass and band-stop filters, especially those with deep notches and steep skirts. This was described in the previous chapter.

Using a signal generator implies that only one frequency can be observed at a time. If a bandpass filter were to be tuned it would be difficult to tune it for a specific characteristic. In the case of a narrow filter where only one frequency is tuned, this may not be difficult. In the case of a single-pole filter, that is, a filter that has only one tuned circuit, only one frequency is required for proper tuning. When a filter has several poles or combinations of poles and zeros, it becomes exceedingly difficult to properly tune the filter.

Without a spectrum analyzer, a sweep generator could be used to tune filters. A diode detector would be used as the output indicator but the detector has a limited dynamic range, usually on the order of 30 to 40 dB. It is not unusual for a filter to have a stop band that is 60 dB deep or greater, which is far beyond the capabilities of the diode detector.

What is desired, in order to use the spectrum analyzer as a detector for tuning filters and other devices, is a signal generator that provides a signal at precisely the same frequency as the input frequency of the spectrum analyzer.

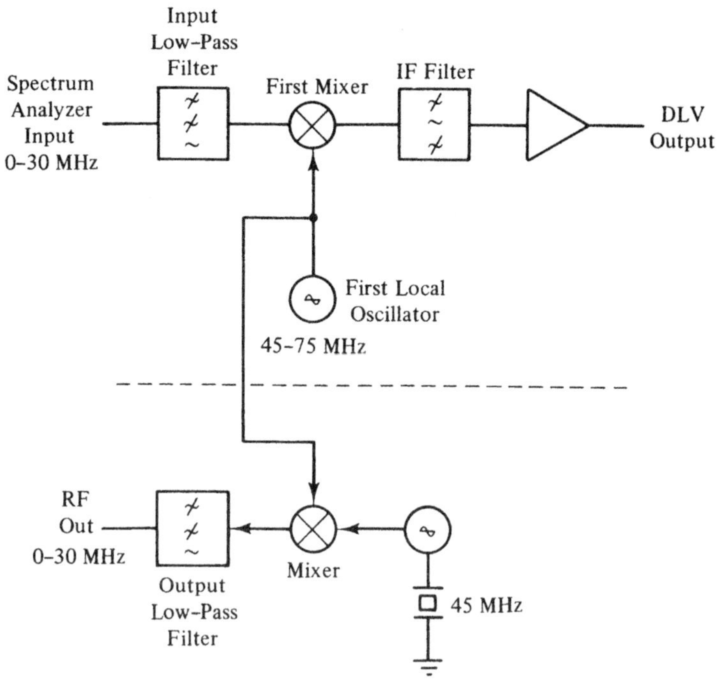

Figure 6-1
Block diagram of a simple tracking generator connected to a single conversion spectrum analyzer.

This device is called the tracking generator because of its ability to provide a signal that tracks the input to the spectrum analyzer.

This tracking signal is generated by essentially operating the spectrum analyzer "in reverse." Figure 6-1 shows a block diagram of a tracking generator connected to a spectrum analyzer. Recall from Chapter 3 that the input frequency of a spectrum analyzer is

$$F_{\text{in}} = F_{\text{LO}} - F_{\text{IF}} \tag{6-1}$$

where F_{in} is the input frequency of the spectrum analyzer, F_{LO} is the local oscillator frequency of the analyzer, and F_{IF} is the IF. If the analyzer in question has more than one conversion, the frequency of the other lcal oscillators are included in Eq. (6-1).

Referring to Fig. 6-1, the tracking generator output is generated by mixing an oscillator at the IF with the local oscillator of the analyzer and filtering the difference frequency to provide the output.

The frequency of the output is

$$F_{\text{out}} = F_{\text{LO}} - F_{\text{IF}} \tag{6-2}$$

Notice that the output frequency of the tracking generator is exactly the input frequency of the spectrum analyzer.

The example of Fig. 6-1 is for the purpose of explanation, and single-conversion spectrum analyzers are rare. However, the features of a tracking generator can be described with a simple example.

The oscillator, A1, operates at the IF. Two important facts concerning this oscillator must be mentioned. First, the frequency must be exactly the IF of the spectrum analyzer and, second, energy must not be allowed to escape from the tracking generator because it could be coupled to the IF amplifier in the spectrum analyzer and cause interference.

A crystal oscillator is usually sufficient to provide an accurate IF frequency generation. Since the local oscillator is the same used in the spectrum analyzer, the output frequency is as close to the input frequency of the spectrum analyzer as the IF oscillator is to the actual IF frequency of the spectrum analyzer.

A very important characteristic of the tracking generator must be examined. The output frequency of the tracking generator is *exactly* the same as the input frequency of the spectrum analyzer. The word exactly is emphasized because it is important to understand what exactly means in this case.

The concept of long- and short-term frequency stability was discussed in Chapters 2 and 3. It is easy to see how the output frequency of the tracking generator is exactly the same as the input frequency of the spectrum analyzer for a long-term frequency drift. It may not be as apparent how this drift-canceling works with a tracking generator and what advantage this serves in the application of the tracking generator.

Consider a spectrum analyzer with a signal generator as an input source. If the frequency span of the spectrum analyzer were reduced to a very narrow value, the phase noise, that is, the short term instability of the signal generator, would be evident. Actually, the phase noise displayed by the spectrum analyzer would be a combination of the phase noise of the input signal—in this case the signal generator—and the local oscillators of the spectrum analyzer. Phase noise is a totally random phenomenon. Therefore, the phase noise power from the input signal simply adds to the phase noise of the local oscillator. As an example, if the phase noise 1 kHz removed from both the input signal and the local oscillator were 80 dB down from the carrier, −80 dBc, the resultant phase noise would be −77 dBc.

Suppose the input signal and the local oscillator frequency moved in exactly the same way as the input signal. For each jump in frequency of the input signal, the local oscillator would jump the same amount. Thus, the signal fed to the IF filter and amplifier in the spectrum analyzer would be free of frequency drift because changes in the input signal frequency would be counteracted by the change in local oscillator frequency.

This characteristic is important. To maximize the dynamic range of the spectrum analyzer, the IF bandwidth should be reduced to the minimum amount. A reduction in IF bandwidth is not effective if the signal that passes through the

IF filter in the spectrum analyzer has any amount of phase noise present. This cancellation of phase noise allows a very narrow IF filter to be used in the spectrum analyzer when the tracking generator is used.

The phase noise is present at the tracking generator output, and this does limit the ability of the tracking generator to sweep very narrow frequency devices. When the noisy output is passed through a narrow device such as a crystal filter, the phase noise from the tracking generator will be converted to amplitude noise and will appear on the spectrum analyzer display.

The simple single-conversion spectrum analyzer was used for the purpose of discussion, and a tracking generator for the example spectrum analyzer will be presented to introduce the practical problems and limitations of this device.

6.2 The Superheterodyne Tracking Generator

Figure 6-2 shows a tracking generator covering the frequency range of 1 to 500 MHz for use with the example spectrum analyzer. Three frequency conversions are used in the example analyzer and the tracking generator has, likewise, three conversions.

A crystal oscillator is used to generate the IF signal, and this is heterodyned with 50 MHz from the spectrum analyzer. The sum frequency, 60.7 MHz, is filtered, amplified, and heterodyned with the second local oscillator from the spectrum analyzer. The sum frequency at 700 MHz is filtered, amplified, and heterodyned with the first local oscillator at 701 to 1200 MHz. The difference, which is from 1 to 500 MHz, is the resulting output.

Amplifiers are provided after each frequency conversion to provide for the loss of signal from the mixer and the filtering. The mixers provide a loss of about 6 to 7 dB, while the filters following the mixers have a loss of 1 or 2 dB, thus requiring a gain of 7 to 9 dB for each frequency conversion.

To insure the 10.7-MHz crystal oscillator in the tracking generator is the last IF frequency in the spectrum analyzer exactly, the frequency is made slightly variable. This is necessary because an IF filter as narrow as 1 kHz or possibly 300 Hz may be employed, which is 0.003% of the last IF. Even small errors will put the tracking generator signal out of the passband of the IF filter.

The 60.7-MHz intermediate frequency in the tracking generator is derived from two crystal sources and is spectrally pure. The 700-MHz intermediate frequency is a result of mixing with a free-running oscillator at 639.3 MHz and will have some phase noise present. This phase noise, just as the phase noise from the last heterodyning process, is canceled in the spectrum analyzer as previously explained.

The biggest hurdle in the design and construction of the tracking generator is to prevent leaking of signals from the tracking generator to the spectrum analyzer.

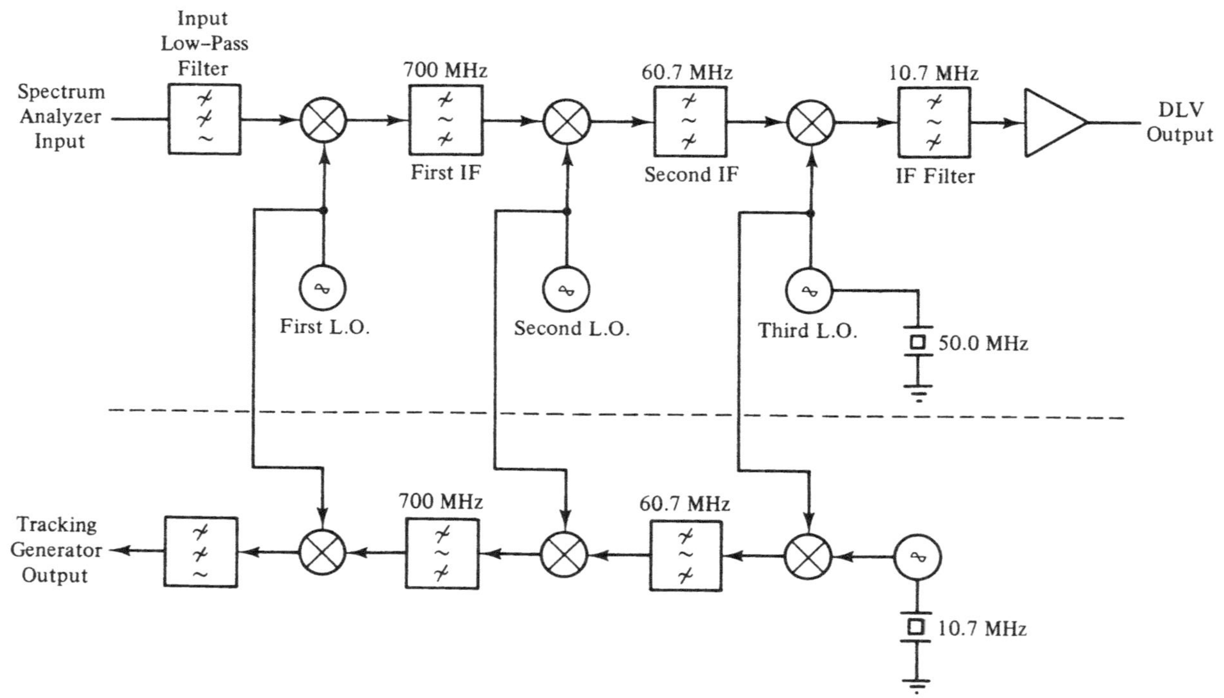

Figure 6-2
Block diagram for a tracking generator for the triple conversion example spectrum analyzer.

There are a multitude of paths for spurious signals to disrupt the spectrum analyzer. A number of these will be investigated with methods for reducing the effect.

Before investigating the effects, the relative level between a potential spurious signal and the sensitivity of the receiving system must be investigated.

The spectrum analyzer is capable of sensitivities of -100 to -115 dBm with the narrowest bandwidths. The tracking generator, on the other hand, would be useful with an output level of from 0 to $+10$ dBm. Providing a higher power would increase the dynamic range. However, many devices are not capable of handling powers greater than $+10$ dBm, and the issue of shielding becomes progressively more difficult. This results in a total loss from the output of the tracking generator to the spectrum analyzer of as much as 125 dB. Very few devices would require a measurement range this great, except an occasional very high-Q notch or bandpass filter.

Spurious responses are not injected into the spectrum analyzer at its input connector, but are radiated from unit to unit and conducted through the interconnecting cables. Therefore, spurious responses may result from various internal frequencies and never appear at the output of the tracking generator.

As an example, the 10.7-MHz crystal oscillator of Fig. 6-2 may be conducted or radiated into the spectrum analyzer. Of course, 10.7 MHz is the last IF of the analyzer, where most of the gain of the unit is obtained and where the lowest level signals are present.

It would appear, on the surface, to be an easy task to carefully shield the oscillator and prevent the 10.7-MHz oscillator energy from entering the IF amplifier and causing spurious responses. But it is not radiation that will be the nemesis making this isolation difficult—it is conduction, as shown Fig. 6.3

The 10.7-MHz oscillator is heterodyned with a balanced mixer to create the 60.7-MHz signal. Some of the 10.7-MHz energy present in all the ports of the mixer is conducted through the mixer and will travel to the spectrum analyzer and be injected into the 50-MHz local oscillator signal. Since this 50-MHz signal is fed to the last mixer in the spectrum analyzer, some 10.7-MHz energy will leak through the mixer and appear at the input of the IF amplifier.

The total leakage path is from the oscillator, through the tracking generator's mixer, through the spectrum analyzer's 50-MHz signal path, and through the last mixer in the spectrum analyzer, finally to the 10.7-MHz IF amplifier. This may seem like a long, complex path where it would be easy to stem the ingress. However, this is the most sensitive part of the spectrum analyzer, where the minimum detectable signal (MDS) could easily be -120 dBm. The local oscillator level for the tracking generator to drive a diode-type balanced mixer is typically $+7$ dBm, making the necessary isolation between the 10.7-MHz oscillator and the input to the IF amplifier 127 dB.

The typical isolation from the LO port to the RF port of a balanced mixer is, perhaps, 40 dB at 10.7 MHz. The isolation is encountered twice, as a bal-

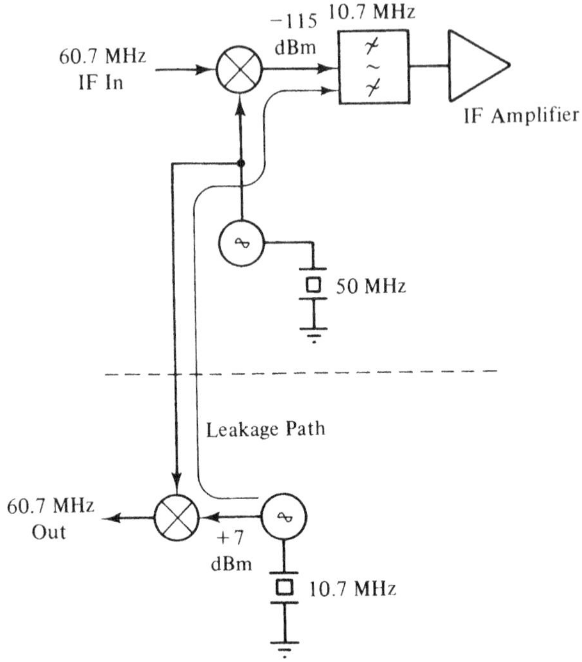

Figure 6-3
The interconnection of part of a spectrum analyzer to a tracking generator showing the potential signal leakage path.

anced mixer is present in the spectrum analyzer before the last IF amplifier. The remaining 42 dB of isolation must be achieved through the 50-MHz source in the spectrum analyzer. Luckily, it is not difficult to achieve this level of isolation with buffer amplifiers, attenuators, and careful shielding. An example of isolation and the resulting amounts is shown in Fig. 6-4.

This potential spurious response path exists for every mixer in the tracking generator. Consider the next mixer in the tracking generator, from 60.7 to 700 MHz. The 60.7-MHz input to the mixer in the tracking generator is the IF in the spectrum analyzer, and this is the potential spurious response. There are some differences in this mixer that work in a positive way for spurious rejection. In this case, the potential 60.7-MHz spurious signal may be the low-level RF input to the mixer and then can be at a much lower level than +7 dBm. The signal cannot be at a ridiculously low level, as noise will become a problem. A level of −10 dBm would be a reasonable amount. A disadvantage, however, is the leakage through the mixer from RF to LO port at the higher frequency. At 60.7 MHz the leakage would typically be 30 dB, which is 10 dB worse than at the 10.7-MHz frequency.

The path of the spurious signal would be similar to the first mix—from the mixer input, through the mixer into the spectrum analyzer, through the local oscillator circuits, and finally through the spectrum analyzer mixer.

It would seem the path were long and rife with barriers that provide isolation. It must be remembered, however, that the frequency involved in this case is six times greater than the 10.7-MHz example, and the isolation of various devices will be considerably less. The techniques and effort required to provide the necessary isolation are about equal to the 10.7-MHz case.

The next frequency mix in the tracking generator is the spectrum analyzer's second local oscillator signal with the 60.7-MHz signal in the tracking generator to produce an IF of 700 MHz, which is, of course, the first IF in the spectrum analyzer.

The path is the same, passing through the mixers and the local oscillator. However, the frequency is now 65 times greater than the 10.7-MHz example,

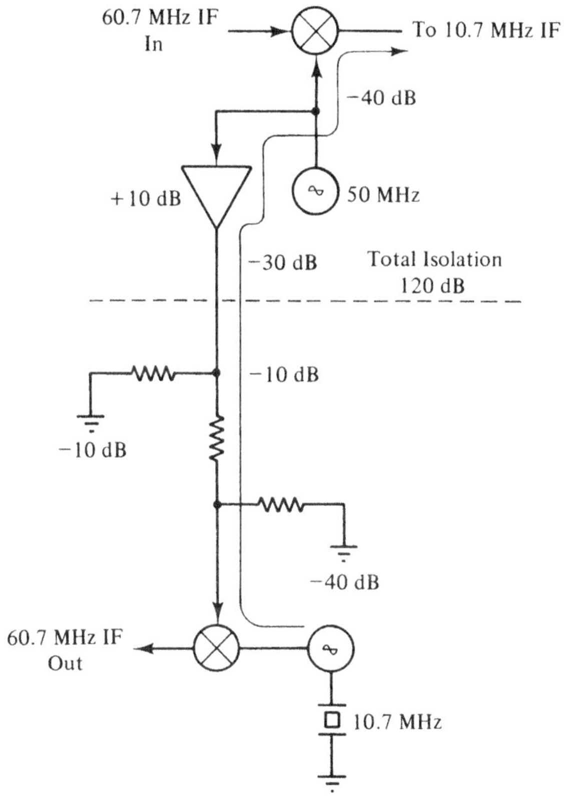

Figure 6-4
An example of improved isolation of the example in Fig. 6-3.

and the task becomes even more difficult. At 700 MHz, mixer isolation becomes only 20 to 25 dB, and little shielded boxes become cavities that may have very little isolation.

Some "shortcuts" may be taken in the design of a tracking generator. If some of the local oscillators of the spectrum analyzer are sufficiently stable, some of the mixes may be eliminated. As an example, the spectrum analyzer used in this text has a crystal-controlled third local oscillator at 50 MHz. In this previous example, the 60.7-MHz second IF was generated by heterodyning the 50-MHz LO from the spectrum analyzer with a 10.7-MHz crystal oscillator to generate 60.7 MHz. It would be simpler to use a crystal oscillator at 60.7 MHz to eliminate one mix and the attendant spurious response paths associated with that mix. It would be necessary to vary the 60.7-MHz signal slightly to center it in the spectrum analyzer passband as previously explained.

Using this technique, only two mixes are required to generate the tracking generator output.

This technique could be expanded to include the second local oscillator at 639.3 MHz, if it were sufficiently stable and if it were not frequency swept. In the example spectrum analyzer, the second local oscillator is neither, and the "shortcuts" are limited to eliminating only one frequency conversion.

If the tracking generator were used only for wide frequency sweeps, a free-running oscillator at a frequency of 700 MHz could be used and only one conversion would be necessary. The tracking generator is a much simpler device, with only one frequency conversion; but it would have a limited sweep range. Typically, a 200-kHz bandwidth would be suited for such a simple tracking generator, which would limit the total frequency sweep to no less than 10 MHz.

There are some alternative methods of achieving spurious isolation which also lead to some flexibility of the tracking generator. Rather than feeding the actual local oscillator signals from the spectrum analyzer to the tracking generator, the frequency is divided with a high-speed frequency scaler and fed to the tracking generator at a much lower frequency. This opens several advantages. Because the frequency is much lower, much simpler cabling and connectors may be used. In the case of the first local oscillator in the example spectrum analyzer, the frequency range is from 700 to 1200 MHz. High-frequency RF connectors must be used in this example. In addition, the length of the cable will be limited as the loss in coaxial cable at these frequencies is significant. Lengths of a few meters, which would be suitable for a tracking generator within the same room, would not introduce any serious problems. However, if the tracking generator were to be separated from the spectrum analyzer by several hundred meters, which would be needed for measuring the frequency response of an antenna or the shielding effectiveness of a shielded room, the loss would have to be made up in amplifiers.

If the local oscillator frequency were divided by a factor of, say, 128, the resultant output frequency for the example spectrum analyzer would be 5.5 to

9.4 MHz. This frequency can be transmitted over coaxial cable or twisted pair for very long distances by using the appropriate line drivers and receivers. The necessary hardware to accomplish this is readily available and rather inexpensive.

Figure 6-5 shows the block diagram of this technique. The frequency of the local oscillator is divided by a factor of 128 and transmitted to the tracking generator. The local oscillator of the tracking generator is, likewise, divided by a factor of 128 and fed to a phase/frequency detector. The other input of the phase/frequency detector is driven from the divided local oscillator from the spectrum analyzer. The phase-detector output is fed to a loop filter and to the tracking generator local oscillator to phase lock that oscillator to the spectrum analyzer.

Thus, the two oscillators are phase locked and will track without the need to transmit UHF signals. However, one of the significant advantages of the track-

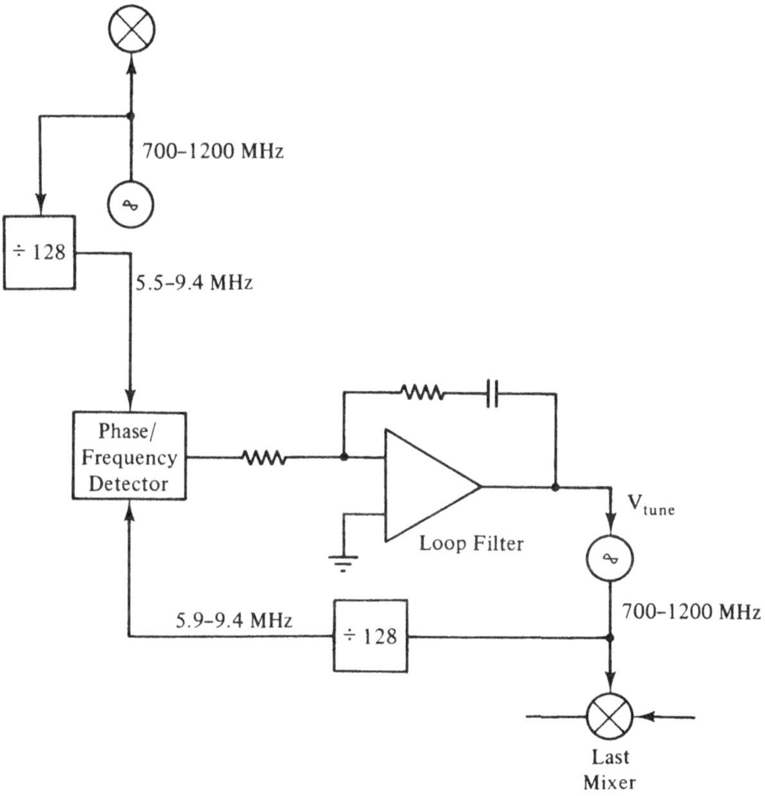

Figure 6-5
A method of phase locking the local oscillator of a spectrum analyzer to the tracking generator to provide increased isolation.

ing generator is the fact that both oscillators have exactly the same long- and short-term frequency drift, which would allow the use of a very narrow IF bandwidth for maximum dynamic range. The phase-locked loop assures that the two oscillators have exactly the same spectrum up to the limits of the loop. Since the loop reference frequency extends from 5.5 to 9.4 MHz, a very broad-band loop filter may be used. If the loop 3-dB bandwidth were at 2 or 3 MHz, the phase-locked loop would be able to track the spectral characteristics of the spectrum analyzer to 2 or 3 MHz from the carrier. This would be more than sufficient for a tracking generator, such as a VCO in the 700 to 1200 MHz range, that was reasonably well designed and would have very little energy in that region. It must be remembered, however, that the tracking generator–spectrum analyzer combination is capable of extreme dynamic range, and even noise sidebands of 80 or 90 dB down at 2 or 3 MHz from the carrier will have a noticeable effect on the performance of the tracking generator.

The price usually paid for a wide loop bandwidth is the presence of sidebands at the reference frequency. Because the spectrum analyzer is responsive only to the output frequency of the tracking generator, the sidebands due to the reference frequency are not received.

It is possible that sidebands, both noise and reference, could cause erroneous indications when used with the spectrum analyzer and therefore a compromise between the two forms would be the best design. A loop bandwidth of about 500 kHz would insure a spectrum similarity between the tracking generator and the spectrum-analyzer oscillators while reducing the reference sidebands to 30 or 40 dBc.

The outputs of the frequency conversions are of a single frequency with the exception of the last frequency conversion, which provides the entire output frequency range. To enable the tracking generator to be effective, the output level should be constant. The single-frequency or narrow-band frequency outputs may be set, and if the devices associated with a frequency conversion are stable over time and temperature, it is most likely that the output level will remain constant. For the broad-band output from the final mixer, the level will not be constant because of the great range of frequencies. For this output an automatic level control (ALC) will be used.

Figure 6-6 shows an ALC system applied to the tracking generator output. A diode rectifies the RF after the low-pass filter, and the resultant DC level is fed to a difference amplifier that controls the input level to the final mixer. The input signal to the final mixer is attenuated with a PIN diode that provides a variable RF resistance as controlled by the forward current through the diode.

The PIN diode current-controlled attenuator is used to control the level of the 700-MHz input to the mixer because the PIN diode is not effective at low frequencies. Therefore, the diode is applied to the 700-MHz signal, which is not only higher in frequency but operating at a constant frequency.

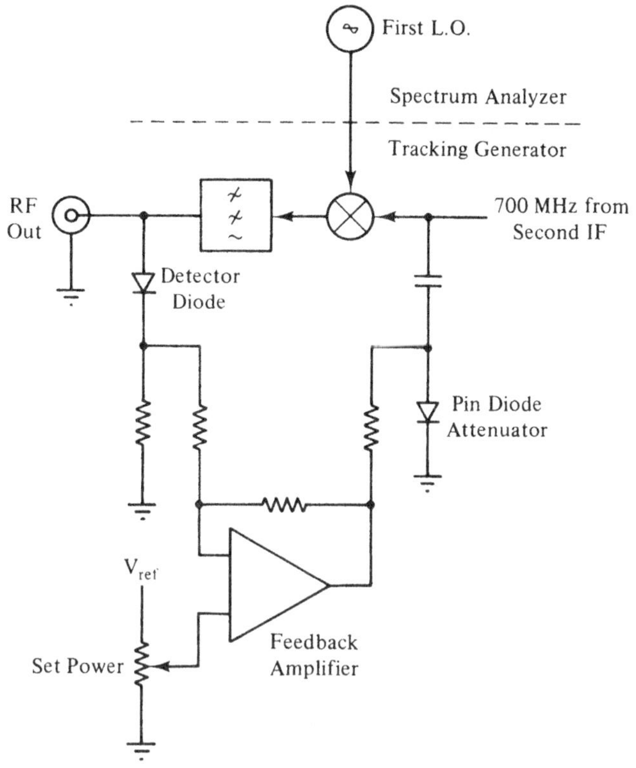

Figure 6-6
An automatic level control applied to the tracking generator.

The ALC system will stabilize the output level due to variations in the mixer and the low-pass filter.

To assist in making accurate measurements, the output of the tracking generator should be a constant 50 Ω. Two mechanisms prevent the output of the tracking generator from appearing as a good 50-Ω source—the ALC system and the low-pass filter. The ALC system will stabilize the output voltage to be a constant, which is the equivalent of a 0-Ω source. Second, the low-pass filter is not a constant impedance.

To overcome these two detractions from a stable 50-Ω source impedance, the output from the low-pass filter is amplified before the detector diode, and an attenuator is applied as shown in Fig. 6-7. The 10-dB attenuator as shown in the figure provides a minimum 20-dB return loss over a broad band of frequencies, even those out of the tracking-generator frequency range. The lack of flat frequency response of the amplifier is overcome in the ALC system. The price

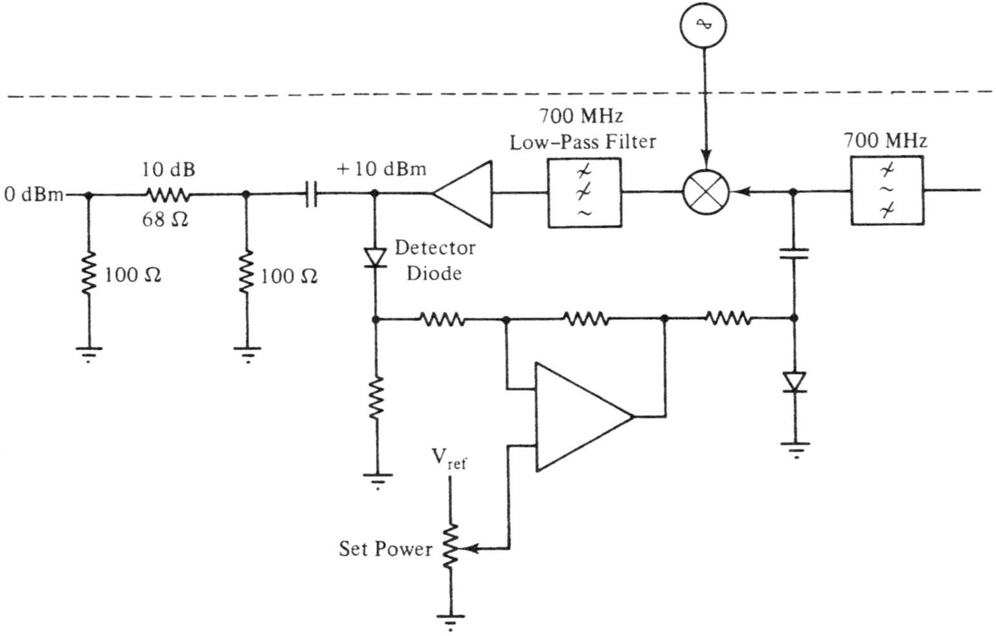

Figure 6-7
An improved automatic level control system for the tracking generator.

to be paid for this stabilized source impedance is the waste of power in the attenuator.

When the definitions of dynamic range were outlined in Chapter 1, three types were explained. The first was display dynamic range, the second was harmonic dynamic range, and the third was nonharmonic dynamic range.

When a spectrum analyzer is used with a tracking generator to analyze a passive device, the only signal present at the input to the spectrum analyzer is the tracking generator. If an active device such as an amplifier is used, harmonics of the tracking generator may exist. There may be some cases in which an active device has other signals present, and this form of testing must be done with great care. Generally, the only signal present at the input to the spectrum analyzer is the tracking-generator signal and some harmonics, some of which may be generated in the tracking generator itself.

The dynamic range of the display, when the spectrum analyzer is used with a tracking generator, is the difference in level between that point where an increase in input signal level causes compression of the display and the noise level of the analyzer. In the discussion of pulse measurements in Chapter 4, the maximum input allowed to the spectrum analyzer when intermodulation was not a problem was the point where the input signal was compressed by 1 dB, or the so-called 1-dB compression point. This point is usually 10 to 15 dB higher than the maximum spurious-free input level of the spectrum analyzer. Therefore, the dynamic range when the tracking generator is used is 10 to 15 dB greater than when the analyzer is used to investigate spectra.

6.3 Network Analysis

The tracking generator, along with a spectrum analyzer, provides the beginnings of a network analyzer. The tracking generator/spectrum analyzer combination is capable of measuring the characteristics of a network that is of the two-port type. A two-port device is one where there is an input and an output terminal with a common, or ground, between the input and the output. A device with an input coaxial connector and an output coaxial connector is a perfect example of a two-port device.

Four basic parameters of the two-port network may be measured: the transfer function that is the output voltage, current, or power as a function of the input voltage, current, or power; the reverse transfer function, which is the voltage, current, or power induced at the input due to a signal applied to the output; the input impedance; and the output impedance.

These four parameters that fully describe a two-port device may be expressed in several ways. Some of the more popular methods are through impedance parameters, admittance or Y parameters, and various hybrid or combination parameters. As an example, to use admittance or Y parameters, the input and output impedance would simply be converted to the equivalent admittance while the transfer function of the device is expressed in transadmittance parameters. A transadmittance parameter is one where the ratio of a current to a voltage is used, but the voltage and current are not relative to the same port.

There are two equations that employ the Y parameters. The input current as a function of the input and output voltages is given by

$$I_{in} = Y_{11}V_{in} + Y_{12}V_{out} \tag{6-3}$$

I_{in} is the input current. The parameter Y_{11} is the input admittance and represents I_{in}/V_{in} with the output short-circuited. Short-circuiting the output insures that V_{out} is zero, and the equation reduces to this ratio. The parameter Y_{12} is the reverse transadmittance and represents the ratio I_{in}/V_{out} with the input short-circuited. Since V_{in} is zero when the input is short-circuited, Eq. (6-3) is reduced to this ratio.

A second equation is based on the output current and is

$$I_{out} = Y_{21}V_{in} + Y_{22}V_{out} \tag{6-4}$$

In this equation, the parameter Y_{21} is the ratio of the output current to the input voltage with the output shorted, or $V_{out} = 0$, and is called the reverse transadmittance. The output admittance with the input shorted is Y_{22}.

These two equations may be written in matrix form where the 2×2 matrix is called the Y matrix.

$$\begin{pmatrix} I_{in} \\ I_{out} \end{pmatrix} = \begin{pmatrix} Y_{11} & Y_{12} \\ Y_{21} & Y_{22} \end{pmatrix} \begin{pmatrix} V_{in} \\ V_{out} \end{pmatrix} \tag{6-5}$$

The discussion of other two-port matrices is beyond the scope of this text, and the reader is directed to a text on network theory.

There is an inherent weakness in the Y-parameter method of defining a two-port network. The Y parameters are measured with the inputs and outputs shorted for various measurements. In general, this does not appear difficult. However, at very high frequencies it is not easy to create precision short circuits or open circuits. Very high frequency circuits are usually categorized and measured into a constant impedance such as 50 Ω. A specialized set of parameters called scattering parameters or S parameters has been defined for very high frequency (RF and microwave), two-port analysis.

All scattering parameters are measured with the circuit under test terminated with a reference impedance. The S-parameter equations and matrix are

$$b_1 = S_{11}a_1 + S_{12}a_2$$

$$b_2 = S_{21}a_1 + S_{22}a_2$$

$$\begin{pmatrix} b_1 \\ b_2 \end{pmatrix} = \begin{pmatrix} S_{11} & S_{12} \\ S_{21} & S_{22} \end{pmatrix} \begin{pmatrix} a_1 \\ a_2 \end{pmatrix} \tag{6-6}$$

The four terms a_1, a_2, b_1, and b_2 are variables involving the input and output voltages by the following relationships:

$$a_1 = \frac{V_{in} + Z_0 I_{in}}{2(\sqrt{Z_0})}; \qquad b_1 = \frac{V_{in} - Z_0 I_{in}}{2\sqrt{Z_0}}$$

$$a_2 = \frac{V_{out} + I_{out} Z_0}{2\sqrt{Z_0}}; \qquad b_2 = \frac{V_2 - I_{out} Z_0}{2\sqrt{Z_0}} \tag{6-7}$$

Solving for S_{11} in terms of the input voltages and currents, the following is obtained:

For $S_{22} = 0$

$$S_{11} = \frac{b_1}{a_1} = \frac{V_{in} - I_{in} Z_0}{V_{in} + I_{in} Z_0} = \frac{Z_{in} - Z_0}{Z_{in} + Z_0} \tag{6-8}$$

This is also known as the voltage reflection coefficient. Because the voltages and currents defining the reflection coefficient are vector quantities, the voltage reflection coefficient is also a vector quantity. Since the spectrum analyzer does not resolve phase, it is not capable of measuring the voltage reflection coefficient. In addition, the spectrum analyzer usually provides a decibel display. Thus, a more appropriate parameter for the spectrum analyzer/tracking generator is the return loss or

$$\text{Return loss} = -20 \log \left| \frac{Z - Z_0}{Z + Z_0} \right| \tag{6-9}$$

A vector network analyzer is capable of resolving phase and, hence, the vector form of the reflection coefficient. The vector network analyzer will be discussed in the following chapter.

The measurement of return loss is achieved using a return-loss bridge. This device is like any other bridge circuit; it is shown in Fig. 6-8.

To analyze this circuit, three nodes are analyzed as shown in the figure. From this, three equations may be written.

$$\frac{V - V_s}{50} = \frac{V_s - V_1}{50} + \frac{V_s - V_2}{50} \tag{6-10}$$

$$\frac{V_s - V_1}{50} = \frac{V_1 - V_2}{50} + \frac{V_1}{50} \tag{6-11}$$

$$\frac{V_s - V_2}{50} = \frac{V_2 - V_1}{50} + \frac{V_2}{Z} \tag{6-12}$$

Solving Eq. (6-10) for V_s:

$$V_s = \frac{V + V_1 + V_2}{3} \tag{6-13}$$

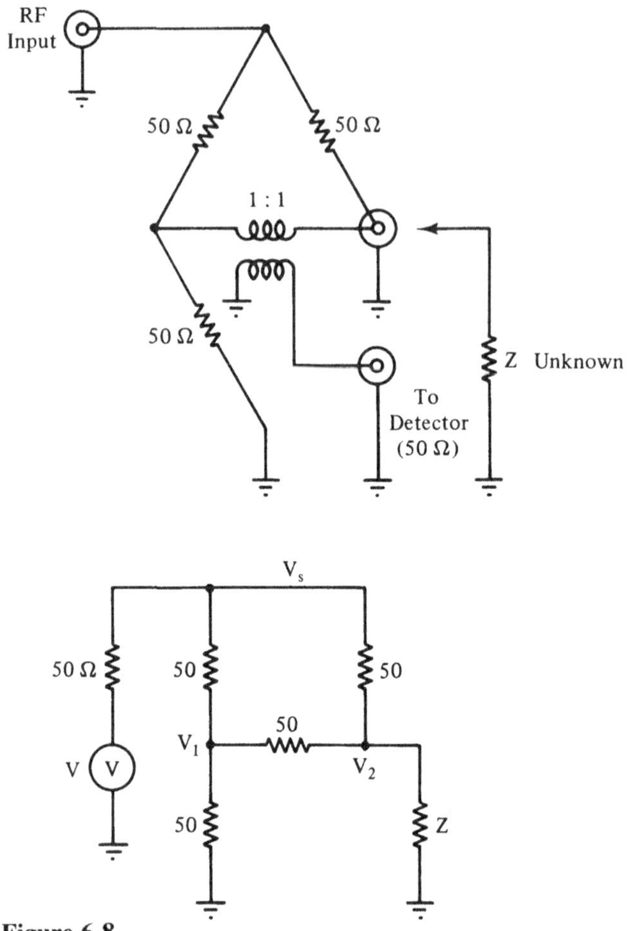

Figure 6-8
An RF-impedance bridge and its equivalent circuit.

Solving Eq. (6-11) for V_s and setting the result equal to (6-13) yields

$$V_s = 3V_1 - V_2 = \frac{V + V_1 + V_2}{3}$$

$$8V_1 = 4V_2 + V \qquad (6\text{-}14)$$

Solving (6-12) for V_s and setting that equal to (6-13) results in

$$V_s = V_2\left(2 + \frac{50}{Z}\right) - V_1 = \frac{V + V_1 + V_2}{3}$$

$$V = V_2\left[5 + 3\left(\frac{50}{Z}\right)\right] - 4V_1 \qquad (6\text{-}14)$$

Eqs. (6-14) and (6-15) are both equations in V_1 and V_2 and may be solved. Solving for V_2,

$$V_2 = \frac{\begin{vmatrix} 8 & V \\ 4 & V \end{vmatrix}}{\begin{vmatrix} 8 & -4 \\ -4 & \left[5 + 3\left(\frac{50}{Z}\right)\right] \end{vmatrix}} \tag{6-16}$$

Solving for V_1,

$$V_1 = \frac{\begin{vmatrix} V & -4 \\ V & \left[5 + 3\left(\frac{50}{Z}\right)\right] \end{vmatrix}}{\begin{vmatrix} 8 & -4 \\ -4 & \left[5 + 3\left(\frac{50}{Z}\right)\right] \end{vmatrix}} \tag{6-17}$$

The absolute value $V_2 - V_1$ is the desired quantity, and thus

$$V_2 - V_1 = \frac{V}{8}\frac{\left(1 - \frac{50}{Z}\right)}{\left(1 + \frac{50}{Z}\right)} = \frac{V}{8}\left(\frac{Z - 50}{Z + 50}\right) \tag{6-18}$$

As it may be seen, the output voltage of the return-loss bridge is directly proportional to the reflection coefficient. When the unknown impedance is an open or short, the output voltage across the detector is $V/8$, which is 12 dB less than the power delivered to the detector from the generator without the return-loss bridge. The normal terminated voltage is $V/2$. Therefore the relationship of the return loss to the detector voltage of the return-loss bridge is

$$20 \log\left(\frac{\text{Detector output}}{\text{Terminated generator}}\right) = \text{Return loss} - 12 \text{ dB} \tag{6-19}$$

The forward transfer function is probably the most important parameter of a two-port network. The tracking generator/spectrum analyzer combination is clearly capable of measuring this parameter. There is one shortcoming, however. As it was explained in Chapter 1, the spectrum analyzer is not capable of resolving phase information. When a spectrum is analyzed, only the magnitude of the signal being analyzed is displayed. The same is true of the display of the transfer function when a two-port network is analyzed. For this reason, the tracking generator/spectrum analyzer combination is often referred to as a "scalar" network analyzer.

6.4 Tracking Generator Applications

Some insight into the applications of the tracking generator was shed in the last chapter. As an example, the five-pole, two-zero elliptical filter shown in Fig. 6-9 will be used. An elliptical filter is made for the purpose of a sharp cutoff, very often more than 70 or 80 dB. To tune such a filter, it is necessary to have a measurement system with at least that much dynamic range.

Most spectrum analyzers have a log-amplifier dynamic range of 70 or possibly 80 dB. Likewise, the display has a similar dynamic range. In other words, the spectrum analyzer can display two signals that differ by no more than the display range at any one time. If a filter to be analyzed has a stop band that is below the on-screen range of the analyzer, the filter passband must be obtained in two passes.

First, the upper half of the trace is displayed by setting the top of the passband of the device under test at the top of the spectrum analyzer display. Since the stop band of the device under test is below the dynamic range of the instrument, part of the passband is below the display range—often below the noise level.

To display the bottom portion of the passband, the input attenuator is reduced to raise the level of the lower portion of the passband. Since the top of the display was at the 1-dB compression point, the top of the display will become compressed and partly off the screen. This is not important, as this portion of the display was viewed in the first pass.

To protect the analyzer, it is imperative that the maximum output of the

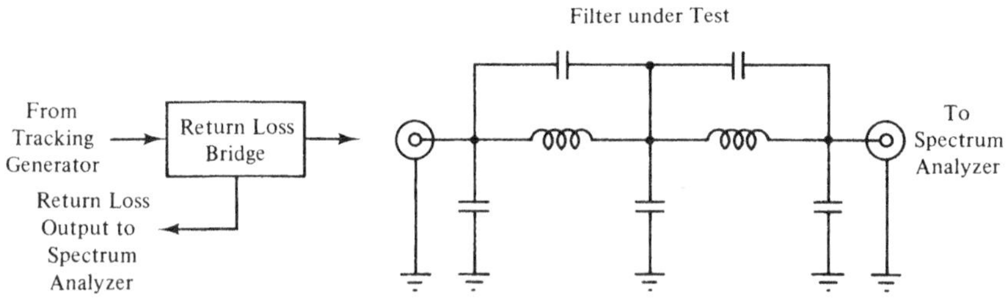

Figure 6-9
The arrangement of a return loss bridge to provide both the filter passband and the input return loss. Reversing the filter would provide the output return loss.

device under test be less than the damage level of the analyzer. The damage level for most spectrum analyzers is on the order of +20 to +30 dBm, while the output of a tracking generator is on the order of 0 to +10 dBm. Therefore, it would be impossible to damage the spectrum analyzer when testing a passive device with the tracking generator. This is not true when testing active devices such as an amplifier. In this case, caution must be exercised.

The output of the tracking generator is connected to the spectrum analyzer, and the level is increased until the tracking generator level is equal to the 1-dB compression level of the analyzer. This level is found very simply by increasing the output of the tracking generator until the spectrum analyzer display is 1 dB below the correct level. Usually a large amount of IF attenuation will result in the noise level of the display resting at either the very bottom or actually below the display and not visible.

The device under test, in this case a filter, is inserted between the tracking generator and the spectrum analyzer, and the output of the tracking generator is increased to return the peak of the passband to the top of the display. This will maximize the display by placing the point of minimum loss at the very top of the display. The amount of the attenuation removed from the tracking generator output is equal to the loss of the filter at the point of minimum loss.

Figure 6-10 shows an example of a bandpass crystal filter where the stop band has a spurious response that is below the normal on-screen dynamic range of the analyzer. In this example, the spurious response is about 65 dB from the passband response, which is about the on-screen dynamic range of the analyzer. Figure 16-10(a) shows the top of the display, where the 1-dB compression point is at the top of screen. In this case the tracking generator was not able to provide sufficient output to place the output of the crystal filter at the 1-dB compression point. Therefore, the top of the filter passband is about 9 dB down from the 1-dB compression point. As Fig. 6-10(a) shows, the noise level is about 50 dB from the filter passband peak and 60 dB from the top of the display. The input attenuation was reduced by 30 dB, which leaves the noise level the same but raises the signal by 30 dB. This places the peak of the passband about 22 dB "off the screen." On the other hand, the spurious response shown slightly above the upper filter skirt is now out of the noise and clearly visible. The total dynamic range of the display taken in two passes is 80 dB, taken with a spectrum analyzer that has a slightly more than 60-dB display range.

If a record of the total passband of the filter were required, two photographs or other hard copies may be made and pieced together.

The significant disadvantage of using the tracking generator for tuning filters with very deep nulls or high-attenuation stop bands is that it is not possible to see the entire passband while tuning the filter. Because intermodulation is the phenomenon that limits the dynamic range of the spectrum analyzer, it is not practical to provide a display range that is much greater than the intermodulation dynamic range. In the network analyzer where only one signal is present, the

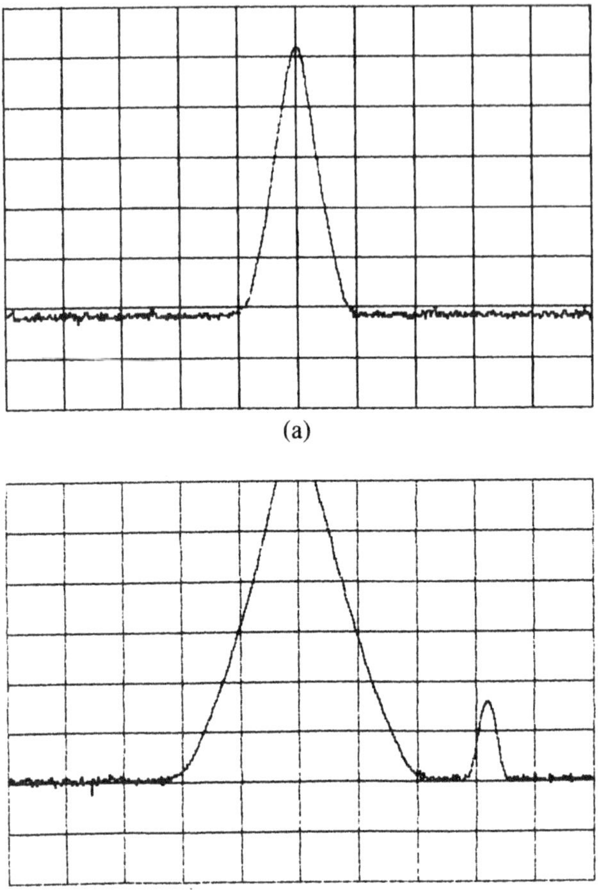

(a)

(b)

Figure 6-10
(a) A passband of a filter where the dynamic range is about 62 dB.
(b) When the input attenuation is reduced by 30 dB, which produces an off-screen display, a spurious response of the filter can be seen about 65 dB down. Even though the display range is still only 60 dB, spurious responses of more than 60 dB are visible because the reference level is above the top of the display.

dynamic range is limited only by the noise level of the receiving section and the maximum power available from the generator section. Very large display ranges, often as great as 100 dB, are common on network analyzers.

In many cases, it is desirable to tune not only the transfer function of a filter but to adjust the return loss as well. In this case it would be necessary to insert the return-loss bridge between the tracking generator and filter under test.

The theory and equations for the return loss bridge were covered earlier in this chapter. Often the return-loss bridge has some errors and should be calibrated before use by removing the device under test and noting the level from the detector port of the return-loss bridge. This level represents zero return loss, or the reference level. If the bridge is accurate, the return loss is measured from the reference.

To check the bridge, known return losses may be connected to the unknown port. An excellent source of known return losses is a step attenuator of the absorption type. The absorption type of attenuator is one that uses resistive pads rather than a piston or a vane.

Connect the attenuator to the unknown port and do not terminate the other end of the attenuator. The return loss of the unterminated attenuator is equal to twice the attenuator setting. As an example, a 3-dB attenuator, unterminated, provides a 6-dB return loss.

The term "return loss" comes about in the following manner. Relative to transmission lines, when a transmission line is shorted or open the energy propagating in that line would be completely reflected when encountering an open or short.

If the discontinuity of the transmission line were not as severe as an open or short, some but not all of the energy would be reflected. The apparent loss of the returned energy is the return loss. If an attenuator were placed ahead of the open or short, the energy would be attenuated by the attenuator, completely reflected and attenuated again. Therefore, the return loss simulated by an open-circuited or short-circuited attenuator is equal to two times the attenuation value.

The filter is tuned for the minimum returned power while the passband loss is periodically checked. Because the return-loss bridge is present only on the input end of the filter, those tuning adjustments that have significant effect on the input impedance match may be tuned. To match the output of the filter, it must be reversed and the output tuned circuits adjusted, all the while checking the transfer function.

The lack of the ability to view both the forward transfer function and the return loss makes the use of the tracking generator difficult. A network analyzer allows for the simultaneous viewing of both the transfer function and the return loss. This is the subject of Chapter 9.

Review Questions for Chapter 6

1. What is a tracking generator and how is the output frequency generated?
2. What does a "tracking" control do and why is it important?
3. What are the more significant problems when designing and building a tracking generator? What are the usual methods of overcoming these problems?
4. What would be a typical insertion loss that may be measured by the spectrum analyzer using the tracking generator as a signal source?

5. What is a two-port device?
6. What are *Y* parameters? What are the four parameters and what do they represent?
7. How is return loss measured? How can return loss be measured?
8. How is the tracking generator used to display a transfer function with a dynamic range greater than the display range?

7

A Practical Spectrum Analyzer

7.1 Overview

Throughout the previous chapters, a specific spectrum analyzer was used for many examples. In this and the next chapter, this example spectrum analyzer will be brought to life as a real piece of hardware. The actual circuits will be presented and some of the considerations for available components and test requirements will be discussed. It will be possible to actually duplicate this analyzer, as it is constructed from parts readily available at the time of this writing.

Constructing the analyzer is an ambitious project but not beyond the grasp of the serious student. The unit is broken down into subassemblies, which could be distributed among groups of students and handled as a class project. The main purpose of presenting an actual working spectrum analyzer is to present some real practical problems and the resulting solutions.

One of the great attractions of a spectrum analyzer as a learning tool are the many important principles that may be learned from the device. Listed below are the devices and principles that may be investigated from the construction and operation of a spectrum analyzer.

Devices	Principles
Attenuators	Attenuation, wideband frequency response, RF switches, impedance matching
Mixers	Conversion loss, image, isolation

Filters	Lowpass filters, bandpass filters, helical resonators, crystal filters, Gaussian filters, impedance matching, frequency response, impulse bandwidth
Log IF amplifiers	Log range, log accuracy
VCOs	Tuning range, frequency stability, phase noise
Sweep voltage generator	Operational amplifier techniques
Frequency readout and frequency control	Phase-locked loop techniques, frequency counter and display, high-speed digital techniques
Power supplies	Low-ripple and low-noise power distribution techniques
General	Noise figure, intermodulation distortion, shielding techniques

This list shows a wide variation of practical techniques that are suited to a broad range of applications. The spectrum analyzer is an ideal vehicle for learning these techniques as it brings together this wide list of subjects into a very useful instrument.

One of the more useful tools in the construction and evaluation of a spectrum analyzer would be another spectrum analyzer. The purpose of constructing this spectrum analyzer is to create such an instrument using lesser tools. The philosophy of the exercise is similar to the chicken and egg paradox. If it takes a spectrum analyzer to make a spectrum analyzer, how was the first spectrum analyzer made?

The spectrum analyzer will be covered in the same order as the signal flow in the unit. Therefore, the discussion of the analyzer circuits will begin with the input attenuator, then the low-pass filter, first mixer, and so on.

7.2 Specifications

The specifications of the example spectrum analyzer were developed using two criteria. First, the analyzer must be useful. This implies that the analyzer must cover a frequency range wide enough to be of practical value in the laboratory. The sensitivity must be such that most measurement tasks may be handled. Phase noise must be reduced to a point where some narrow-band measurements may be made. In general, the specifications were to be comparable to a low-to-medium-priced spectrum analyzer. The on-screen dynamic range was chosen to be 70 dB for several reasons. First, many oscilloscopes have eight major divisions in the vertical axis which, at a scale factor of 10 dB per division, would allow the noise level to fall at the bottom half of the display while the maximum permitted input would fall at the very top of the screen—which is a very desirable situation. Second, the choice of the log IF amplifier can provide a reasonably accurate log display over 70 dB but is capable of reduced accuracy to 80 dB. Finally, a 70-dB dynamic range may be achieved without resorting to very expensive high-level mixers or low-noise amplifiers. The example spectrum analyzer is invaluable as a learning tool, but it must have some practical use. The resulting analyzer has a spurious-free 70-dB dynamic range and can be pushed to 80 dB with some increased error, which is certainly a practical range.

Other important considerations are the availability of parts, the need for very sophisticated test equipment to align the unit, and the ultimate cost. There will affect certain other specifications such as the IF filters.

The specifications of the spectrum analyzer adhere to IEEE Standard 748-1979. (See the following table.)

Specifications

Frequency range	500 kHz to 500 MHz
Frequency spans	50 MHz/div 20 MHz/div 10 MHz/div 5 MHz/div 2 MHz/div 1 MHz/div 500 kHz/div 200 kHz/div 100 kHz/div 50 kHz/div 20 kHz/div 10 kHz/div 5 kHz/div zero
Resolution bandwidths	300 kHz 15 kHz 3 kHz
Frequency readout	0–499 MHz center frequency 1 MHz resolution 0.2% accuracy
Display	80 dB, on screen ±1 dB; 16 dB, on screen ±0.2 dB differential accuracy Frequency axis ±1% of selected frequency span
Nonharmonic dynamic range	70 dB, on screen
Input third-order intercept point	+16 dBm
Input impedance	50 Ω
Input return loss	20 dB min., 0–500 MHz
Maximum input power	1 W average, 100 watts peak
Noise figure	25 dB max.

Residual FM	1 kHz in a 20-kHz BW
Internally generated spurious signals both power supply related and reference sidebands on phase lock	Down 70 dB

7.3 Attenuator

The purpose of the input attenuator is to reduce the input signal level to a safe value so that the maximum dynamic range of the analyzer may be used without danger of destroying the input mixer. An attenuator must accomplish a simple task—reduce a signal power level by a fixed amount. Simple resistor networks are used for this purpose. However, the power level must be reduced while maintaining a constant input impedance and over a large range of frequencies.

Figure 7-1 shows a simple attenuator using pi-pads and a double-pole, double-throw switch. Because there are nó reactances in the attenuator, there would be no frequency dependencies of the attenuator. Figure 7-2 shows one step of the same attenuator, except with the parasitic reactances that may be encountered in real components.

To gain an insight into the effects of real reactances, consider a carbon composition resistor. The equivalent circuit of this component varies depending on the construction of the resistor. Typically, a 1/4-W composition resistor has an equivalent parallel capacitance of 0.4 pF. At a frequency of 500 MHz, the capacitive reactance is 796 Ω. If the capacitive reactance were considered, particularly in the high-attenuation steps, the frequency response would rise dramatically at the high-frequency end of the input range. It is nearly impossible to eliminate capacitive reactance within components, and this focuses attention to the high-attenuation steps.

Several problems are associated with the high-attenuation steps, such as a 40-dB step. First, 98% of the power dissipiated by the 40-dB step is handled by the first resistor in the attenuator. Therefore, either a 1-W resistor or four 1/4-W resistors will be required for the first, shunt, resistor. The remaining power is only 20 mW; for any of the remaining resistors, 1/4 W or even 1/8 W resistors will be sufficient. The shunt capacitance of four 1/4 W resistors is 199 Ω which when placed in parallel with a 25-Ω resistance (the 51-Ω resistor in parallel with the 50-Ω source), does not have a great effect on the attenuation. However, the effect on the attenuation due to the series resistor is more dramatic. As an example, the voltage attenuation of a single 40-dB resistive attenuator (with the effects of the 0.4-pF capacitance of each resistor considered) at 500 MHz is 29.7 dB, an error of 10.3 dB of the total of 40 dB!

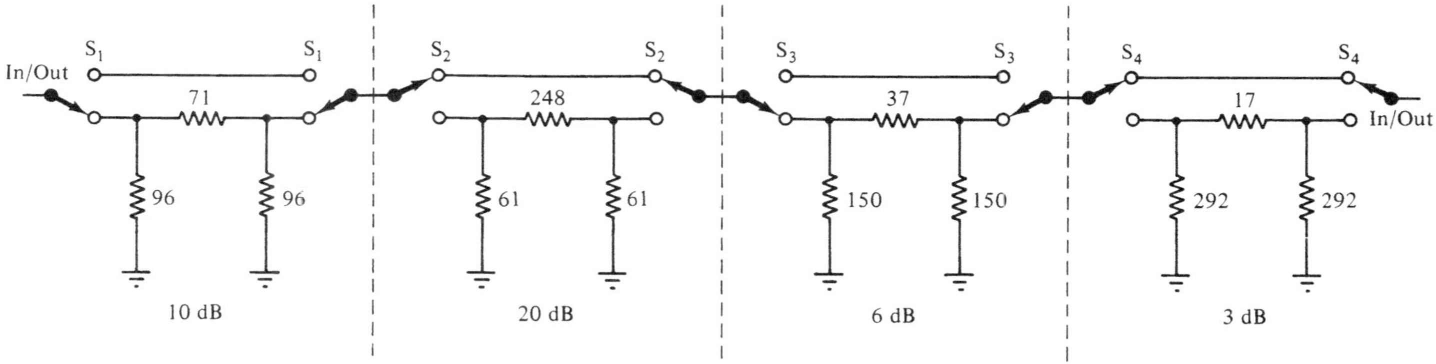

Figure 7-1
A schematic of a step attenuator using resistance pads. The values shown are for a 50-Ω attenuator.

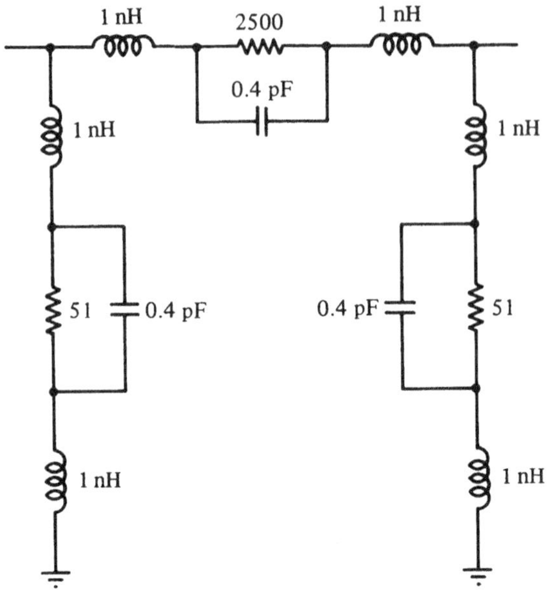

Figure 7-2
The equivalent circuit of a 40-dB attenuator showing the parasitic reactances of the resistors.

One method of reducing the error due to the parallel capacitance is to generate a 40-dB attenuation using two 20-dB attenuators, as shown in Fig. 7-3. In this case, the attenuation at 500 MHz is 39.3 dB, which is only a 0.7-dB error.

Additional improvement may be obtained with the inclusion of inductances in series with the series resistance. Using a computer aided design package, an optimum value of 60 nHy in series with both series resistors of the two 20-dB sections reduced the 0.7-dB error to only 0.1 dB maximum throughout the 0 to 500 MHz input frequency range.

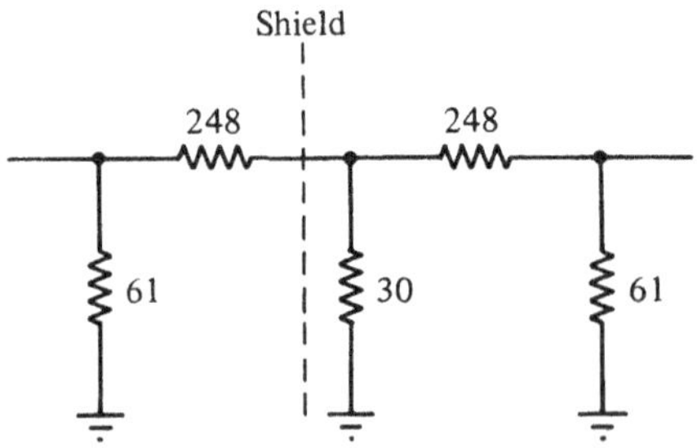

Figure 7-3
Generating a 40-dB attenuator for high frequencies involves using two 20-dB attenuators in tandem with a shield between the two.

There are more mechanisms for signal leakage from the input of an attenuator to the output—for instance, inductive coupling from one resistor to another, leakage through the switches due to capacitance, and inductance within the resistors and so on. Consequently, attenuator design is more an art than a science.

The resistor attenuators are mounted in individual shielded compartments so that energy does not leak around the attenuation. At VHF frequencies and above, an empty conductive box may look more like a resonant cavity, and it offers very little attenuation between the input and output connectors. Therefore, it is necessary to provide adequate shielding in the form of baffles and shielded compartments to achieve the necessary attenuation.

There are some sure-fire methods of improving attenuator design, such as the use of specially designed switches and relays for attenuator use. In addition, thick-film attenuator networks produce broad-band attenuator steps inexpensively. Companies that specialize in attenuator design produce high-performance attenuators at attractive prices. Therefore, for the example spectrum analyzer, a commercially available attenuator was used.

A 10-dB-per-step attenuator is typically used in the front end of a spectrum analyzer. A nice addition to a spectrum analyzer is an additional attenuator with 1-dB steps. This is particularly useful when a 1- or 2-dB-per-división vertical scale factor is used.

The required attenuation range may be calculated from the noise floor and the maximum power the attenuator can handle. The example spectrum analyzer has a maximum input power before serious intermodulation distortion of about −20 dBm. For an attenuator capable of handling 1 W, which is +30 dBm, 50 dB of attenuation would place the top-screen reference at 1 W, the maximum level the attenuator could handle.

Typically, 10-dB-per-step attenuators have more attenuation than 50 dB, and the additional attenuation is useful for handling pulse power. The power handling of an attenuator is usually relative to the CW power that will not cause damage to the attenuator, but the power handling of a spectrum analyzer is instantaneous power. The damage to the spectrum analyzer is usually the destruction of the input mixer, which takes mere microseconds to accomplish. When a pulsed-carrier spectrum is measured, the peak power may be considerably greater than the average power, requiring additional attenuation beyond the 50 dB previously discussed; but the average power would be comfortably below the power rating of the attenuator. With all factors considered, a 100-dB step attenuator with 10-dB steps would be suitable for the input of a spectrum analyzer.

7.4 Input Low-Pass Filter

The characteristics of the input low-pass filter were discussed in Chapter 2. The general rule of thumb is that the low-pass filter must reject any out-of-band signals that are capable of producing a spurious response by as much as the on-screen dynamic range of the analyzer, which, in this case, is 70 dB. It would be prudent to provide an additional attenuation, perhaps 10 dB, to insure a spurious-free display.

Of course, it is not possible to provide a filter with an infinite attenuation at the highest input frequency. Thus, some transition region between the highest input frequency and the lowest potential spurious-response frequency will exist where the attenuation will increase from less than 1 dB to the needed attenuation to reduce the spurious response to an acceptable level. In the case of the example spectrum analyzer, the region is between 500 MHz, being the highest input frequency, and 700 MHz, the first IF feedthrough.

An elliptical filter, as discussed in Chapter 2, provides attenuation at the IF of 700 MHz by placing one of the zeros of the transfer function of the filter at the IF. The filter must provide 80 dB of attenuation at 1400 MHz, the low point of the image frequency band.

Constructing the input low-pass filter is not difficult. If must be remembered, however, that the components used in the low-pass filter must be usable at frequencies well above the desired passband frequency range. Although the filter is to *pass* frequencies from 0 to 500 MHz, the filter is to *stop* frequencies to a region of nearly 2 GHz. If the capacitors and inductors used in the filter are not good quality components at 2 GHz, the filter stop band will be compromised.

The input filter for the example spectrum analyzer is shown in Fig. 2-4 and again, with the other front-end elements, in Fig. 7-4. The inductors used in the low-pass filter are conventional wire solenoids, and the capacitors are disk ceramic with the leads cleaned of insulation until they are essentially leadless. For those shunt capacitors that connect to ground, a leadless disk or chip capacitor would be preferable. The filter is constructed in a brass box with a partition between the sections of the filter, to prevent coupling from the input to the output. A connector is provided for the input to the filter, but the output is connected directly to the first mixer, which is located in another compartment of the brass box.

The values shown for the input low-pass filter are the closest standard value and do not represent the design center value. Therefore, it is necessary to adjust the filter slightly to achieve a flat passband and to place the transfer-function zero at 700 MHz. This is done by adjusting the inductors, by crushing or expanding the coils. To reduce the inductance slightly, bend the end turn so that its center axis does not correspond to the axis of the remaining turns. This removes one of the turns from the magnetic flux of the remainder of the coil and reduces the mutual inductance. The inductance can be further reduced by pushing two turns from the end of the coil. The inductance can be increased by pushing the turns of the coil together, which not only increased the mutual inductance slightly but adds distributed capacitance. The amount of adjustment should be slight.

A sweep generator with a broad-band crystal detector, as shown in Fig. 7-5, is used to sweep the low-pass filter for a passband ripple of no more than

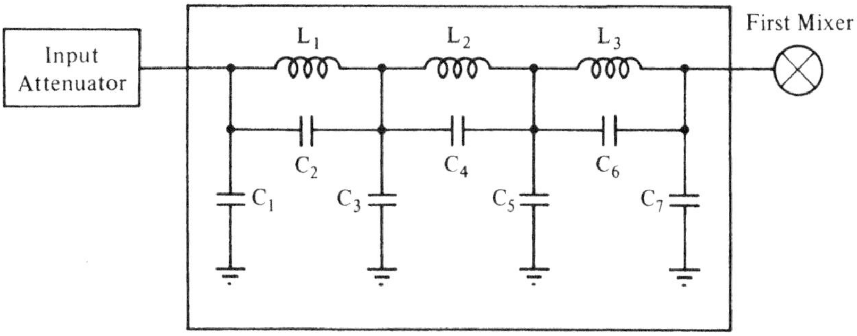

$C_1 = 8.6$ pF
$C_2 = 0.62$ pF
$C_3 = 12$ pF
$C_4 = 3.3$ pF
$C_5 = 10$ pF
$C_6 = 2.2$ pF
$C_7 = 6.8$ pF
L_1 $1\frac{1}{2}$ turns #22 $\frac{3}{16}''$ diameter
L_2 $1\frac{1}{2}$ turns #22 $\frac{3}{16}''$ diameter
L_3 $1\frac{1}{2}$ turns #22 $\frac{3}{16}''$ diameter

Figure 7-4
The schematic and placement of an imput low-pass filter for a spectrum analyzer.

± 1 dB and sufficient attenuation at the IF to remove the spurious response at that frequency. It will be necessary to temporarily disconnect the output of the low-pass filter from the first mixer and install an RF connector or length of cable to make this measurement. The actual bandwidth of the filter or the 3-dB point is somewhere in the range of 600 MHz. This 3-dB point is not critical; only the passband ripple of ± 1 dB and the IF rejection needs to be adjusted.

The potential spurious response at the IF is due to leakage through the first mixer to the first IF amplifier. The theoretical attenuation of the input low-pass filter at the IF is more than 70 dB. Using the crystal detector will make it somewhat difficult to measure an insertion loss of this amount. A typical diode detector has a tangential sensitivity of about -40 dBm. Using a signal or sweep generator with an output of $+13$ dBm, which is a typical maximum RF output level, an insertion loss of only 53 dB can be measured. The critical alignment of the input low-pass filter is the passband flatness, which can easily be checked using the sweep generator and a crystal detector.

The notch at 700 MHz in the low-pass filter transfer function may be adjusted to be centered around 700 MHz, using the crystal detector. The design of

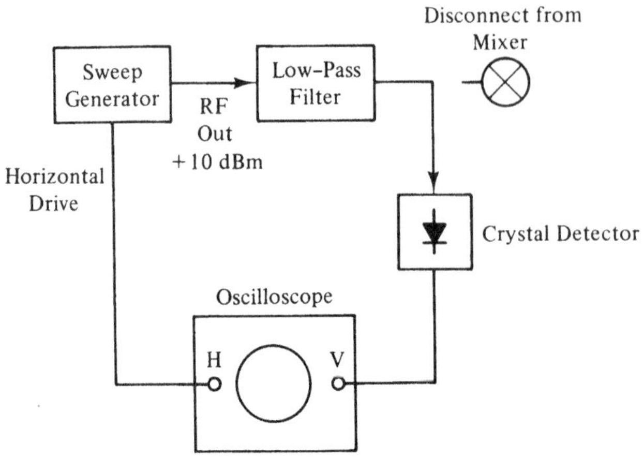

Figure 7-5
Test equipment setup for sweep frequency testing of the input low-pass filter.

the filter is such that this notch is at least 50 dB and is theoretically much greater. The mixer will supply about 30 dB of isolation at the 700-MHz IF. This is about 23.5 dB relative to the output of the first mixer, having suffered a 6.5-dB loss relative to the input due to the conversion loss. Therefore, the IF feedthrough must be reduced by 46.5 dB to place it below the 70-dB on-screen dynamic range of the spectrum analyzer. Simply centering the notch around 700 MHz is a near-guarantee that the attenuation at the IF is at least 50 dB. A final check and slight adjustment may be made after the entire analyzer is constructed using the analyzer itself as an indicating device.

An elegant method of tuning the input filter would be use of a network analyzer or a spectrum analyzer and a tracking generator. However, the philosophy of constructing the analyzer is to create a more sophisticated instrument from lesser instruments.

7.5 First Mixer and Local Oscillator

The first mixer is a commercially made double-balanced mixer. Although a double-balanced mixer may be constructed from discrete components, the manufacturers of these devices have developed such finely honed skills that it is hardly worth the effort to make a balanced mixer from transformers and diodes.

The balanced mixer is placed in the circuit such that the normal IF port is the input and the RF is the output, as shown in Fig. 7-6. this is done because of the need for the input frequency to extend down to 500 kHz. The balanced-mixer

RF port is a winding of one of the transformers, and these transformers cannot pass frequencies as low as 500 kHz. The normal IF port connects to the diodes and is essentially flat to DC. The local oscillator frequency is from 700 to 1200 MHz, while the IF is a constant 700 MHz, both of which can easily pass through the transformers.

The local oscillator power requirement for a balanced mixer depends on the mixer type. For the example spectrum analyzer, a mixer with the normal local oscillator power rating of +7 dBm was chosen, which provides a third-order intercept point of about 9 dB above the local oscillator when the mixer is used in the conventional manner.

When a double-balanced mixer is used with the IF port as an input, the intermodulation performance is not as good as it might be if the input were connected to the RF port. Typically, when the RF port is used, a third-order intercept point of about 6 dB above the local oscillator level results. If a local oscillator slightly higher than rated power, in this case +10 dBm, is used, the third-order intercept point may be raised by an additional 3 dB.

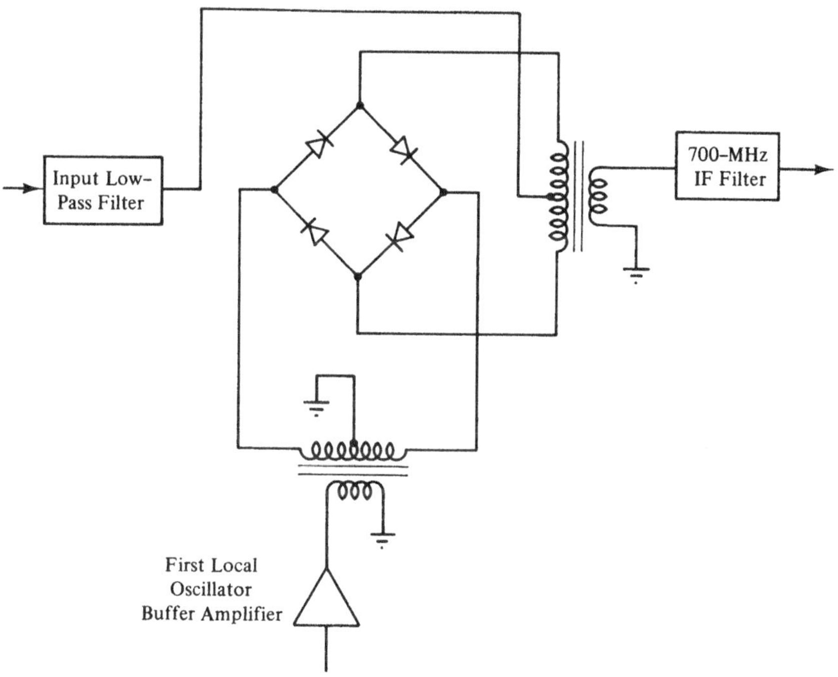

Figure 7-6
The connection of the input mixer showing the unusual connection of the mixer with the IF port as the input.

The first local oscillator is a Colpitts type using a bipolar transistor and tuned with a varactor. When the tuning range of a varactor-tuned oscillator approaches an octave, it is extremely important that parasitic reactances be kept to a minimum. This and other design criteria for voltage-tuned oscillators was covered in Chapter 2.

A second varactor is included in the oscillator for the phase-locked loop.

The local oscillator is followed by two stages of broad-band amplifiers to provide isolation to the oscillator from the mixer and the frequency prescalers. Lack of sufficient isolation will cause the first local oscillator frequency to be pulled by the input signal, causing distortion of the spectrum.

In this analyzer, the third-order intercept point for the input balanced mixer will set the dynamic range of the spectrum analyzer. (It will be shown that the dynamic range of the other parts of the analyzer do not significantly affect the dynamic range of the entire analyzer.) The dynamic range is the difference in signal level, in decibels, between the highest pair of signals, each of the same level, producing a third-order intermodulation distortion equal in level to the minimum detectable signal level of the spectrum analyzer.

As an example, if the local oscillator level of +10 dBm is used, which will not damage a +7-dBm mixer, the third-order intercept point is +16 dBm.

The level of a third-order intermodulation product is

$$P_3 = 3P_{\text{in}} - 2\text{IP} \qquad (7\text{-}1)$$

where P_3 is the third-order intercept point in dBm, P_{in} is the input power in dBm, and IP is the third-order intercept point in dBm.

From Eq. (7-1) it can be seen that every increase of 1 dB in the intercept point results in an increase of 2 dB in the dynamic range of the spectrum analyzer. For the example spectrum analyzer, the on-screen display range is 70 dB, which implies that for two signals at the very top of the display not to produce a visible intermodulation distortion, the third-order intermodulation distortion is 70 dB down from the input signals, or

$$P_{\text{in}} - 70 = 3P_{\text{in}} - 2\text{IP} \qquad (7\text{-}2)$$

The low-pass filter inserts an additional 1 dB of loss before the mixer, making the intercept point of the analyzer, including the low-pass filter, +17 dBm. When this value is inserted into Eq. (7-2), the maximum input level for a display without a visible intermodulation distortion is −17 dBm.

Since every 1-dB increase of the local oscillator level will produce a 2-dB increase in dynamic range, why not increase the local oscillator level? This is a valid method of increasing the dynamic range, and mixers that permit higher local oscillator levels, up to +27 dBm (0.5 W) are available. There are several disadvantages to increasing the local oscillator level. First, the amount of IF feedthrough at "zero" frequency will become proportionally higher. This will reduce the low-frequency versatility of the analyzer. Second, considerable power may be able to leak into the circuit under test. The input low-pass filter was designed to reject the IF and the image frequency and also not to provide extreme isolation to the local oscillator frequency. Finally, very high level mixers are expensive, being 5 to 10 times the cost of their lower power counterparts.

The lower line of the display will represent the noise level of the analyzer and is a function of the bandwidth and the noise figure of the analyzer. The minimum detectable signal is a signal that is visible above the noise level and is typically taken to be 3 dB above the noise level. This level is given by

$$\text{MDS} = -111\ \text{dBm} + 10\log(\text{BW}/1\ \text{MHz}) + \text{NF} \qquad (7\text{-}3)$$

where MDS is the minimum detectable signal, BW is the IF bandwidth, and NF is the noise figure of the spectrum analyzer. In Eq. (7-3), −111 dBm is the power of the thermal noise, or KTB, for a bandwidth of 1 MHz at 290K. In this case, K is Boltzmann's constant, T is the absolute temperature in Kelvins, and B is the bandwidth of 1 MHz. The term 10 log(BW/1 MHz) is a correction term for bandwidths other than 1 MHz.

Applying this to the example spectrum analyzer, the limitation of the spectrum analyzer would occur when the IF bandwidth is the maximum available, thus producing the greatest MDS, which in turn causes the top of the display to represent the greatest signal level. The maximum IF bandwidth of the example analyzer is 300 kHz, which produces an MDS of

$$-111\ \text{dBm} + 10\log(.3) + \text{NF} = -116\ \text{dBm} + \text{NF} \qquad (7\text{-}4)$$

Since the maximum input signal to produce a third-order intermodulation product more than 70 dB down from the input signal was calculated to be −18 dBm, the maximum MDS is −88 dBm, which will permit a noise figure of up to 28 dB.

The noise figure of every element in the signal path of the spectrum analyzer will contribute to the overall noise figure. It is necessary to evaluate the equation for the noise figure for cascaded elements to locate those devices that contribute significantly to the overall noise figure. Devices with high gain will isolate later elements in the signal flow, so that only the first elements contribute anything significant to the noise figure. In the example spectrum analyzer the first IF amplifier is the first element with gain in the signal path and will isolate the remaining elements from significant contributions to the overall noise figure.

To calculate the noise figure of cascaded elements, it is easier to use the noise factor rather than the noise figure. The noise figure is simply 10 log(Noise Factor). The cascaded noise factor of cascaded elements is given by

$$\text{NF}_{1,n} = \text{NF}_1 + (\text{NF}_2 - 1)/G_1 + (\text{NF}_3 - 1)/G_1G_2 + \cdots + (\text{NF}_{n-1})/G_1G_2 \cdots G_{n-1} \qquad (7\text{-}5)$$

where $\text{NF}_{1,n}$ is the noise factor of a cascaded system of n devices having noise factors NF_1, NF_2, NF_3 . . . G_n is the gain of each device.

The noise figure of the example spectrum analyzer is calculated from the following parameters:

Device	Noise factor	Gain
Input low-pass filter	$NF_1 = 1.26$	$G_1 = 0.8$
Input mixer	$NF_2 = 5.01$	$G_2 = 0.22$
First IF filter (A)	$NF_3 = 2.00$	$G_3 = 0.5$
First IF amplifier	$NF_4 = 4.0$	$G_4 = 20.0$
First IF filter (B)	$NF_5 = 2.0$	$G_5 = 0.5$
Second mixer	$NF_6 = 5.01$	$G_6 = 0.22$
Second IF filter	$NF_7 = 1.59$	$G_7 = 0.63$
Third mixer	$NF_8 = 5.01$	$G_8 = 0.22$
Third IF filter	$NF_9 = 2.5$	$G_9 = 0.4$

Substituting the above data into Eq. (7-5) results in a cascaded noise factor of 194 or a cascaded noise figure of 22.9 dB.

Each totally passive device has a noise factor equal to the loss of the device. This can be proven in the following way. A perfectly noise-free signal of power P from a resistive source has a signal-to-noise ratio of P/KTB, where KTB is the thermal noise power of the resistive source. When this signal is attenuated with a passive device such as an attenuator, the signal is reduced a factor of A, which is the attenuation, while the noise power remains KTB. Therefore, the signal-to-noise level at the output is $P/AKTB$. The signal-to-noise ratio has been reduced by a factor of A, which is the definition of noise factor.

The diode-balanced mixers are "quasi-passive." The input signal is not increased in power, but power is supplied to the mixer from the local oscillator. Because of this, a small amount of noise is added to the signal as converted by the mixer. This additional noise can generally be ignored.

It is concluded that the 22.9-dB noise figure of the spectrum analyzer will provide the necessary 70-dB dynamic range required by the specifications.

In a similar fashion, the intercept point of the analyzer must be considered relative to the intercept points of the cascaded elements.

In the previous calculation of the spectrum analyzer dynamic range, the third-order intercept of the system was treated as the third-order intercept of the first mixer alone. The first mixer is the most critical of the devices in the spectrum analyzer, as it is subject to the entire frequency range of the spectrum analyzer and has the greatest chance of generating spurious responses. The first IF amplifier, as well as any other amplifier or mixer in the analyzer, is also capable of generating spurious responses. However, each amplifier has some measure of filtering ahead of it and is subject to increasingly narrower frequency ranges. As an example, the input mixer is subject to the entire 600-MHz passband of the input low-pass filter while the first IF amplifier is subject to the passband of half the first IF filter, or about 6 MHz. However, if two signals were present in the passband of the first IF filter so that they produced a visible intermodulation, this would reduce the dynamic range of the analyzer. This would be true for all the remaining IF amplifiers as well.

In the case of the example analyzer, there is no amplifier at the third IF and clearly there is no intermodulation to be generated. There is, however, a second and third mixer. All mixers in the spectrum analyzer are of the same type, and the input level at each mixer is less than at the input mixer. Thus the level of intermodulation generated at the second and third mixers will be less than at the first mixer.

However, there is an amplifier present early in the signal path at the 700-MHz IF, and it is imperative that the effects of intermodulation due to this amplifier be calculated. The amplifier used for the first IF is a Mini-Circuits MAR-3 monolithic integrated circuit that has a gain of about 12 dB at 700 MHz. The amplifier is operated at a slightly higher current than the specified operating point to improve the gain and intercept point slightly at 700 MHz. The input return loss is excellent at the 700-MHz IF, ensuring a good impedance match for the first IF filter. The output third-order intercept point of this amplifier is +23 dBm, which translates to an input intercept point of +11 dBm. Since there is 9.5 dB of loss ahead of the amplifier due to the input low-pass filter, the first mixer and the first 700-MHz IF filter, the third-order intercept point of this amplifier relative to the input of the spectrum analyzer is +20.5 dBm.

The equivalent third-order intercept of the analyzer, considering the distortion of the first mixer only, was calculated to be +17 dBm. Since third-order intermodulation products rise 3 dB for each decibel increase of the input signals, the intermodulation generated from the +20.5-dBm intercept point due to the IF amplifier is 10.5 dB below those generated by the first mixer at the largest input level and are not visible. Therefore, the dynamic range of the spectrum analyzer is a function of the intercept point of only the input mixer.

The overall signal loss from the input connector to the second mixer was calculated to be 0.5 dB, implying that the intermodulation generated by the second mixer would be 1 dB higher than that generated by the first mixer, but only when the signals are close enough in frequency to fall within the passband of the first IF filters. However, in a pragmatic sense, the losses of connectors and cables and any possible impedance mismatches between the connections of the modules of the spectrum analyzer would more likely result in a loss of a fraction of a decibel rather than an overall gain of a fraction of a decibel. This would place the intermodulation distortion of the first mixer above that generated in the second mixer.

The third and final IF amplifier does not contribute to the generation of intermodulation. Since it is a logarithmic amplifier, not a conventional linear amplifier, it would be, in fact, a great generator of intermodulation. By definition, only one signal exists after the final IF filter. If this were not the case, spectrum analyzer analysis would not be possible as the filter would have insufficient bandwidth to resolve the spectrum. Because there are no multiple signals in the log amplifier to generate intermodulation, the intermodulation characterics of the final IF amplifier are not a factor in spectrum analyzer design.

7.6 First IF Amplifier, Second Mixer, and Second Local Oscillator

The first IF amplifier is a broad-band amplifier preceded by a helical resonator filter, as shown in Fig. 7-7. The output of this amplifier drives a second helical resonator filter, which drives the second mixer. The effects of the gain, dynamic range, and noise figure of this amplifier were covered in detail in the previous section.

The second mixer is a commercially made double-balanced mixer that receives its drive from a free-running oscillator operating at a frequency of 639.3 MHz and one stage of buffer amplification.

This oscillator has a varactor diode so that the oscillator may be swept for

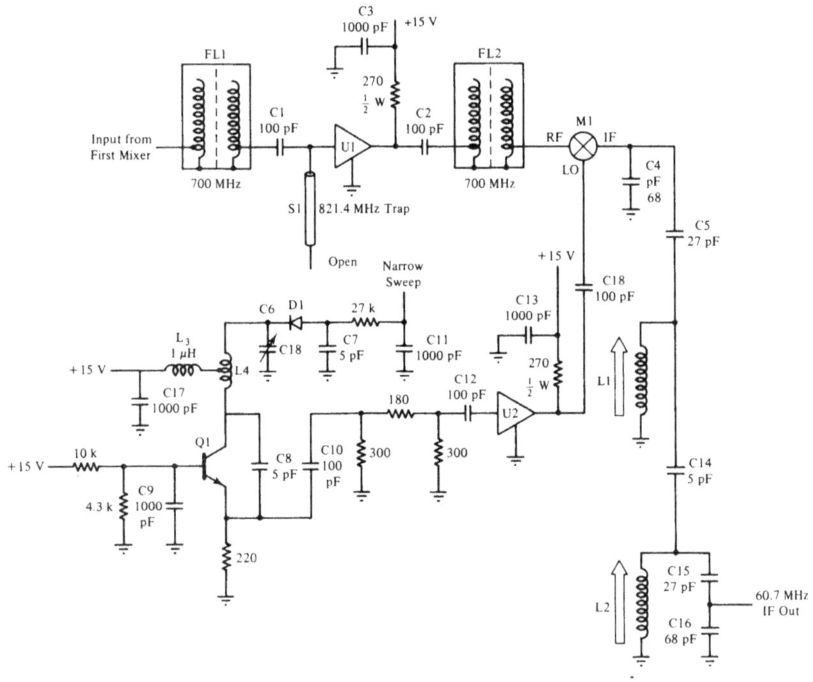

Figure 7-7
Schematic of the first IF filter/amplifier, the second local oscillator, the second mixer, and the second IF filter.

the narrow spans. Since the total frequency sweep is only 500 kHz and the oscillator frequency is 639.3 MHz, the proportional frequency sweep is very small.

The most important characteristic of this oscillator is its frequency stability. Since there is no phase lock, the accuracy of the analyzer's center frequency is a function of this oscillator. Therefore, it is important that stable components be used to create this oscillator.

The output of the second mixer is 60.7 MHz, and it is filtered with a conventional L-C two-section bandpass filter.

7.7 The IF Filters

The three IF filters are shown in Fig. 7-8 (a), (b), and (c).

As previously explained, the ultimate selectivity of the spectrum analyzer is dependent on the passband of the last IF filter. The three IF bandwidths chosen for the example spectrum analyzer were based on a compromise between need and economy. The broadest IF bandwidth is set by the minimum bandwidth necessary to provide a flicker-free display at the maximum frequency span. For a scan rate of 50 MHz per division, the maximum at a scan rate of 50 sweeps per second with an 18-ms scan time and a retrace time of 2 ms, the scan rate is 27.8×10^9 Hz/s. Substituting this value into Eq. (2-32) results in a minimum filter bandwidth of 14.5 kHz. This results in spectral lines that are only 0.003% of the full scan, which is unnecessarily small. A filter bandwidth of 300 kHz provides a spectral line width of 0.06%—quite suitable and allowing the use of an inexpensive and near-Gaussian shaped ceramic filter. In addition, the broader filter will be useful in pulse and noise-band measurement where its wider impulse bandwidth will be needed.

Two ceramic filters are used with additional L-C tuning, providing impedance matching as well as additional attenuation of spurious responses from the ceramic filter. Ceramic filters tend to have a number of spurious responses, including the odd harmonics of the filter center frequency.

The next filter bandwidth is 30 kHz, which uses a pair of two-pole crystal filters. These filters are designed for VHF communications systems and are made to have sharp skirts. By deliberately detuning the filters, it is possible to achieve a more rounded characteristic, making the filter suitable for spectrum analyzer use.

The narrowest filter is a 3-kHz crystal filter. This filter is constructed using two conventional quartz crystals. The effects of the leakage through the parallel reactance of the crystal is nulled by using a bridge circuit with a trimmer capacitor. This was discussed in detail in Chapter 2. The resulting filter has a nearly Gaussian characteristic.

The IF filters are switched by the use of small relays. The relays are connected in such a way that a filter that is not selected is grounded, preventing signal leakage through a nonselected filter.

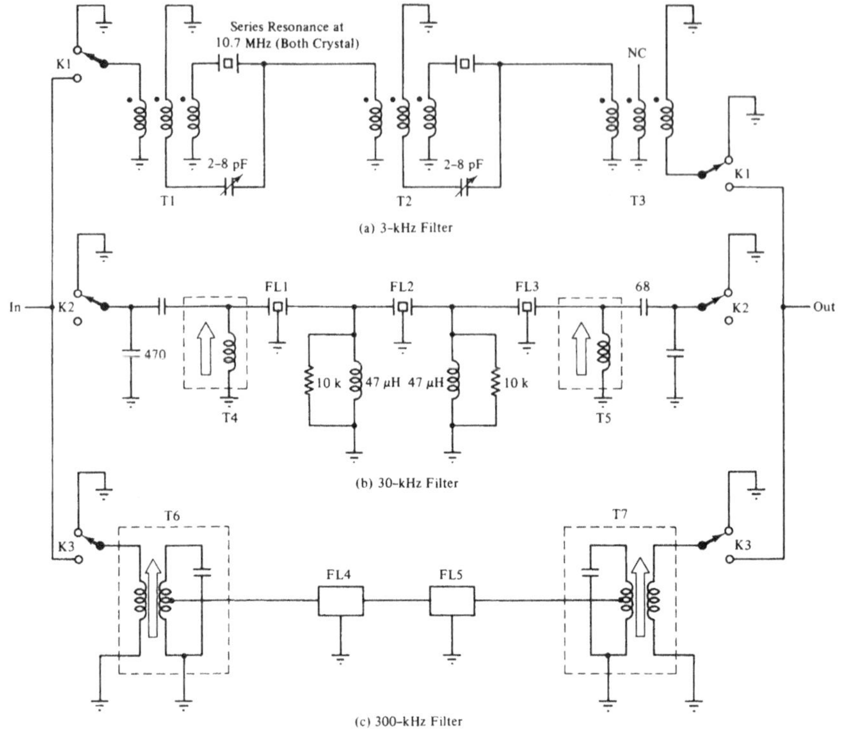

Figure 7-8
The schematic of the three IF filters for the spectrum analyzer. In actual construction, the filters would be separated by metal shields to prevent signal leakage.

The reason for the use of relays rather than a switch may not be readily apparent. It is difficult to connect the filters to a conventional wafer switch without significant feedthrough. When a mechanical switching arrangement is used for the IF filters, switch sections are placed at the input and at the output of the filter. An insulated shaft passes through the filter area and mechanically connects the two switch wafers. An insulating shaft is required, as energy can be coupled inductively through a conducting shaft.

There are several disadvantages to the mechanical switch arrangement. First, the switch must be carefully and correctly made to prevent signal leakage. Second, it is not possible to switch the filters electronically. This would be desirable for coupling to the frequency-span control, in which a mechanical arrangement would be nearly impossible.

The IF filters are aligned using a sweep generator and a diode detector for a preliminary alignment; final alignment, if required, is made using the spectrum analyzer itself.

As it was in the case of the input low-pass filter, the sweep generator/crystal detector method of frequency response measurement is not capable of a wide dynamic range. Only the passband of the filter may be adjusted. The insertion loss of the 300-kHz filter is adjusted for minimum loss by adjusting T6 and T7 as shown in Fig. 7-9. The passband ripple should not be more than 1 dB. If it is not possible to adjust either T6 or T7 for a 1-dB maximum ripple while maintaining a reasonable insertion loss, it will then be necessary to select the 10.7-MHz filters for a closer frequency match. Manufacturers of this type filter have sorted the filters by center frequency and identified the filter center frequency with a color dot. These dots have a resolution of as much as 60 kHz, and therefore it can be expected that filters within a color dot category would vary in center frequency by as much as 60 kHz. Since these filters are very inexpensive, it would not be unreasonable to sort from as many as 10 filters for the best passband characteristics.

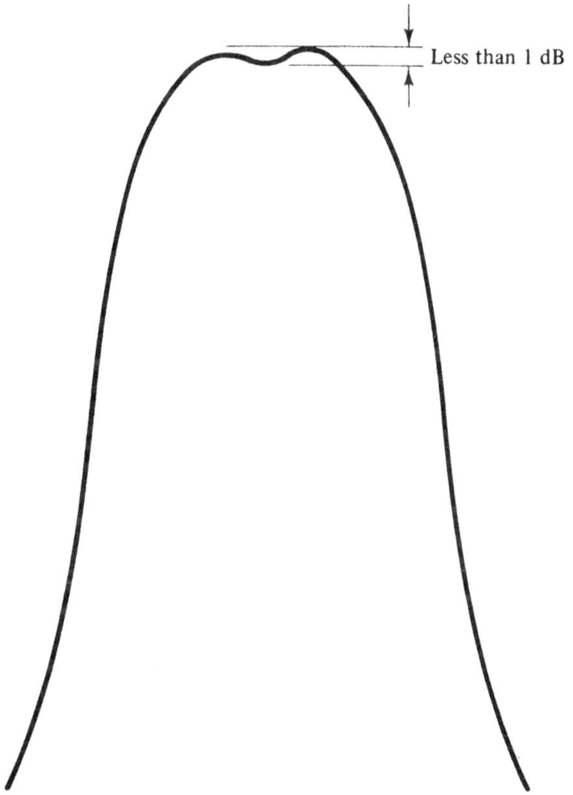

Figure 7-9
The IF filter is adjusted for a pass-band ripple of no more than 1 dB, as shown here.

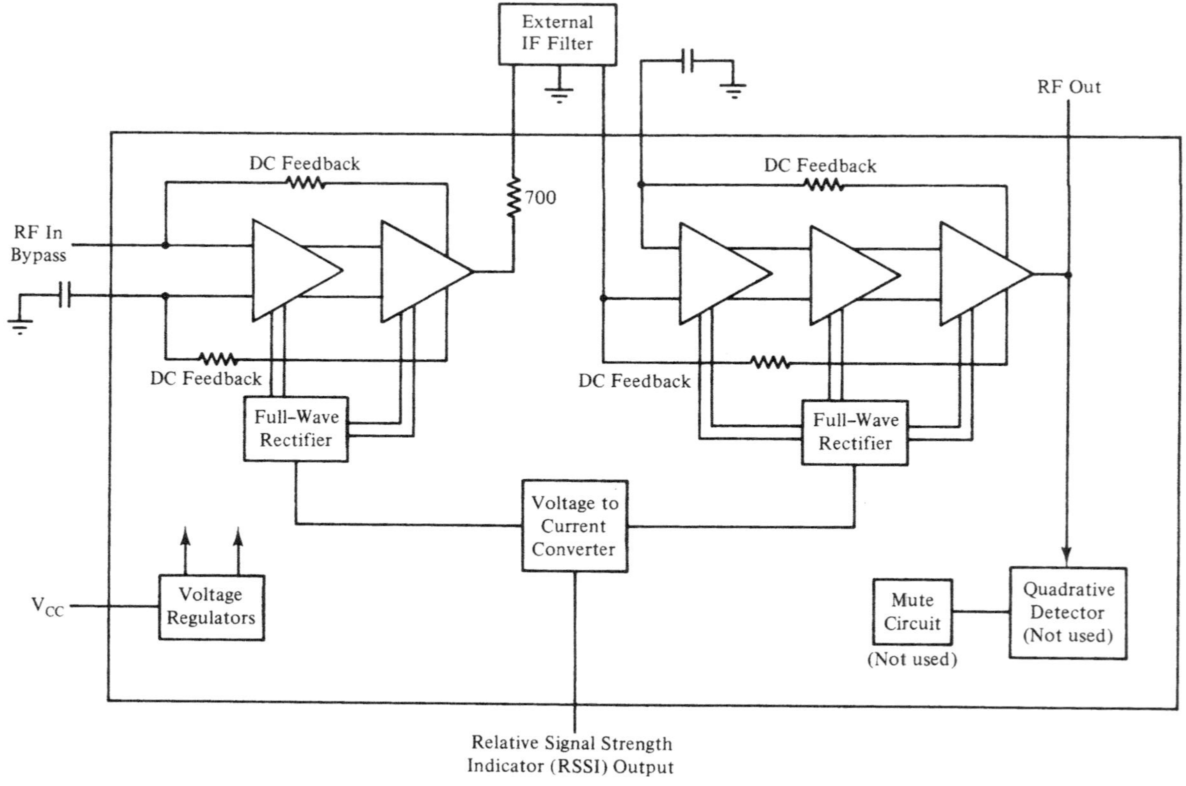

Figure 7-10
Schematic of the FM IF amplifier chip used as the log amplifier for the spectrum analyzer. (*Figure continues.*)

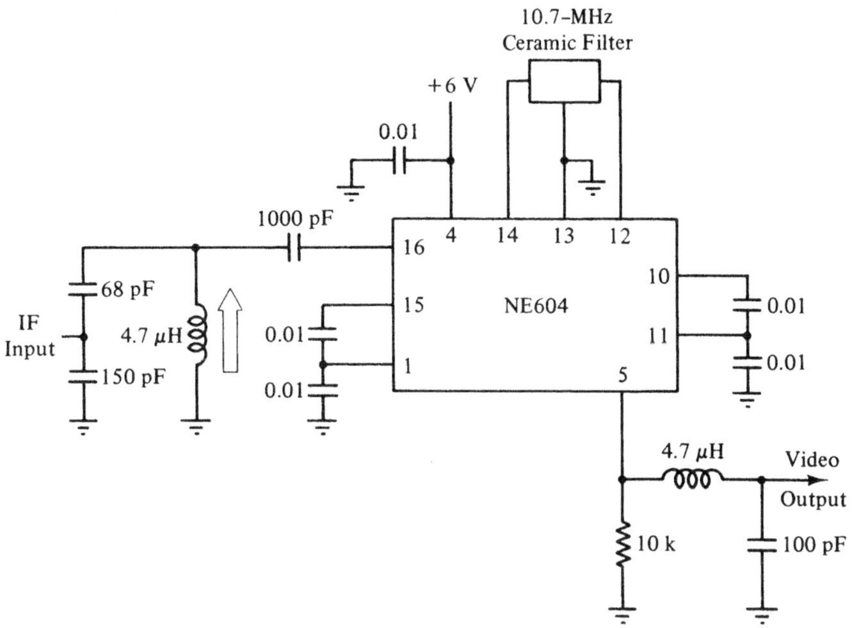

(b)

Figure 7-10 *(continued)*

7.8 Log IF Amplifier and Video Display Amplifiers

The log IF amplifier uses an IF chip normally intended for an FM receiver. As shown in the block diagram in Fig. 7-10(a), the Signetics NE614 chip has a five-stage limiting amplifier that includes a full-wave rectifier for each limiter stage. Full-wave rectification is achieved by operating differential amplifiers throughout the chip and including two half-wave rectifiers for each amplifier stage. The basic operating technology is identical to that discussed in Chapter 2. When applied in a mobile telephone application, the rectified output provides a relative signal-strength indicator (RSSI) used in the system for control of the transmitter power for the mobile units. This output is used as the detected log video for the spectrum analyzer. The FM demodulator is not used.

The log accuracy of the FM radio chip is about ± 1 or ± 2 dB over a 70-dB signal range. The IF chip is capable of operating over an 80-dB range, but the log accuracy deteriorates at high signal levels.

As shown in Fig. 7-10(b), the log output from the FM radio chip is amplified and filtered to remove any 10.7-MHz energy.

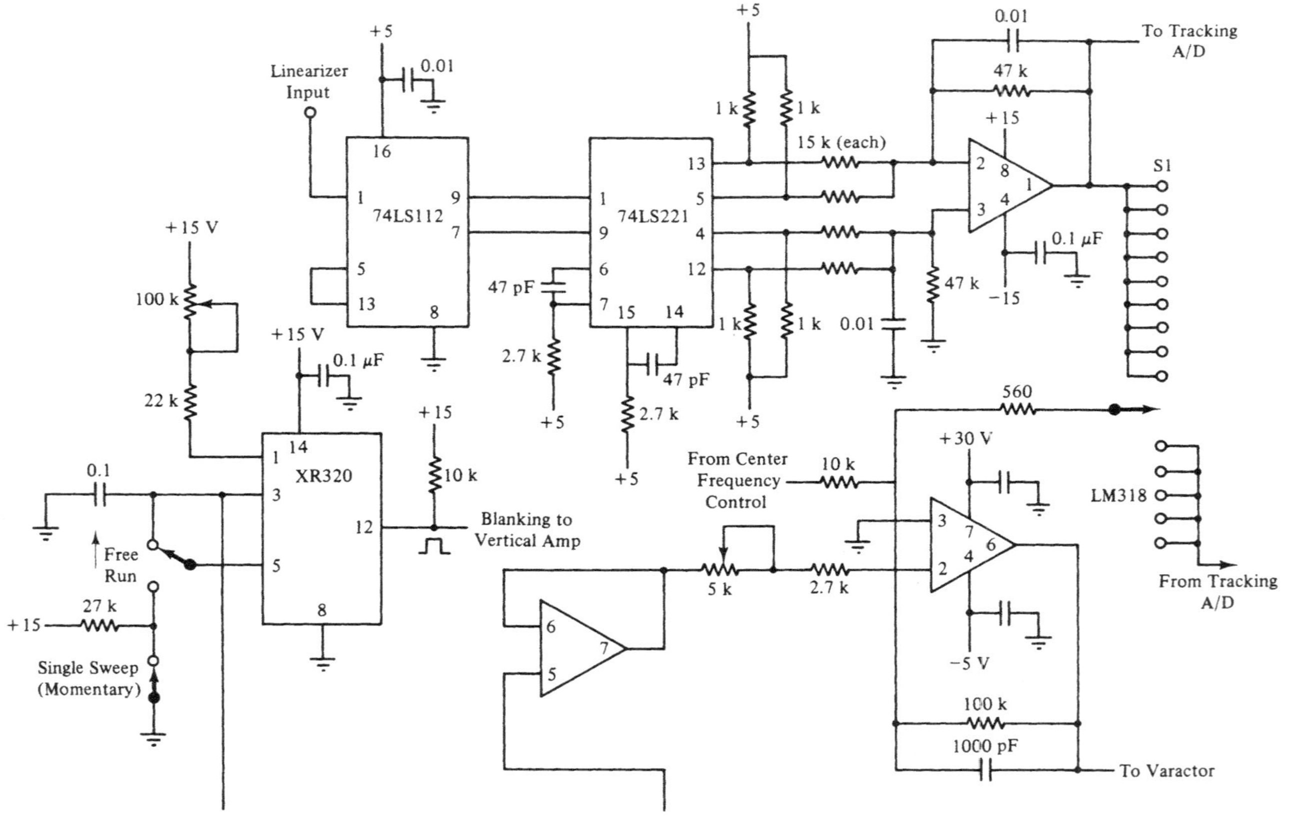

Figure 7-11
(a) The schematic of the saw-tooth generator, the span switch, and the feedback linearizer circuits. (*Figure continues on the following page.*) (b) The schematic of the tracking D/A for holding the VCO tuning voltage when the analyzer is in phase lock. (*See page 162.*)

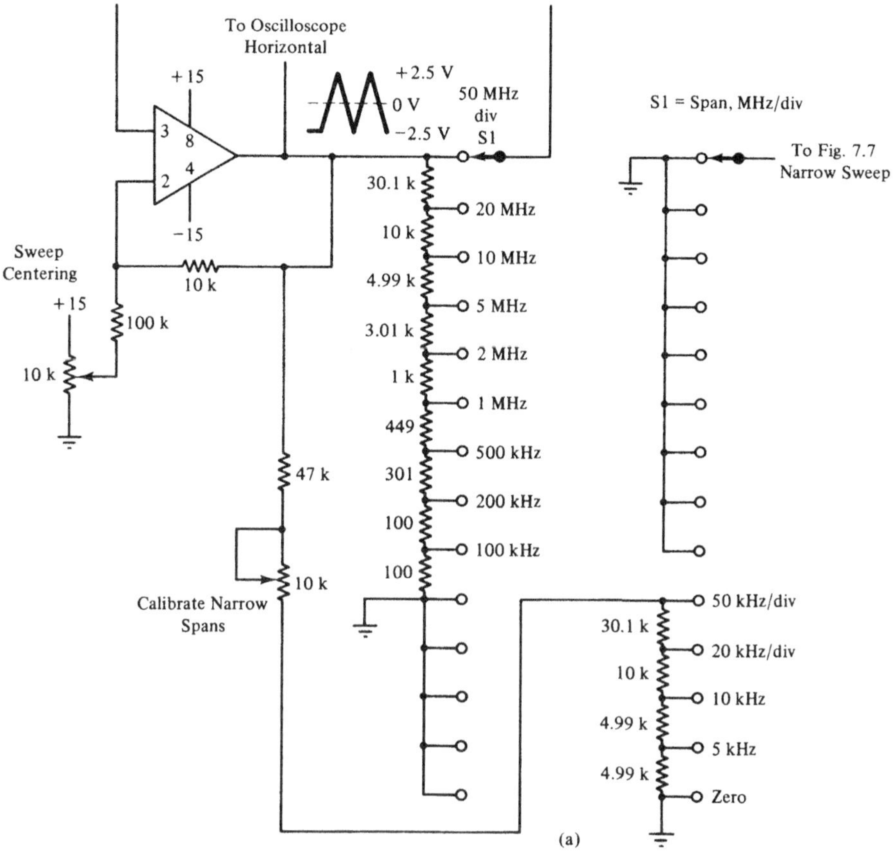

Figure 7-11 (*continued*)

7.9 Horizontal Sweep Generator and Amplifiers

The sweep voltage generator of the sweep system shown in Fig. 7-11(a) uses a simple timer chip, XR-320, to provide the basic sawtooth waveform for the spectrum analyzer. Often the sweep voltage generator is calibrated so it may be used as a time base for time domain analysis with spectrum analyzer in the zero span position. The example spectrum analyzer will use an oscilloscope in the X-Y mode without a time-base calibration from the sweep voltage generator, since the example spectrum analyzer is to drive a conventional oscilloscope in the X-Y mode. For time domain analysis with the spectrum analyzer, the oscilloscope time base may be used.

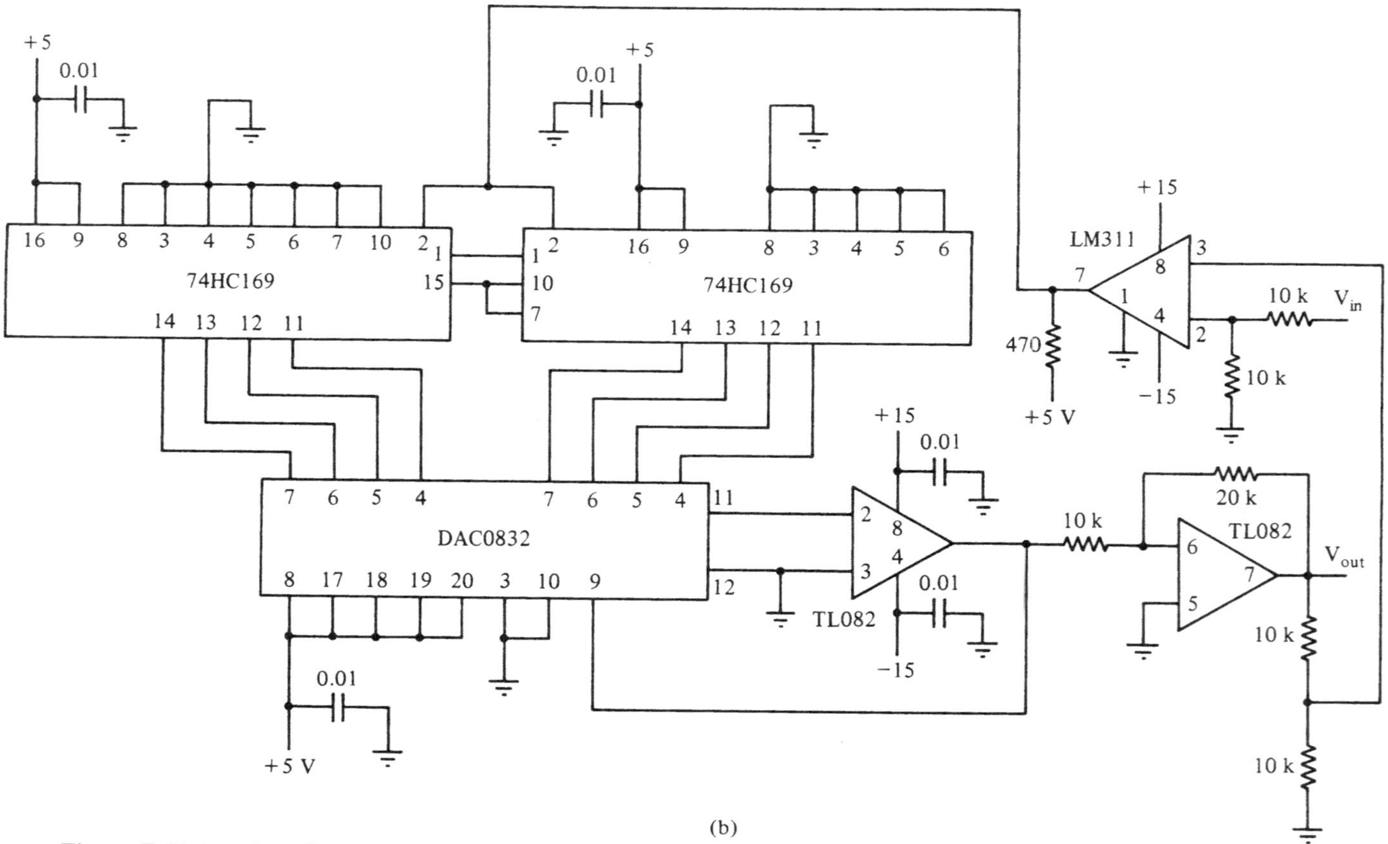

(b)

Figure 7-11 *(continued)*

The output of the sawtooth generator drives a noninverting amplifier where the sawtooth waveform is adjusted to ensure that the center of the ramp is exactly zero volts. The importance of this was explained previously.

The output of the amplifier feeds the span switch attenuator where nine of the spans are generated. These wider spans, 50 MHz/division to 100 kHz/division, are buffered with a unity gain amplifier to prevent loading of the span attenutator and fed to the frequency-linearizer circuit which, in turn, sweeps the frequency of the first local oscillator.

At the output of the frequency linearizer is a digital sample-and-hold circuit, as shown in Fig. 7-11(b). This circuit is a form of A/D converter called a tracking converter, which uses an up–down counter to step a D/A converter; so the output of the D/A tracks the input voltage. This converter is disabled when the phase-locked loop is enabled, so the VCO control voltage is "frozen" at the value immediately preceding the switch from the non-phase-locked condition to phase lock.

If the frequency linearizer were left operating, the linearizer, being a feedback system, would attempt to counteract the actions of the phase-locked loop circuit. As an example, if the phase-locked loop attempted to raise the frequency, the linearizer would attempt to lower the frequency. This lowering of the frequency would cause the phase-locked loop to attempt to raise the frequency even more, until the phase-locked loop ran out of range. The linearizer, having a range equal to the full range of VCO frequency, would win out and essentially render the phase-locked loop ineffective.

The tracking A/D converter tracks the error voltage from the linearizer; when the frequency sweep is switched from the first local oscillator, the error voltage is "remembered" by the tracking A/D converter. The feedback from the linearizer is disabled, and the output of the tracking A/D is substituted. This disables the feedback without the varactor tuning voltage making a great jump.

The phase-locked loop stabilizes the oscillator with a dedicated varactor diode for this purpose. The reason for using a dedicated varactor diode is so that a wide bandwidth may be provided for the phase-locked loop.

Two amplifiers are used to interface with the horizontal and vertical channels of the oscilloscope. In the case of the horizontal, a sawtooth waveform is supplied to drive the oscilloscope display. It is desirable that the amplitude of this sawtooth waveform overdrive the display by about 20%, so the display will be certain to fill the entire screen and any transients that occur due to the retrace will be outside the display and not visible. What is most important, however, is that the center of the display be the exact center frequency of the analyzer. This is important, for should the center of the display not be the actual center of the frequency range of the analyzer, changing the span will cause the display to move to the left or right and will require constant correction. Generally, this is assured by supplying a bipolar sawtooth voltage for the oscilloscope where the center frequency of the display corresponds to zero volts, exactly.

The actual amplitude of the oscilloscope drive depends on the oscilloscope used for display. Typically, a drive level of .05 V per division is used, which requires a 600-mV peak-to-peak horizontal drive, providing a full-screen deflection plus the desired 10% overdrive for full left and full right deflection, assuming a ten-division horizontal display.

7.10 Vertical Amplifiers and Video Filter

The vertical output to the oscilloscope is a bipolar voltage similar in amplitude to the horizontal output. Many oscilloscopes have only eight divisions of vertical deflection while some have 10, requiring a 400 or 500-mV drive, respectively. Relative to the vertical output to the oscilloscope, the center of the display should correspond to zero volts. However, within the spectrum analyzer, where the scale factor is changed, the zero-voltage point should be equivalent to the top of the screen. The top line is called the reference level; when the scale factor is changed from 10 dB per division to 2 dB per division, the top of the display should remain stationary. Thus, the reference level is equal to zero volts of the inverted vertical display as shown in Fig. 7-12, before the scale factor switch and an offset are added at the output amplifier to allow the center of the display to correspond to zero volts as presented to the oscilloscope. An adjustment that is summed with the output of the log amplifier is supplied to ensure this zero-voltage reference.

Retrace blanking may be added to the vertical amplifier. The retrace of the frequency sweep of the spectrum analyzer is blanked so that it is not visible. If the retrace were not blanked, a faint spectrum would appear, superimposed on the desired display. Because the retrace rate is so much more rapid than the trace, the retrace spectra would be severely distorted. Even if the trace and retrace time were made the same, hysteresis in the circuits within the frequency sweeping of the analyzer would cause the retrace to be slightly different and cause a "ghost" trace.

There are two basic methods of blanking the trace. The classic method is to blank the electron beam of the oscilloscope so that the oscilloscope does not write during retrace. When the spectrum analyzer has a built-in display, this is the preferred method.

When the display is an external oscilloscope, in order to use the conventional blanking technique an external blanking input must be available in the display oscilloscope. Not all oscilloscopes have this input, and there tends to be a lack of standardization of those inputs that are available.

An alternative method is to clamp the video output and offset the vertical retrace signal so it is below the bottom line of the display. This is shown graphically in Fig. 7-13. The trace is simply "pushed" below the display and out of

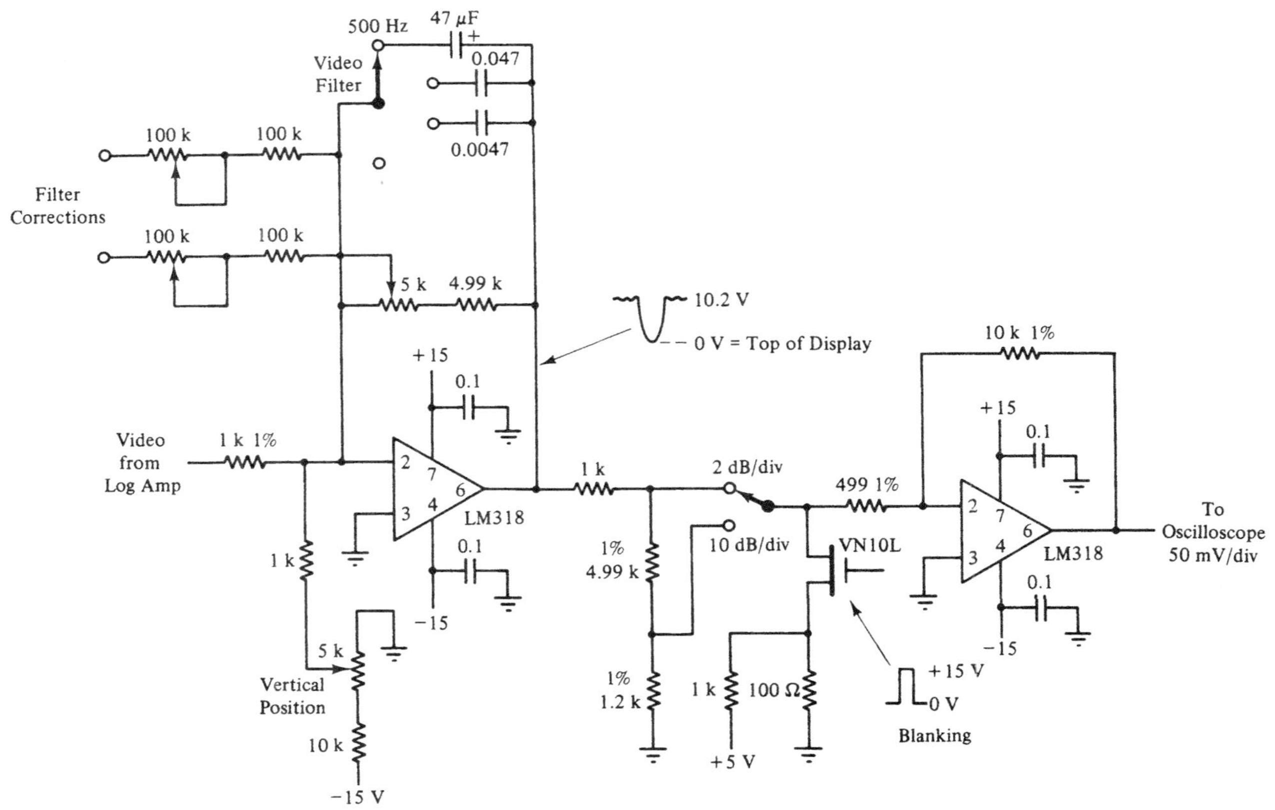

Figure 7-12
Schematic of the video filter and blanking circuits for the vertical portion of the spectrum analyzer.

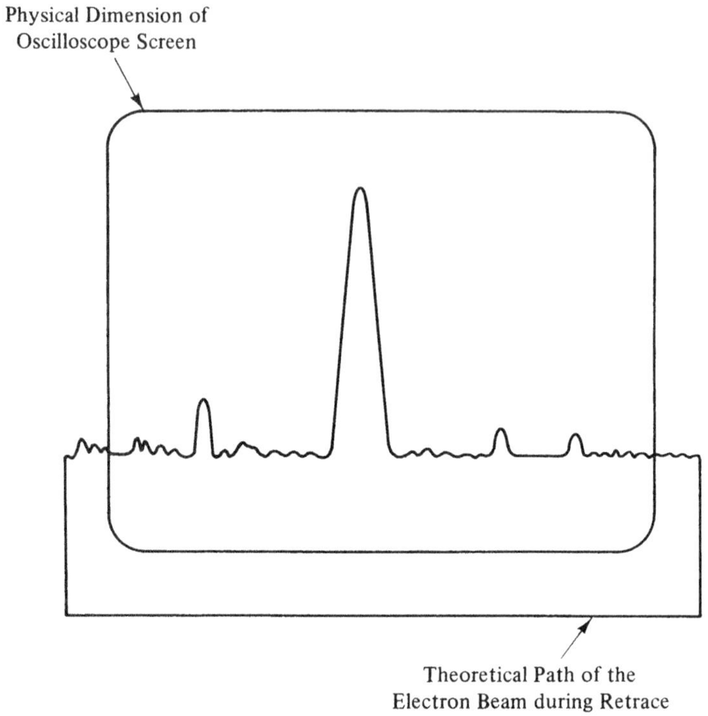

Figure 7-13
A graphical representation of the method of blanking where the retrace is "pushed" below the screen during retrace.

sight. This technique requires no external blanking signal from the spectrum analyzer, and any oscilloscope that can be driven in the X-Y mode may be used as a display for the spectrum analyzer.

The frequency response of the display amplifiers should be commensurate with the bandwidth of the widest IF filter. This is necessary so that the analyzer can handle broad-band spectral analysis accurately. In the previous chapters, the impulse bandwidth of the spectrum analyzer was related to only the IF filter bandwidth. This is only true if the video amplifier, as well as the display oscilloscope, has a bandwidth significantly greater than the IF filter's impulse bandwidth.

In the case of the example spectrum analyzer, the widest IF bandwidth is 300 kHz, and thus a video bandwidth of 500 kHz would be sufficient.

An inexpensive high-frequency operational amplifier is suitable for the video amplifier, as shown in Fig. 7-12. In addition, the figure shows the method of blanking.

The video filter is a simple single-pole RC filter, which may reduce the video bandwidth. This device is used to find the average value of noisy displays. It essentially smoothes the display so the center of the "fuzz" may be seen when viewing noise spectra. It can also be used to retrieve weak signals from the baseline noise by averaging the noise level.

For a video filter to be useful, it must have a bandwidth significantly less than the bandwidth of the IF filter in use. This is just the opposite of the requirement that the video bandwidth of the analyzer be significantly greater than IF filter bandwidth in order to accurately display pulse and noise spectra. To effectively reduce the effects of noise, the video bandwidth must be significantly less than the IF bandwidth.

In the example analyzer, the video filter is equipped with three bandwidths and employs an integrator for the filter. The widest video bandwidth, which achieves bandwidth reduction from the capabilities of the amplifier, is 500 kHz. Three other video bandwidths are available: 50 kHz, 5 kHz, and 500 Hz.

7.11 Frequency Readout and Control

The practical spectrum analyzer uses a full feedback method of frequency linearity. Some of the devices used for the frequency linearity circuits are used for the frequency readout and the phase-locked loop frequency control.

The frequency range of the first local oscillator VCO is from 700 to 1200 MHz. Although technology is constantly improving, at the time the example analyzer was designed, very few reasonably priced dual-modulus prescalers were available for this frequency range. Most dual-modulus prescalers that approach the frequency and price objectives are high-division prescalers such as 128/129. Using a prescaler of this division requires a minimum programmable divider of 16,385. This, in turn, dictates a reference frequency of 43 kHz, which is too low for the phase locking of the first local oscillator. A goal of 125 kHz for the reference frequency was set for the analyzer. This value will allow a reduction of phase noise of the first local oscillator so that the 3-kHz IF filter can be successfully used.

Using a 125-kHz reference and a dual modulus prescaler so that the first local oscillator may be locked every 125 kHz would require a maximum dual-modulus prescaler of 75/76. A typical modulus would be 64/65, which was not available at the time of the design. Therefore, a compromise was decided upon. A fixed divide-by-eight prescaler would be used with the 125-kHz reference and would allow the local oscillator to be phase locked at 1-MHz multiples.

This divide-by-eight prescaler will be shared among the frequency linearizer, the frequency display, and the phase-locked frequency stabilizer.

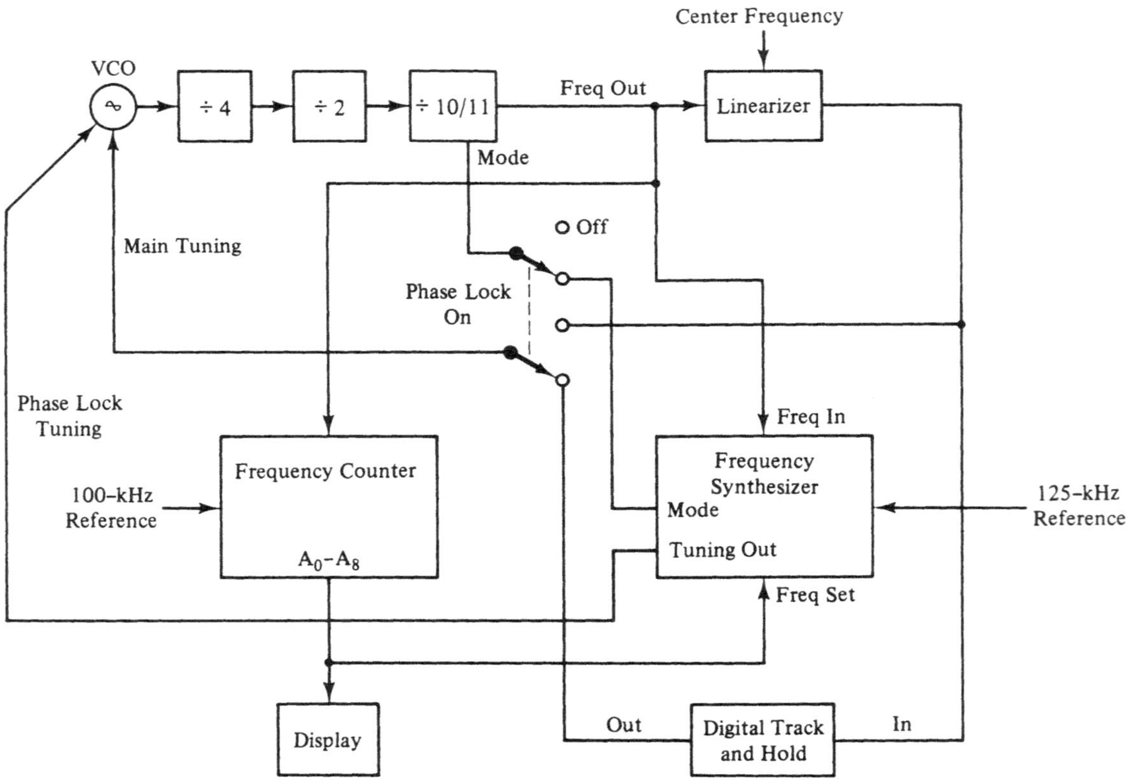

Figure 7-14
The interconnection of the various subsystems for the frequency control and display for the first local oscillator.

Figure 7-14 shows a block diagram of how these three systems interconnect.

The VCO frequency is divided by using a 2.5-GHz divide-by-four followed by an ECL toggle flip-flop for a total division of eight. The 2.5-GHz chip is an inexpensive prescaler used for satellite television receivers.

This divided output feeds a 10/11 dual-modulus prescaler, which is also shared among the frequency linearizer, the frequency display, and the phase locked loop. The choice of a 10/11 prescaler rather than division based on binary values such as 32/33, 15/16, etc., was for the convenience of the manipulation of binary-coded decimal required for the frequency readout.

For wide spans, those greater than 100 kHz per division, the first local oscillator is swept in frequency while the second local oscillator is fixed. For frequency spans of 100 kHz per division or less, the first local oscillator is phase locked and the second local oscillator is swept. This technique was thoroughly covered in Chapter 3.

For the narrow spans where the first local oscillator is phase locked, the dual-modulus prescaler is a part of the phase-locked loop's programmable divider. For the narrow spans, the frequency readout and the linearizer are inoperative. Since the second local oscillator is swept, the frequency linearizer is unnecessary; and since the first local oscillator is phase locked, its frequency is known and thus there is no need to count the local oscillator frequency.

The frequency linearizer shown in Fig. 7-11(a) uses the technique shown in Chapter 2. The VCO is divided by a total of 80 with high-speed ECL frequency dividers external to the linearizer, which includes the divide-by-four prescaler, the toggle flip-flop for an additional division of two, and the 10/11 prescaler dividing only by 10. An additional division of four is provided and produces a frequency range from 2.1875 to 3.75 MHz.

This frequency drives a one-shot multivibrator with a period of 150 ns. This provides a duty cycle from 33% to 56% that is filtered with an integrator. The output of the integrator is adjusted with a potentiometer to provide an output in which the center of the maximum span, 700 to 1200 MHz, occurs at exactly zero volts. Any other voltage may be used here, but using zero as the absolute center of the maximum simplifies the design.

The frequency is counted "on the fly," as explained in Chapter 3. The schematic of the frequency counter section is shown in Fig. 7-15. A frequency resolution of 1 MHz was desired, which would provide a frequency readout to within 0.2% of the maximum span, which is reasonable for a medium performance spectrum analyzer. The same fixed division used by the frequency linearizing circuit will be used, which provides a sample of the local oscillator frequency divided by 80. To count this frequency to within 1 MHz, a count gate of 80 μs is required. This is obtained by dividing a 100-kHz reference frequency by 8.

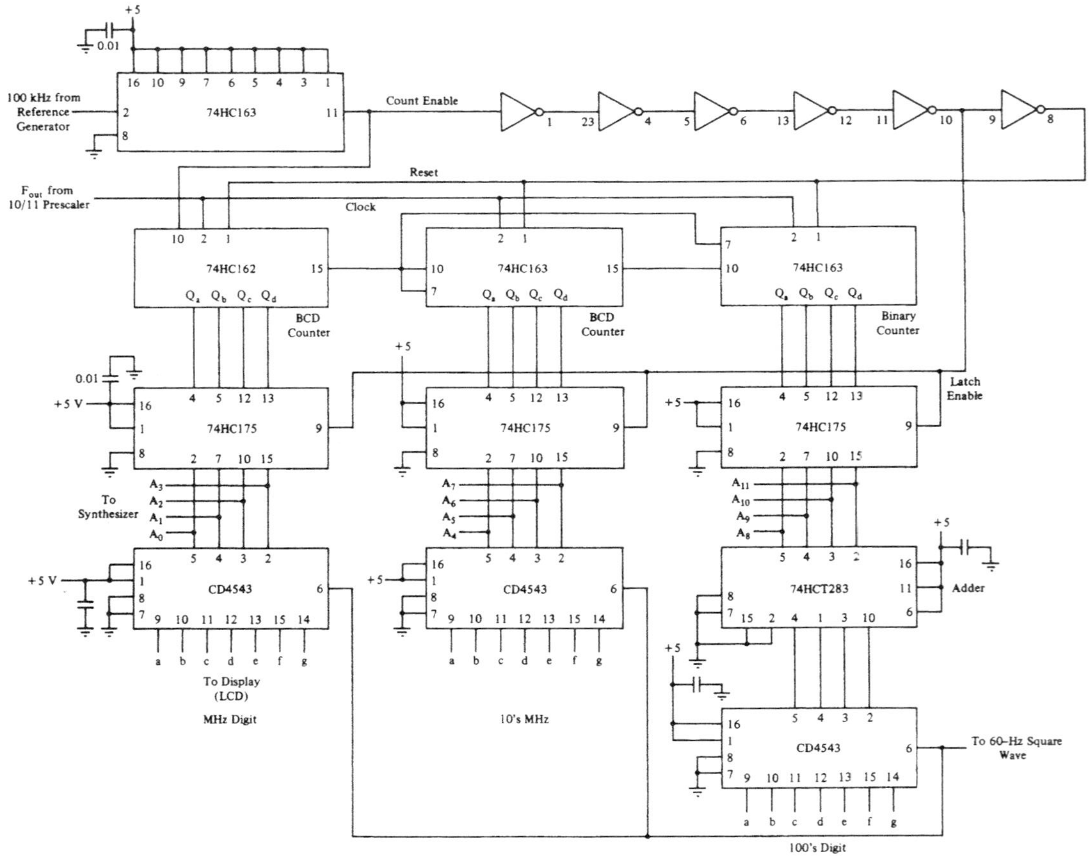

Figure 7-15
Schematic diagram of the frequency counter section of the first local oscillator frequency control and display.

Three digits of frequency display is required for the spectrum analyzer. In addition, 700 MHz must be subtracted from the displayed frequency for the input frequency to be displayed. Three decade counters and one binary counter are used to count the local oscillator frequency. The binary counter is used for the most significant digit, as it ranges from 7 to 12, corresponding to 700 to 1200 MHz. The use of the binary counter saves one additional decade counter. The frequency display is the counted frequency minus 700, which is achieved by adding 9 to the most significant digit and ignoring the carry from the addition. Ignoring a carry is the same as subtracting 16, and every addition involves a carry when the frequency is above 700 MHz. Therefore, the result is adding 9 and subtracting 16, or the same as subtracting 7. Since the weight of the most significant bit is 100, the result is the subtraction of 700, which is the desired result.

It is possible for the local oscillator to go below 700 MHz. This is an improper operation of the analyzer, as it involves "negative" frequency that in the spectrum analyzer is meaningless. When the most significant digit is less than 6, indicating the analyzer is below the "zero" frequency, the addition of 9 produces 15, which is not a valid BCD code. The 4543 LCD seven-segment decoder produces a blank for non-BCD codes and indicates the analyzer is operating in the "negative" frequency region.

When the spectrum analyzer is switched from a span of 100 kHz per division to 50 kHz per division, the frequency of the first local oscillator is phase locked and the second local oscillator is swept in frequency. The frequency at which the first local oscillator is locked is the actual counted center frequency. Therefore, the frequency counter is stopped and the last counted frequency is used to program the divider in the phase-locked loop.

The counter latches that hold the display frequency for the frequency counter are connected to the display decoders and the phase-locked loop. Therefore, the phase-locked loop is constantly programmed to the center frequency of the first local oscillator, to the nearest 1 MHz.

The displayed frequency will shift slightly, as the actual center frequency before the phase-locked loop is engaged is not necessarily a precise multiple of 1 MHz. Since the phase-locked loop must lock the center frequency to a precise multiple of 1 MHz, the frequency could change by as much as 0.5 MHz.

The capture range of the phase-locked loop using the phase/frequency detector shown in the block diagram of Fig. 7-16 has a capture range limited only by the tuning range of the varactor diode used for the phase-locked loop. However, since the free-running frequency of the first local oscillator is very close to the desired frequency when the span switch changes to phase-locked operation, the loop requires very little capture range.

The precision time-base generator is required for the frequency counter, and the phase-locked loop is shown in Fig. 7-17. A 50-MHz oscillator is used as

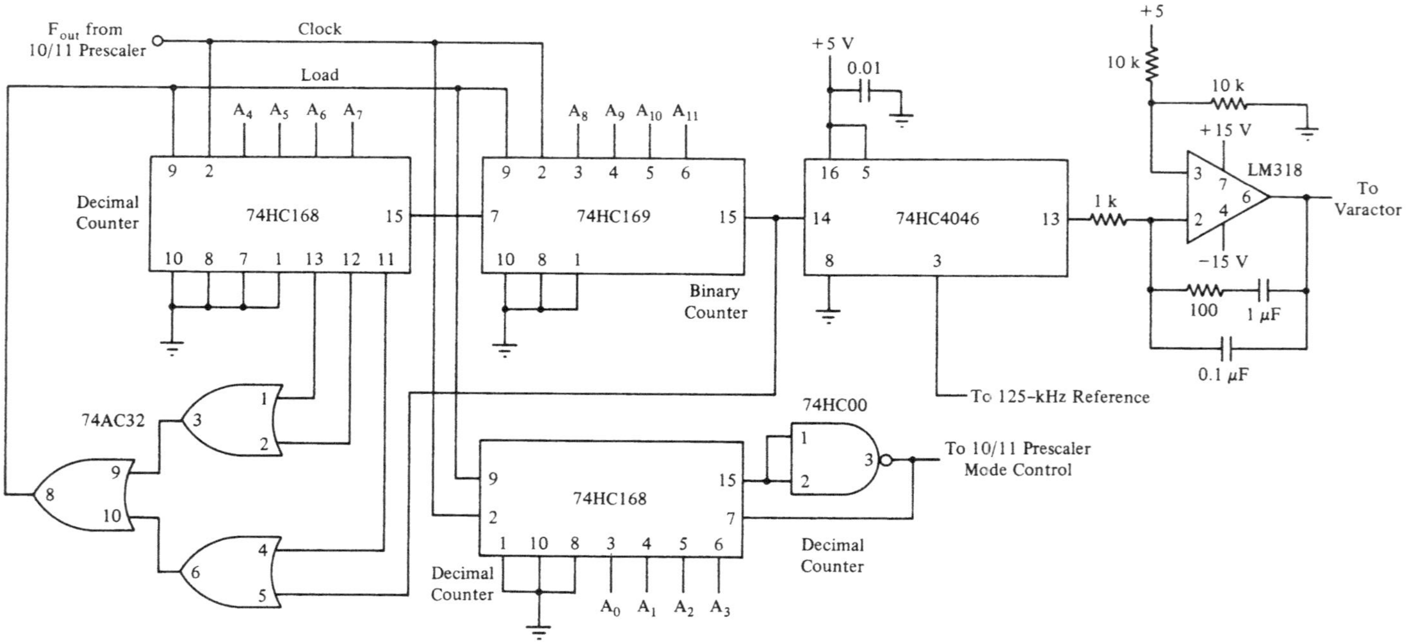

Figure 7-16
Schematic diagram of the frequency synthesizer for the first local oscillator.

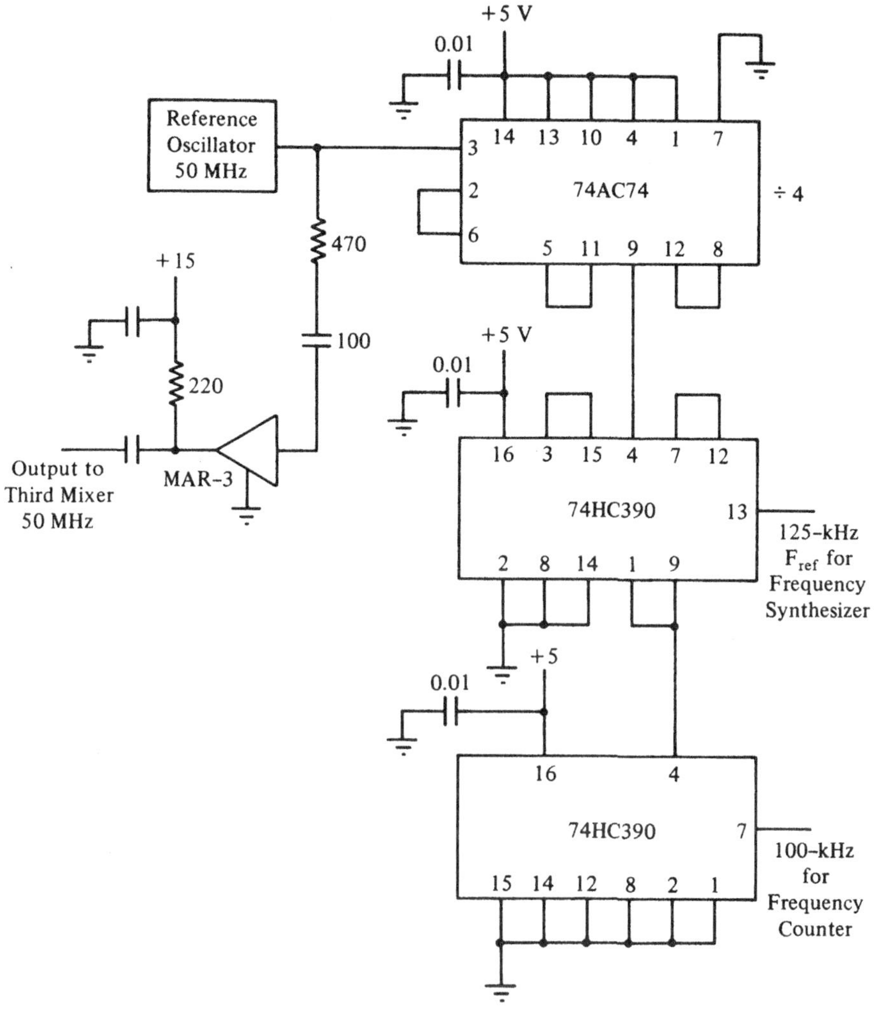

Figure 7-17
The reference frequency generator for the spectrum analyzer.

the master oscillator and is divided by four to obtain 12.5 MHz. This is divided by 25 to obtain 500 kHz. Dividing the 500 kHz waveform by 4 produces the 125-kHz reference for the frequency synthesizer, and dividing by 5 produces the 100-kHz reference required for the frequency readout.

The 50-MHz oscillator frequency is used for the third local oscillator of the analyzer.

Review Questions for Chapter 7

1. What are some of the error sources in a high-frequency attenuator? What are some of the techniques used to reduce these error sources?
2. Why is it necessary to shield the sections of an attenuator? Would this be more necessary with the high-attenuation steps or the lower attenuation steps?
3. What are the important characteristics of an input low-pass filter for spectrum analyzer?
4. Why is it necessary to choose components for the input low-pass filter that have good qualities well above the frequency range of the analyzer?
5. What is the significant advantage of using an elliptical filter as the input low-pass filter?
6. What instrumentation set-up would be suitable for adjusting the flat portion of the input low-pass filter? Why is the method not suitable for adjusting the stop band of the filter?
7. Why is the "IF" port of a balanced mixer used as the input to the spectrum analyzer? Is there a similar problem with the other mixers in the analyzer?
8. What is the third-order intercept point?
9. For a diode type of mixer, how is the third-order intercept point affected by local oscillator power?
10. If a mixer has a third-order intercept point of +15 dBm and two input signals each have a level of −20 dBm, what is the level of the intermodulation products?
11. If the two input signals described in the problem above were at frequencies of 102 and 104 MHz, what would be the frequencies of the third-order intermodulation products?
12. What is noise figure? How does the noise figure of a spectrum analyzer affect the dynamic range?
13. What is the noise level of a spectrum analyzer with a noise figure of 25 dB with an IF bandwidth of 1 MHz?
14. If the third-order intercept point were +10 dBm for the analyzer described in problem 13, what would be the dynamic range?
15. What would be the cascaded noise figure of an IF subsystem with a filter of 3-dB loss, followed by an amplifier with 15-dB gain and a 2-dB noise figure followed by a second IF filter of 3-dB loss?
16. It is often necessary to measure a signal level below the maximum sensitivity of a spectrum analyzer. To do this a preamplifier is added ahead of the spectrum analyzer. What signal level would be 3 dB greater than the noise level if a preamplifier with 20-dB gain, a 2.5-dB noise figure, and a third-order intercept point of −15 dBm were placed ahead of the spectrum analyzer described in problem 13? Compare this level to the signal 3 dB greater than the noise level of the analyzer described in 13.

17. Would the addition of the preamplifier described in the previous problem increase or decrease the dynamic range of the analyzer? Calculate the new dynamic range.

18. Why is there no intermodulation distortion generated in the last IF amplifier of the analyzer?

19. What filter technology is used for narrow-frequency filters, medium bandwidths, and very large bandwidths?

20. What advantage does an IF filter serve? How does the video filter affect the impulse bandwidth of the analyzer?

21. Where is the reference level of a spectrum analyzer usually placed?

22. Why is retrace blanking used in a spectrum analyzer? Describe some methods of providing blanking.

8

Spectrum Analyzer Performance Determination

8.1 Overview

The need to establish standards for spectrum analyzers and other test equipment was discussed in Chapter 2. The advantages of maintaining a common set of nomenclature for the front panel of a spectrum analyzer so that an operator will be able to properly operate any instrument is clear. Common definitions of terms, particularly those used to specify the capabilities of the analyzer, are also needed.

When evaluating the performance of any instrument, the test method can influence the measurement. Therefore, in many instances, it is desirable to have a standard set of preferred test procedures for the evaluation of the spectrum analyzer.

The IEEE standard for spectrum analyzers, STD 748-1979, contains a complete set of measurement techniques for spectrum analyzer evaluation. Because spectrum analyzer technology has taken great strides since the publication of STD 748-1979, the tests outlined in this chapter are based on the IEEE standard but have been updated to include modern spectrum analyzers. In addition, the order of tests presented in this chapter is different than the order appearing in the IEEE standard. The test methods appearing in the IEEE standard are in simple alphabetical order and are not presented in a way that would facilitate aligning a spectrum analyzer.

The order of tests in this chapter is such that, for most spectrum analyzers, the minimum test time and equipment are required. As an example, the center-frequency readout and span accuracy are checked and adjusted, if necessary, before the filter bandwidth is measured. Thus, the frequency readout and span calibration may be used to measure the filter bandwidth.

8.2 Spectrum Analyzer Tests

8.2.1 Center-Frequency Display Accuracy

This parameter is called "frequency linearity" in the IEEE standard 748-1979.

Apply an input signal from a calibrated signal generator. A spectrum analyzer center-frequency display typically has a frequency accuracy of 1000 PPM to about 100 PPM (parts per million). A signal generator with a calibrated output frequency of 10 PPM, which does not represent either an expensive or unusual signal generator, would provide an adequate calibration signal.

Using the signal generator, provide an input signal and display the signal generated at the center of the spectrum analyzer display. Check the accuracy of the center frequency display and adjust if necessary.

In many spectrum analyzers, measuring the center-frequency display at one frequency does not imply the frequency accuracy at any other part of the analyzer's frequency range. Therefore, the center-frequency display must be checked at various points of the input frequency range.

Some spectrum analyzers allow the display of the start frequency and in some cases, generally spectrum analyzers that have microprocessor control, both start and stop frequencies may be specified. Start and stop frequencies should be calibrated in the same manner as the center frequency readout.

When the spectrum analyzer under test involves harmonic mixing, it is not necessary to check the center-frequency display accuracy for all of the harmonic bands. It is important, however, to take the harmonic number into account when the center-frequency display accuracy is specified as an absolute rather than a percentage of the displayed frequency.

As an example, if the center-frequency display accuracy is specified as 10 kHz, this accuracy must be five times better at the fundamental than when operating at the fifth harmonic mix. Generally, the accuracy is specified as a percentage of the center frequency, which does not involve the harmonic number.

The actual center-frequency accuracy involves the IF filter and the frequency-span circuits. As an example, if the center frequency of the IF filter were in error, the displayed frequency would be in error. In addition, the wider the span, the more difficult it is to determine the actual center. Therefore, a typical center-frequency display accuracy would be 10 PPM of the center frequency plus 1% of the span plus 10% of the resolution bandwidth.

Using the above example, when the span is wide, the center-frequency display accuracy is a function of the span. As an example, for a 1000-MHz span with a 300-kHz resolution bandwidth, the inaccuracy due to the span would be 10 MHz and the IF filter would contribute 30 kHz. As it can be seen, for wide frequency spans, the inaccuracy is dominated by the span. For a very narrow span such as 10 kHz with a 1000-Hz resolution bandwidth, the inaccuracy from the span is 100 Hz plus another 100 Hz from the resolution bandwidth plus 10 PPM of center frequency. At a frequency of 1000 MHz, the 10 PPM inaccuracy is 10 kHz and is clearly the controlling factor of the center-frequency display accuracy in this example.

8.2.2 Frequency Span Readout

The accuracy of this parameter is usually specified as a percentage of the span. As an example, for an analyzer where the frequency span accuracy is 10%, when the selected span is 1 MHz per division the actual span would lie between 0.9 and 1.1 MHz per division.

The accuracy of the frequency span is a function of the span voltage divider, the frequency-linearizing circuits, and the VCO. The span voltage divider is a fixed circuit and is usually constructed from 1% or better resistors. Therefore, it is neither likely to be more than 1% in error nor adjustable if it is more. The frequency linearizer, on the other hand, is often an adjustable circuit and is subject to considerably more error.

Because the frequency linearizer approximates a linear voltage/frequency function using straight-line segments, the frequency span accuracy will be a function of the display frequency. This is because the accuracy of each line segment may be different, and thus the span accuracy depends on the line segment the spectrum analyzer is operating on. Therefore, it is necessary to check the frequency span accuracy on several frequencies of the spectrum analyzer frequency range.

Perhaps the simplest technique to use for checking the frequency span accuracy is a comb generator. This circuit was described in Chapter 3 in conjunction with a phase-locked method of frequency stabilization. Essentially, a very nonlinear device such as a step-recovery diode is driven with an RF source. This produces a very large number of harmonics, which may be displayed on the spectrum analyzer.

Frequency-span accuracy can be measured very easily with a frequency comb. As an example, a 1-MHz comb—that is, harmonics of an accurate 1-MHz frequency source—would provide 10 frequency markers when used in conjunction with a 10-MHz-per-division span. Every tenth spectral line would fall directly on a major division at the frequency span.

At 5 MHz per division, every fifth harmonic would fall on a major division. At 1 MHz per division a harmonic would be present at every division, and at 500 kHz per division. At 100 kHz per division a harmonic would appear at every tenth division. This would place a harmonic at the far left and the far right of the display. This is not a fair assessment of the frequency-span accuracy, and other methods should be employed for these narrow spans.

If would appear that to change the comb frequency to harmonics of 100 kHz would be a reasonable solution. However, the 100-kHz comb, when used with a 1000-MHz analyzer, would involve harmonics up to the 10,000th, which is difficult. If, on the other hand, a 30-MHz analyzer were being checked, the use of a 100-kHz comb would allow a reasonable assessment of frequency-span accuracy to 10 kHz per division.

The major advantage of using the frequency comb is the simplicity of the measurement. Because it is necessary to measure the frequency-span accuracy at several center frequencies, it is a simple matter of selecting several center frequencies throughout the frequency range of the analyzer and quickly observing the span error.

For measuring narrow frequency spans, it is necessary to use a signal generator. The generator used must have an accurate frequency display, as it will be necessary to vary the frequency of the generator to assess the frequency-span accuracy.

An alternate, and superior, method is to either frequency or amplitude-modulate the signal generator. In this method, only the modulating frequency needs to be accurate and not to the extent required of the center frequency.

Amplitude-modulating the signal generator would produce a carrier and two sidebands. If the signal generator introduced any distortion, or if the modulating signal were distorted, a few more than two sidebands would appear. If the signal generator were frequency modulated, a large number of sidebands would be generated depending on the modulation index. Therefore, the frequency-modulated generator would appear more like a frequency comb except the frequency resolution could easily be made quite narrow, perhaps as low as 100 Hz, depending on the modulation capabilities of the generator.

The measurement technique is essentially the same as when using a frequency comb. The center frequency of the analyzer is set, and the signal generator frequency is set to place the modulated sidebands in the analyzer display.

8.2.3 Resolution Bandwidth Accuracy

This is an important parameter to evaluate, particularly to calculate an accurate impulse and noise bandwidth.

Measuring the resolution bandwidth is very simple provided the frequency span of the analyzer is sufficiently accurate to make the measurement. This is a case where one performance test—frequency-span accuracy—should be performed before another—resolution bandwidth.

Apply a stable signal from a signal generator. Display the passband of the filter to be evaluated on the spectrum analyzer display using either the linear scale or 1-dB-per-division scale. Verify the 3-dB down point from the peak of the passband by attenuating the signal generator by 3 dB. It is usually more precise to find the 3-dB point with the signal generator attenuator rather than rely on the spectrum analyzer decibel scale.

Read the frequency difference between the two 3-dB points using the spectrum analyzer display.

This method produces a 3-dB bandwidth with an accuracy no greater than the frequency-span accuracy for that frequency span and center frequency. If the results of the frequency-span calibration did not produce a span accuracy sufficient to make this measurement directly, an alternate method must be employed.

Note the position on the display of the 3-dB down point of either the upper or lower filter edge. Change the frequency of the signal generator until the opposite filter edge appears at the point. The diffference in frequency of the signal generator is the 3-dB bandwidth of the IF filter.

8.2.4 Shape Factor

The shape factor of a filter is the ratio of the 6-dB bandwidth to the 60-dB bandwidth and is a measure of the filter's ability to resolve signals with large amplitude differences.

The 6-dB bandwidth of the filter to be measured is determined using the technique described in the previous step. Measuring the 60-dB bandwidth often involves increasing the input signal level such that it is above the reference level and off the display. To measure the 60-dB bandwidth, set the signal generator attenuator to provide a peak of the display about 30 or 40 dB from the top of the display. Using this level as a reference, increase the signal by 60 dB and observe the bandwidth at the same reference level.

8.2.5 Display Vertical Accuracy

The accuracy of the vertical display depends on two parameters: the display deflection factor and the reference level.

The deflection factor refers to the scale of the display such as 10 dB per division or, in the linear mode, volts per division. Usually, with a spectrum analyzer, the linear mode is microvolts or millivolts per division. The reference level is usually the absolute level that produces a signal at exactly the top of the display.

A signal generator with a calibrated attenuator is used to evaluate both the deflection factor and the reference level.

An input is applied to the reference level and the display should produce a signal with a peak at the top of the screen. It is very important to ensure that the output level of the signal generator is exact. Some signal generators have excellent amplitude calibration and may be used without external calibration. To ensure the greatest accuracy, the signal generator output level should be checked with a bolometer-type or other accurate power meter.

Often, the reference level may be adjusted from the front panel of the spectrum analyzer. If necessary, adjust the reference level to coincide with the very top of the display.

It is also necessary to check the reference level for each IF filter in the analyzer. It is possible that the losses through the IF filters are not matched, producing differences in the apparent reference levels between IF bandwidths. In the example analyzer, adjustments were provided to equalize the display for the varying losses, which is true of other spectrum analyzers.

When checking the reference level match between IF bandwidths, be certain that the scan rate is not excessive and does not cause scan loss.

Assuring the accuracy of the reference level at the top of the display does not ensure precise displays of levels below the reference level. The deflection factor is either a logarithmic display such as 10 dB per division or a linear display where the bottom of the display is zero, the top is the reference level, and the scale is in volts. Some analyzers have a square-law display where the display is volts squared or proportional to power.

The deflection factor of a linear display is given as a percentage of the deflection. It is necessary to view the deflection as starting at the top of the screen and going down. Therefore, the accuracy of a linear display is given as a percentage of deflection from the top down.

For the log display, the deflection factor accuracy is given as the error, in decibels, per dB deflection from the reference level. As an example, for a 10-dB per division display, the accuracy could be given as 1 dB/10 dB. In addition, there is often a limit to the amount of accumulated error for the display. To cite an example, the accuracy of 1 dB/10 dB could claim a maximum error of 2 dB. Thus, if two signals differ by 10 dB the level difference would be a maximum of 1 dB in error. If the signals were 20 dB different, the error would be a maximum of 2 dB. On the other hand, if the signals differed by 30 dB the displayed difference would be in error by no more than 2 dB.

Measuring the displayed error with a signal generator is easy, especially when checking the logarithmic ranges. This is a simple matter of providing a signal at the reference level, reducing the output in steps of 1 or 10 dB, and checking the display.

For the linear display, it is necessary to convert the logarithmic difference in signal levels to linear relationships. As an example, if -10 dBm represents the reference level of the analyzer, with a 10-division display, -30 dBm—that is, 20 dB down from the reference level—represents a 1/10 deflection. A level 3 dB from the reference level is 7.07 divisions of deflection, while 6 dB down represents half deflection. Usually six or seven levels are sufficient to fully check the linear display.

The square-law display is checked in a similar fashion. In this case, the decibels must be converted to power difference. Three dB down from the reference level is half deflection. Six dB down is 25% deflection, while 10 dB down is 1/10th deflection. As in the linear display, six or seven points are sufficient to check the square-law display.

8.2.6 Frequency Response

The measurement of the frequency response of a spectrum analyzer is a matter of measuring the actual reference level over the full input frequency range of the spectrum analyzer.

To measure the frequency response, apply a signal from a signal generator at a frequency near the center of the input frequency range and adjust the output level of the signal generator to place the peak of the response at the top of the display, or the reference level. The position of the input attenuator may have some effect on the frequency response. The frequency response will be a function of the input attenuator, the low-pass filter, and the input mixer. Placing some attenuation at the input of the spectrum analyzer will improve the impedance match between the input from the signal generator and the low-pass filter. In the general use of a spectrum analyzer, it is prudent to make all measurements with the maximum possible amount of input attenuation consistent with a reasonable measurement. This is to protect the input mixer from damage should excess power be applied to the analyzer. All input attenuation may be removed for only the most sensitive measurements. Therefore, when measuring the frequency response of the analyzer, unless it is specified otherwise, insert 10 dB of input attenuation.

Raise and lower the frequency of the signal generator from center frequency, and note the deviation from the initial reference level. Raise or lower the signal generator output power to return the peak of the display to the top of the display.

The number of points required to make this measurement is on the order of 10. Typically, the variation of reference level is gradual and there are no deep holes in the response that may be overlooked using only 10 measurement points.

8.2.7 Display Flatness

The measurement of display flatness is very similar to frequency response except the measurement involved covers only the frequency range of the display. In most modern spectrum analyzers, the maximum span is also the entire frequency range of the analyzer. Therefore, the frequency response and display flatness are the same. In older spectrum analyzers, especially the so-called swept IF analyzer, the display flatness and frequency response may be quite different.

The measurement technique for display flatness is exactly that for frequency response, except the center frequency tuning is not changed for the measurement.

8.2.8 Sensitivity

The sensitivity of the spectrum analyzer is the instrument's ability to display low-level signals. Sensitivity is essentially the noise level of the analyzer. Measuring the sensitivity of the analyzer is an important step that must be performed before the dynamic range of the instrument is measured.

Apply a signal generator to the spectrum analyzer. Display the signal generator response at the center of the display using a moderate-resolution bandwidth. Reduce the signal generator level until the displayed signal is 3 dB greater than the noise level.

The use of the video filter will be a help in this measurement. The video filter will average the noise level and transform a "fuzzy" picture to a smooth trace.

Reduce the resolution bandwidth and the span until the narrowest resolution bandwidth is being used. Reduce the signal output further until the displayed signal, once again, is 3 dB above the noise. This level is the analyzer's sensitivity.

8.2.9 Dynamic Range

Two types of dynamic range involved in the specifications of the spectrum analyzer were discussed in Chapter 2. The first type is harmonic dynamic range and refers to the generation of a spectrum response at a harmonic of the input signal, which renders it difficult or impossible to observe the real harmonic distortion.

The choice of signal generator for providing an input signal is very critical for measuring harmonic dynamic range. The signal generator must have very low harmonic distortion. Typically, the level of harmonic distortion in a spectrum analyzer will be 60 to 80 dB down from the fundamental. Many signal generators are not capable of providing an output with this level of distortion, and a low-pass filter will be required. The dilemma with this measurement is that the instrument that would be used to determine the level of harmonic distortion from the signal generator is the very instrument being measured. The technique employed is to measure the harmonic distortion of the signal generator using the spectrum analyzer. This level may be 40 to 80 dB down from the fundamental and may be partially generated in the spectrum analyzer. What is important is that the true harmonic level of the signal generator is less than that displayed. A low-pass filter is added which, depending on the order of the filter, will reduce the harmonic level from the signal generator is less than that displayed. A low-pass filter is added which, depending on the order of the filter, will reduce the harmonic level from the signal generator by an additional 40 to 60 dB. This will reduce the level of the harmonics from the signal generator to below the level of internally generated harmonics.

Apply the signal generator followed by the low-pass filter and observe the spectrum analyzer display at the harmonic frequencies. Increase the level of the input signal until any harmonic appears about 3 dB above the noise level. It may be difficult to determine an exact 3 dB above the noise level. However, the generation of harmonics is a second-order or greater effect. This means for each 1-dB increase of input level the harmonics increase by 2 dB or more. Therefore, only a slight increase in input level will cause a significant increase in the displayed peak.

The signal level required to produce a harmonic above the noise level may require an input well above the reference level and thus will cause the peak of the fundamental signal to be above the display. This is permissible and is the sign of a good spectrum analyzer, where a signal within the confines of the display will produce no visible harmonics.

8.2.10 Intermodulation Dynamic Range

Intermodulation is the generation of spurious signals from the interaction of two or more input signals and was explained in Chapter 3. Many different types of intermodulation are described by their mathematical formulas. The most troublesome is called third order and has a frequency of

$$f_3 = f_1 \pm 2f_2 \tag{8-1}$$

where f_3 is the frequency of the third-order intermodulation, f_1 is the frequency of one of the two input signals, and f_2 is the frequency of the other of the two input signals. Since the equation has both plus and minus signs, there are two intermodulation products. One intermodulation product appears above the two generating frequencies while the other appears below the two generating frequencies.

To test a spectrum analyzer for third-order intermodulation, two signal generators are used to supply input signals to the spectrum analyzer. The level of the two generators are set to be equal, and the combined levels are increased in level until the intermodulation product is visible just above the noise. It is very important to ensure that the two generators do not create an intermodulation product of their own. If insufficient isolation is provided between the two signal generators, intermodulation may be generated within the signal generators. The method of combination shown in Fig. 8-1 provides sufficient isolation for most signal generators. Two amplifiers are used to provide a high signal level from the generator. Then the output of the amplifier is reduced in level by using an attenuator. This allows for a high degree of isolation between the two signal sources.

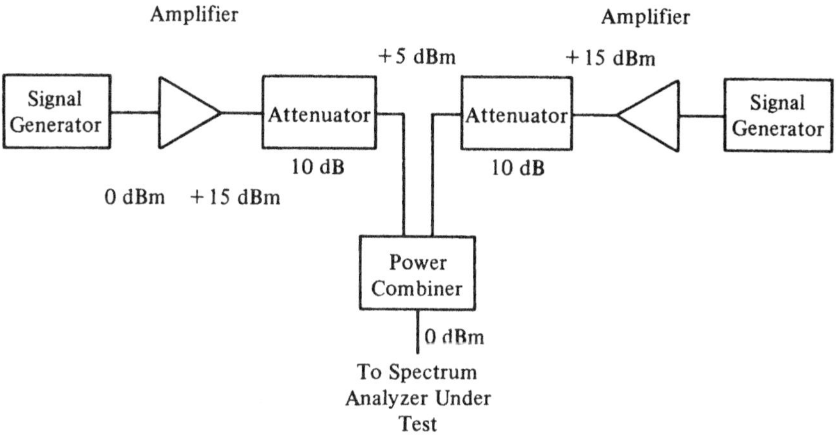

Figure 8-1
Method of combining two signal generators without generating intermodulation within the signal generators.

8.2.11 No-Signal, Internally Generated Spurious Responses

The use of the term "no-signal" is to separate this test from the intermodulation and harmonic tests where an input signal is required to produce a spurious response. This is perhaps the easiest spectrum analyzer test to perform. No input signal is required. To reduce the amount of potential spurious inputs from radiated signals the spectrum analyzer input should either be terminated or the maximum amount of input attenuation should be applied.

With no signal applied, simply observe the display for signals other than the "zero frequency" response. It will be necessary to minimize the noise level by using the narrowest IF filter available. Because of this, it will be necessary to use a relatively narrow frequency span and to manually tune the spectrum analyzer slowly through its entire frequency range, while observing any spurious responses.

8.2.12 Residual Frequency Modulation

The most effective method of measuring the residual frequency modulation of the spectrum analyzer is to use the analyzer's IF filter as a frequency discriminator. To achieve this, it is necessary to characterize the slope of the IF filters.

Which IF filter to use for measuring the residual frequency modulation depends on the expected amount of residual frequency modulation. There may be more than one specification for residual frequency modulation. One major reason for this is the application of phase lock to enhance the noise performance of the analyzer. When the phase-locked circuits are enabled, the residual frequency modulation will be reduced. It may be necessary to measure the residual frequency modulation with the phase-lock circuits activated and off.

An input signal is applied to the spectrum analyzer. It is important that the phase noise and residual frequency modulation of the input signal be significantly better than the expected residual modulation of the spectrum analyzer. If the input signal has its own residual frequency modulation, the measurement will be the sum of the spectrum analyzer and the signal source.

Using the linear mode of the spectrum analyzer, reduce the frequency span so that the upper or lower slope of the IF filter appears as an angled line on the display. Adjust the center frequency so that the line covers as much of the display and is as straight as possible.

Calculate the constant

$$k = \Delta f / \Delta d \tag{8-2}$$

where k is the filter slope constant and $\Delta f / \Delta d$ is the slope of the line in terms of hertz per division of deflection. This constant is measured at the center of the display.

Using the same input signal, reduce the span to zero and adjust the center frequency so that the horizontal line of the display is at the center of the screen. The peak-to-peak deviation of the horizontal line multiplied by the constant k calculated by Eq. (8-2) gives the peak-to-peak incidental frequency modulation.

8.2.13 IF Feedthrough

To measure the amount of feedthrough, the first IF must be known. Apply a signal from the signal generator at the first IF. It would be advantageous to use the widest IF filter for this measurement, as any mismatch between the signal generator frequency and the actual IF would cause an error of measurement. The wider IF would minimize this error. Increase the signal generator until the response of the IF is seen. This would not be a spectrum peak but a raising of the baseline, as the first IF is not swept at this point. Adjust the signal generator to maximize the rise in baseline.

The difference in the level of the baseline and the signal generator level is the IF rejection.

In many spectrum analyzers the IF rejection is so great that an input signal level at the IF well above the reference level of the analyzer would be required to obtain a visible shift of the baseline. It is possible that the signal generator in use may not have sufficient output level to provide a visible baseline shift. Use caution when increasing the signal generator level to a point where the IF feedthrough would be visible, as this level may be sufficient to cause damage to the analyzer's input circuitry.

8.2.14 Other Tests

There are a number of other tests that may be performed on a spectrum analyzer; it would not be possible to outline all of the possible tests. Practically any parameter specified by the manufacturer may be tested. If there is need for a complete performance check, the manufacturer's service manual will usually provide a test procedure.

Review Questions for Chapter 8

1. Why must the center-frequency accuracy be measured at several points within the spectrum analyzer frequency range?
2. What elements of the spectrum analyzer affect the center-frequency accuracy?
3. What is a frequency comb? How may this signal aid the evaluation of a spectrum analyzer?
4. What are the limitations of a comb generator?
5. Why is it important to measure the resolution bandwidth of a spectrum analyzer accurately?
6. What is shape factor?
7. How is the vertical-display accuracy of a logarithmic display specified?
8. What is the difference between display flatness and frequency response?
9. What are the three types of dynamic range applied to a spectrum analyzer?
10. What are the requirements of the signal generator used to measure the dynamic range of a spectrum analyzer?

9 The Network Analyzer

9.1 Introduction

It was made abundantly clear throughout the discussion of the spectrum analyzer that the instrument was not capable of resolving any phase relationships of the signals displayed. Furthermore, it was made clear in Chapter 6 that complete network analysis requires the knowledge of the phase relationship between the stimulus and the output of two-port networks. The tracking generator, although a very important tool for some network analysis, is deficient in this phase information. The true network analyzer described in this chapter is capable of providing a display of amplitude and phase of a signal relative to a reference signal. This instrument is often referred to as a "vector" network analyzer as compared to a "scalar" network analyzer, which would be an instrument such as a spectrum analyzer in conjunction with a tracking generator.

The vector network analyzer is also distinct from the spectrum analyzer in that the display, being a vector quantity, is presented as a vector display. This can take the form of a polar display or a specialized polar display such as a Smith chart. There are scalar forms of vector displays such as a Bode plot, which is a simultaneous display of amplitude and phase, both presented as scalar quantities.

From the previous discussion of network analysis in Chapter 6, it was shown that a two-port network could be represented as a matrix of four quantities that described the forward and reverse transfer, and the input and output impedance or admittance functions. All four of these parameters are vector quantities.

The heart of the network analyzer is a sensitive measuring system that is capable of measuring and displaying an input signal as a vector quantity. A second input is provided to establish a phase reference for the vector measurements. In addition, some network analyzers are capable of comparing, as a ratio, the amplitude of the unknown input to the amplitude of the reference. This allows an accurate measurement of the forward and reverse transfer functions of a device.

Many newer network analyzers have built-in signal sources for stimulating the device under test, whereas most earlier network analyzers required a sweep generator or signal generator to provide the stimulus. One of the characteristics that distinguishes a network analyzer from other types of vector impedance measuring instruments, such as bridges and vector voltmeters, is that impedance is measured and displayed over a broad range of frequencies. Although the network analyzer is certainly capable of measuring a network at a single frequency, the real advantage of the instrument is the ability to observe the network characteristics over a band of frequencies.

The addition of an internal signal source is not only a convenience but also offers more flexibility in the design of the network analyzer.

Figure 9-1 shows a block diagram of a network analyzer. A signal source is shown in this example, covering the frequency range from 10 to 400 MHz. The detector portion of the analyzer has two input ports, called the unknown and the reference. The network analyzer can handle these two ports in several ways. First, the two levels may be displayed simultaneously. Using the reference signal as a phase reference, the magnitude and angle of the unknown port input may be displayed as two scalar quantities, or the phase and magnitude can be combined into a vector display. A relative value in the form of a ratio of the magnitude of A to B along with the phase difference may be displayed as a vector quantity.

To measure impedance and admittance, external directional couplers or impedance/admittance bridges are necessary. Usually, the signal source is supplied at one port, which requires an external power splitter. This is done with a simple power divider, shown in Fig. 9-2. At first look, it may appear that this method of power splitting is very inefficient and crude. In network analysis it is very important to insure that the power is split without any significant phase shift. Many more elegant power dividers have inherent phase shifts that would be a function of frequency and would not be suitable for the network analyzer.

Figure 9-3 shows a block diagram of the set-up for measuring the forward transfer function of a device. In this set-up, the power divider provides a driving source for the device under test and provides the input for the reference input of the network analyzer. The other input channel, the unknown, is connected to the output of the device under test. The forward transfer function of the device under test is a vector quantity, where the magnitude is the ratio of the input to the output signal levels and the angle is the phase difference between the input and output. The reverse transfer function may be measured by simply reversing the device in the test setup.

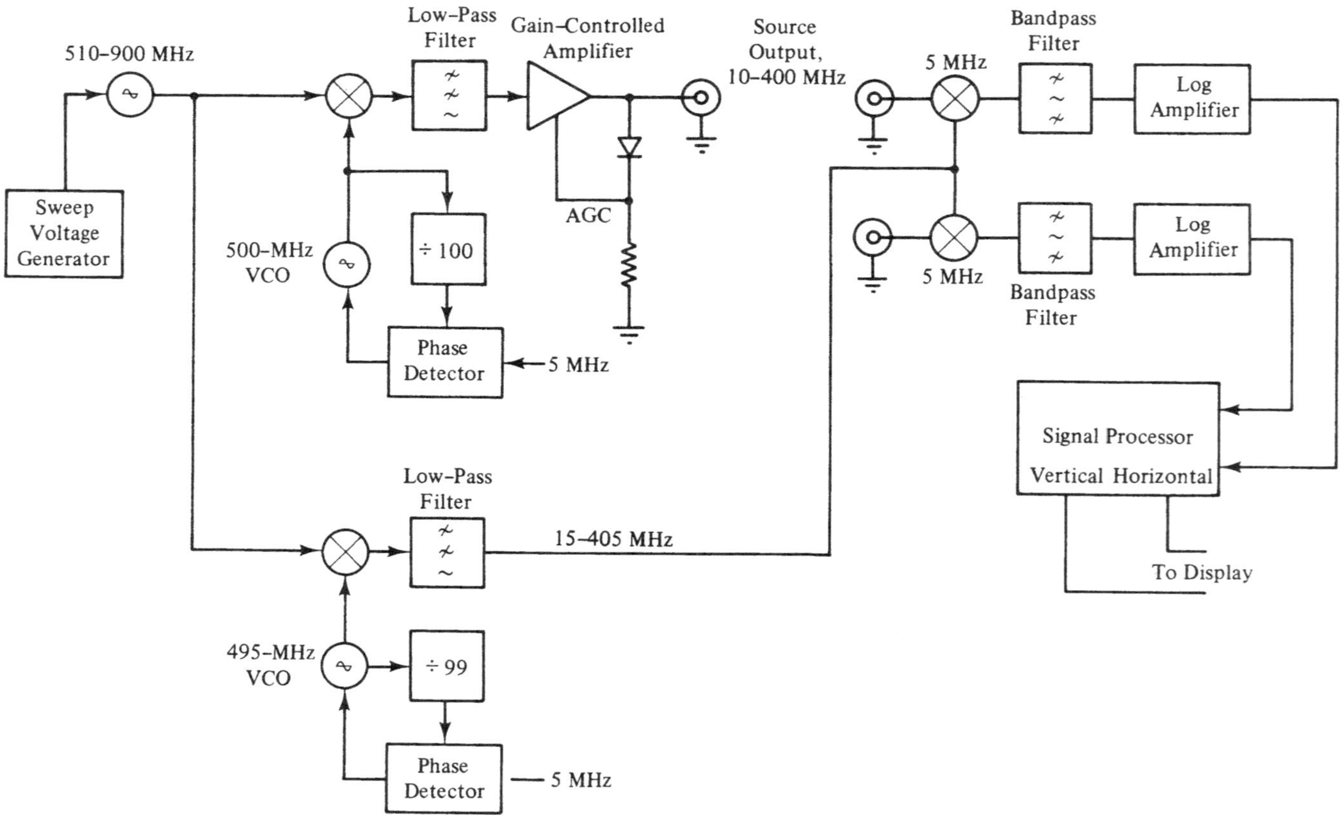

Figure 9-1
Block diagram of a simple network analyzer with an integral signal source.

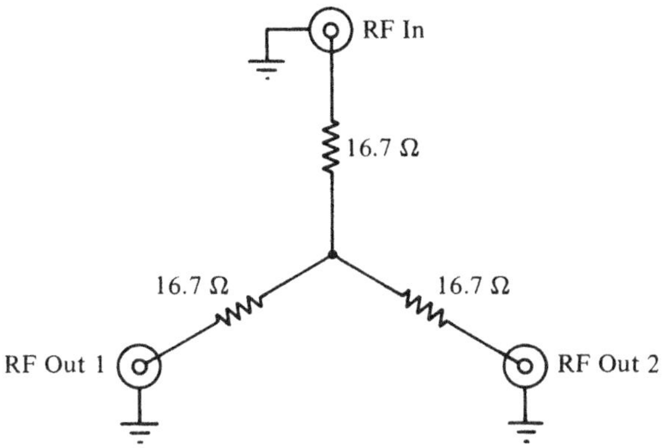

Figure 9-2
A power splitter suitable for use with a network analyzer.

The block diagram shows a simple connection from the power splitter to the reference input of the analyzer. This is all that is involved for many measurements. When a precision measurement is required, or when measurements take place at a high frequency, the simple connection must be made with extreme care.

The addition of a coaxial cable introduces a phase shift between the signal source and the reference input of the analyzer. On the other hand, the interconnecting cables used to connect the device under test will also introduce a phase

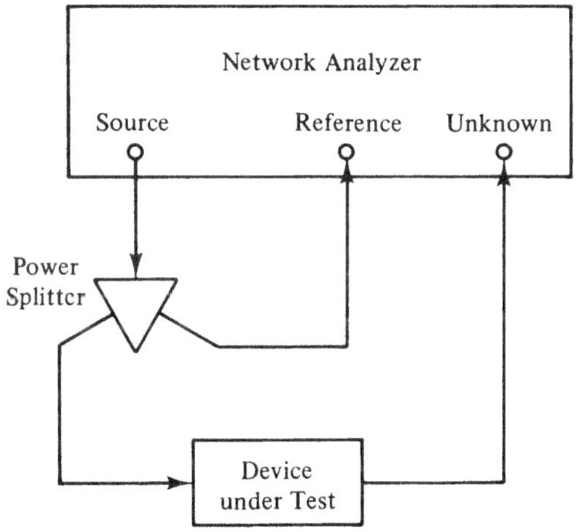

Figure 9-3
The interconnection for the measurement of a vector transfer function of a device using the network analyzer.

shift to the unknown measurement signal path. The ideal situation in many cases is to create equal phase delays for both the reference and unknown signal paths.

As an example, assume the network analyzer is to be used to characterize an amplifier. The amplifier is connected to the network analyzer with two cables, one for the input and a second for the output, each being 50 cm in length. Therefore, the cable connecting the reference input to the signal source should be 1 m. The phase shift must be checked for accurate measurement by removing the device under test, connecting the input and output connectors together, and checking the display for phase error. Often the input and output connectors of the unit under test will not mate, and some form of adapter must be used. In this case, there will be some additional phase shift due to the electrical length of the adapter. Generally, this will be quite small and may be ignored. On the other hand, for higher frequencies or precision measurements, this adapter may introduce an unacceptable error.

The amount of phase shift introduced by cables and adapters is described by the electrical length of the item in question. The electrical length of a device depends on the physical length, the frequency of operation, and the velocity of electrical energy in the device relative to the velocity of electromagnetic energy in space. The electrical length of a coaxial cable, in degrees, is

$$l = \frac{f}{3 \times 10^8 \text{ m/s}} \times \frac{360^\circ}{\text{(velocity factor)}} \times L \qquad (9\text{-}1)$$

where l is the electrical length in degrees, L is the physical length of the cable in meters, f is the frequency of the measurement, and the velocity factor is the ratio of the velocity of energy transfer in the cable divided by the velocity of light.

As an example, to calculate the electrical length of 1 m of teflon dielectric cable with a dielectric constant of 2.5 and a velocity factor of 0.63, Eq. (9-1) is evaluated.

$$1 = \frac{360^\circ \times 1}{3 \times 10^8 \text{ m/s} \times (0.63)} (f) = 1.9 \times 10^{-6} \text{ degrees/Hz}(f)$$

As Eq. (9-1) shows, the phase shift introduced by a length of coaxial cable is dependent on the frequency of measurement. Therefore, there will be a variable error of phase if the lengths of cables are not matched in a measurement setup. Because of this, various devices such as "line stretchers" and phase adjusters may be used to equalize the line lengths.

The phase measurement accuracy is a function of the length of coaxial cables, the existence of adapters, and so on. The situation becomes extremely complex when devices are being measured that have no convenient connectors but some sort of text fixture. A good example of a fixture would be for the measurement of the S parameters of a transistor. This requires the use of concept called the reference plane.

To gain an understanding of the reference plane, consider the previous example of the measurement setup with the 1-m cable connecting the signal generator to the reference input and the two 50-cm cables that interconnect the amplifier to the system.

The network analyzer would measure zero degrees if the amplifier were removed and the cables connected together. If one of the cables were removed and the unknown port were connected to the signal source with the 50-cm cable, the network analyzer would read $+42.5°$. This is because the measured signal would be 42.5° earlier than the reference. What if the remaining 50-cm cable were replaced with a 1-m cable? In that case, the analyzer would read zero degrees with the reference input cable connected to the signal source. If the interconnecting cable to the reference input were less than one meter, the zero-degree reference plane would be inside the signal source. Now, there is a serious problem and this situation should be avoided.

For this reason many network analyzers have "line stretchers" or other methods of synthesizing an increased line length. This "line stretching" may be done either at the input frequency or at the IF of the network analyzer.

The situation of the reference plane being at the signal source is an advantage, as the device under test may be connected directly to the signal source without an interconnecting cable, and there is some advantage to this.

The concept of the reference plane becomes really significant when more than just cables are involved. A test fixture is an example of where the electrical length involves more than just cables. Consider the example of a test fixture for measuring the characteristics of transistors. The reference plane would be adjusted using the line stretcher to correspond to the plane of the transistor test socket.

Most network analyzers have an attenuator to reduce the level of the signal generator output. If the level were changed, theoretically the network analyzer display would not change, since the display is the ratio of the input of the device under test to the output. However, to maximize the dynamic range of the measurement, the largest signal possbile should be used to increase the signal-to-noise level of the display. On the other hand, excessive signal level can cause overload in active devices such as amplifiers.

Figure 9-4 shows the setup for measuring the input impedance of the device under test. Since the device output is now removed from the analyzer, as that channel is required for the output of the impedance bridge, it will be necessary to terminate the output of the device under test with a terminating resistor equal to the output impedance of the device.

The impedance bridge has an internal loss that depends on the type of bridge used. A resistive bridge was described in Chapter 6, wherein the internal

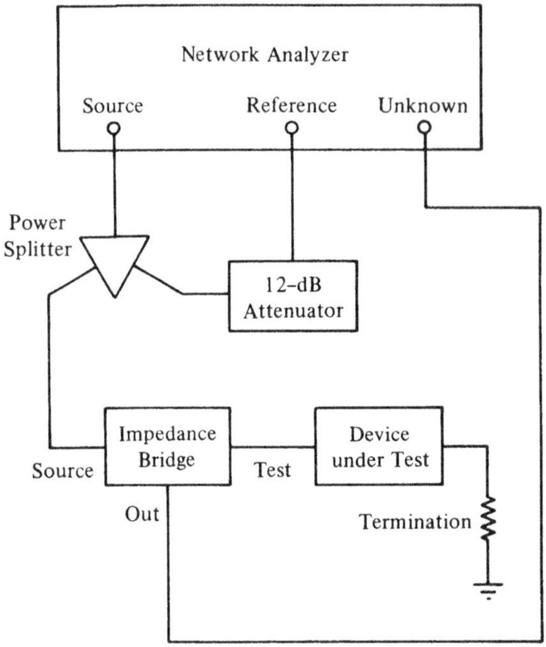

Figure 9-4
The interconnection for the measurement of input impedance of a device using the impedance bridge.

loss was about 12 dB. This 12-dB loss means that when the test port of the impedance bridge is terminated with either an open or a short, representing a 0-dB return loss, the output of the bridge is 12 dB below the signal generator input port. For the network analyzer to display return loss directly, a 12-dB attenuator may be installed between the power splitter and the reference channel of the network analyzer.

9.2 Group Delay Measurements

The concept of group delay is one that is not well understood by many engineers.

To understand group delay, it is important to consider a signal as a set of components, each at a specific frequency. As an example, a normal voice signal such as that used on a telephone circuit would have a very complex set of components at various frequencies. However, all the components are contained within a band of frequencies from 300 to 3000 Hz.

If the telephone signal were transmitted through a device, typically a filter, there would be a time delay from input to output. Ideally, the signal components would be delayed, as a group, by a fixed amount, but in many systems not all frequency components are delayed by the same amount. Perhaps the higher frequencies would be delayed by more than the lower frequencies or vice versa. Due to the difference in time delay, the signal passing through the system will become distorted. The phenomenon is called group delay distortion.

Imagine that each frequency component of the composite signal is separated by frequency, passed through the device, and reassembled at the output. The result would be a distorted signal if the emerging frequency components did not leave the filter with the same relative time relationships they had when entering.

Voice signals can encounter considerable group delay distortion and still be useful, which is largely because the ear is not a phase-sensitive device. However, digital data, for one, is very susceptible to group delay distortion.

It is very important to measure group delay for filters used in digital systems, and the network analyzer is a suitable instrument for the task.

One method of measuring group delay is to apply pulsed carriers to the input of the device under test and measure the time delay from input to output. This would be the time domain method. The spectrum analyzer and network analyzer are frequency domain instruments and group delay is, essentially, a time domain parameter.

To find the relationship between the time domain and the frequency domain for measuring group delay, consider the delay of a device at one frequency. Consider the device as a piece of cable that introduces a simple time delay.

To measure the time delay at any one frequency, consider the device under test as a constant time delay, such as the length of transmission line. The relationship between the time delay and the phase angle between input and output was given by Eq. (9-1). The difficulty of this equation is that the network analyzer cannot resolve the difference between an angle and the same angle plus $2n\pi$ radians. As far as the network analyzer is concerned, Eq. (9-1) must be rewritten as

$$1 = \frac{\omega/2\pi}{3 \times 10^8} \times \frac{2\pi}{\text{(velocity factor)}} \times L + 2\pi n$$

$$= \frac{\omega}{3 \times 10^8 \text{(velocity factor)}} \times L \times 2\pi n = \theta \qquad (9\text{-}2)$$

where n is an unknown integer and θ is the electrical length in radians.

Equation (9-2) may be modified by taking the derivative of both sides of the equation and solving for Δt.

$$d\theta = \frac{d\omega}{3 \times 10^8(\text{velocity factor})} \times L$$

$$\frac{d\theta}{d\omega} = \frac{L}{3 \times 10^8(\text{velocity factor})} = \Delta t \qquad (9\text{-}3)$$

where Δt is the time delay of the cable. As it can be seen, the unknown, n, is no longer in the equation. Equation (9-3) is the connection between the time domain and frequency domain for the measurement of group delay.

To measure the group delay, the frequency of the signal source is modulated, and the resulting change in phase angle is measured. The frequency modulation may be a step change or it may be simple sine modulation, where the peak of the modulation envelope is compared to the peak of the variable phase angle.

As an example, consider a video filter operating at a carrier frequency of 41.25 MHz and having a passband from 40 to 46 MHz. At the center of the passband, 43.0 MHz, the phase shift is 2° peak for a frequency modulation of 100 kHz peak. Calculate the group delay at that frequency.

$$\Delta t = \frac{d\theta}{df} = \frac{(2/360) \times 2\pi}{100 \times 10^3 \times 2\pi} = 55 \text{ ns}$$

It must be remembered that it is not group delay that is the nemesis of electrical communications, but group delay distortion. A filter that has a constant delay throughout the passband has no group delay distortion. On the other hand, a filter with a varying group delay throughout the passband will suffer from excessive distortion. In the stop band and the skirts of a filter, the group delay is quite variable and thus group delay distortion is great. Since this is not the working part of a filter, it is not important.

9.3 Network Analyzer Circuits

A network analyzer contains two basic elements, the signal generator and the receiver or measuring circuits. The local oscillator for the receiver section requires a tracking local oscillator with an offset frequency that is equal to the receiver IF. Usually, the local oscillator frequency is above the input frequency of the receiver, to reduce the amount of spurious responses of the receiver, especially at lower frequencies.

Unlike the spectrum analyzer, the receiver section of the network analyzer does not filter the image response of the frequency conversion. In the spectrum analyzer, the first IF was chosen to be very high so that the image frequency range was above the highest input frequency and a low-pass filter might have been used to remove the image band.

The first IF, and usually the only IF, of the network analyzer is a relatively low frequency, typically below the lowest input frequency, and no input tracking filter is used. A low-pass filter is provided before the input to prevent harmonics of the input from affecting the measurement. Therefore, the receiver is sensitive to the desired input as well as to the image. Since the signal generator provides only the desired frequency and there is no energy at the image frequency, there will be no spurious responses. This assumption is based on a device under test that does not generate its own signals. If signals are generated within the device under test, when the image passes through the frequency of those internally generated signals, the display will become distorted as the image responds to the spurious signal.

In the example network analyzer shown in Fig. 9-1, a 510–900-MHz voltage-controlled oscillator is heterodyned with a 500-MHz oscillator. The difference frequency is extracted by low-pass filtering the output of the mixer to produce an output from 10 to 400 MHz. This output is amplified and amplitude-stabilized with an AGC system to provide the sweeping signal source for the network analyzer.

A second oscillator at 495 MHz is heterodyned with the same voltage-controlled oscillator to produce an output from 15 to 405 MHz, which is exactly 5 MHz above the sweep frequency generator. This signal source is used as the local oscillator for the receiver.

It is important that the local oscillator signal be a constant and accurate 5 MHz above the signal generator frequency. This is necessitated by the narrow-bandwidth IF required by the receiver for large dynamic range measurements. To ensure an accurate 5-MHz difference frequency, the 500-MHz oscillator is divided by 100 and phase locked to a 5-MHz crystal oscillator. The 495-MHz oscillator is divided by 99 and locked to the same crystal oscillator. With a reference frequency as high as 5 MHz, the phase noise of the 500 and 495 MHz free-running oscillators may be reduced considerably, as well as ensuring an accurate 5-MHz difference frequency.

It is important to note that the 5-MHz crystal oscillator is exactly the frequency of the IF. There is no escaping this frequency using a phase-locked technique, as each oscillator must be an integer multiple of the crystal, and the difference frequency must be the IF. Therefore, if any energy from the oscillator should find its way to the IF, interference would result. The techniques of preventing this interference are exactly those used in the tracking generator; they are described in Chapter 6.

The local oscillator signal is routed to two mixers, one for the reference input and the second for the unknown input. The output of the mixer feeds an IF filter with a center frequency of 5.000 MHz. The noise floor of the receiver is dependent on the IF bandwidth, as in any receiver. Because the phase noise of the 500 and 495 MHz oscillators has been reduced and because the phase noise of the sweeping voltage-controlled oscillator appears the same on both the signal generator output and the receiver local oscillator, the receiver bandwidth may be quite narrow. Chapter 6 described how the effects of phase noise were mitigated when using a common voltage-controlled oscillator for both the signal source and the receiver.

Following the IF filters is an eight-stage log IF amplifier. This is very much like a spectrum analyzer with the exception that a greater dynamic range will be encountered, as the receiver is not susceptible to intermodulation distortion. Therefore, a larger log amplifier is found in the network analyzer.

Generally, a limiting type of log IF amplifier is used. This type of log amplifier is preferred, as the limited output from the amplifier is used for the phase detector.

The phase detector is one of the "zero degree" types where the nominal center of the dynamic range is at zero degrees. These phase detectors contain flip-flops and are best constructed from logic elements. Figure 9-5 shows a representative phase detector with a zero-degree operating point constructed from flip-flops.

Before proceeding further in the discussion of the network analyzer, the mathematical basis of the instrument will be presented.

Referring to the block diagram of Fig. 9-6, assume two devices are connected between the power divider and the network analyzer. Usually "device 2" in the reference path is a simple coaxial cable. However, for accurate measurements and for a full understanding of the network analyzer, the phase shift of this piece of cable must be considered.

The output of the two devices are reduced in amplitude by a value of k_1 and k_2 and shifted in phase by θ_1 and θ_2 for device 1 and 2, respectively.

The driving signal from the power divider is

$$B \cos \omega_c t \tag{9-4}$$

The output of device 1 is

$$Bk_1 \cos \omega_c t + \theta_1 \tag{9-5}$$

The output of device 2 is

$$Bk_2 \cos \omega_c t + \theta_2 \tag{9-6}$$

These two inputs are mixed with the local oscillator, which is above the input frequency by an amount equal to the IF. The resulting output is

$$\frac{Bk_1}{2} \cos\left[(2\omega_c + \omega_{IF})t + \theta_1\right] + \frac{Bk_1}{2} \cos(\omega_{IF} t + \theta_1) \tag{9-7}$$

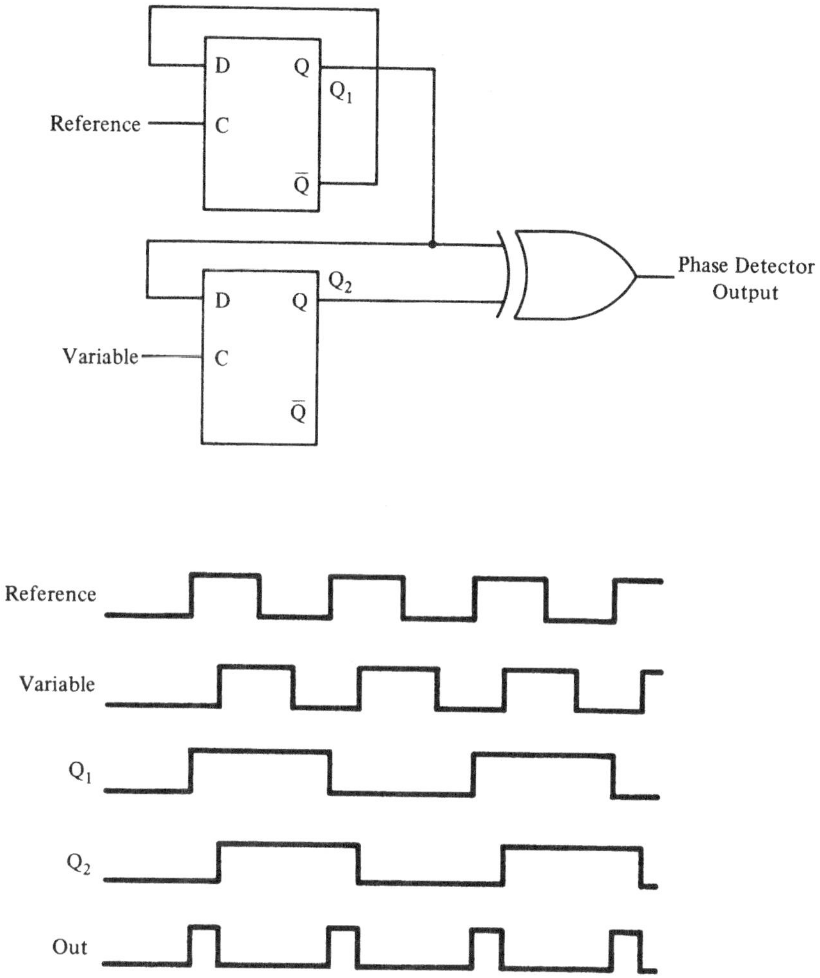

Figure 9-5
The logic diagram and waveforms for a "zero-degree" phase detector suitable for the measurement of phase in a network analyzer.

for the unknown channel and

$$\frac{Bk_2}{2}\cos\left[(2\omega_c + \omega_{IF})t + \theta_2\right] + \frac{Bk_2}{2}\cos(\omega_{IF}t + \theta_2) \qquad (9\text{-}8)$$

for the reference channel.

The IF filter removes all signals outside the IF bandwidth. After the IF filter, a logarithmic amplifier provides a log output that is proportional to the log

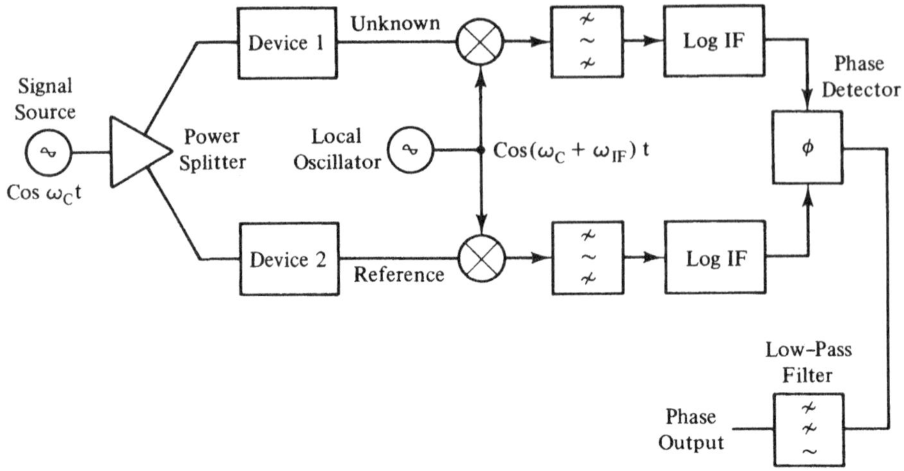

Figure 9-6
The block diagram for the mathematical analysis of a network analyzer.

of the input amplitude. In addition, the log amplifier provides a limited output. For ease of calculation, the amplitude of the limited output will be set to be $\sqrt{2}$. Therefore, after filtering and limiting, (9-7) becomes

$$\cos(\omega_{IF}t + \theta_1 + \sigma) \quad (9\text{-}9)$$

and (9-8) becomes

$$\cos(\omega_{IF}t + \theta_2 + \sigma) \quad (9\text{-}10)$$

where σ is a phase shift due to the IF filter.

If is important to note that the two IF filters are identical in that the phase shift and insertion loss are the same. In addition, the conversion losses of the mixers are also matched. In general, the insertion losses or gains and phase shifts of every component of the IF signal flow must be identical to the other channel. If identical components are not capable of achieving this match, it will be necessary to trim these parameters until they are matched.

The magnitude of these two IF signals is proportional to the amplitude of the input levels. Thus, the detected log video will represent the amplitude of the inputs. To determine a ratio, one log video voltage is simply subtracted from the other.

The phase angle must be obtained from these signals. To find this phase angle, the limited output of the log amplifiers are multiplied together to obtain the following result,

$$\sqrt{2}\cos(\omega_{IF}t + \theta_1 + \sigma)\sqrt{2}\cos(\omega_{IF}t + \theta_2 + \sigma) = \cos(2\omega_{IF}t + \theta_1 + \theta_2 + 2\sigma) + \cos(\theta_1 - \theta_2) \quad (9\text{-}11)$$

When this is fed through a low-pass filter to remove harmonics of the IF, the following results:

$$\cos(\theta_1 - \theta_2) \tag{9-12}$$

In reality, the outputs of the log amplifiers are less than a sine wave and more on the order of a square wave, and the multiplication can be done more effectively using a digital phase detector. The result is the same; after low-pass filter the resulting voltage is proportional to the phase difference between the reference and unknown.

9.4 Network/Spectrum Analyzers

A trend in recent years has been to combine the functions of a spectrum analyzer with that of a network analyzer. In Chapter 6, it was shown how a tracking generator with a spectrum analyzer could serve as a scalar network analyzer. In this chapter some of the similarities of the spectrum analyzer and the vector network analyzer were outlined. With the addition of a few circuits, the network analyzer may be configured into a spectrum analyzer.

Figure 9-7 shows the example network analyzer of Fig. 9-1 reconfigured as a 0–400-MHz spectrum analyzer. The network analyzer with its single conversion and low IF was susceptible to spurious responses for input signals other than its own source. Therefore, a first IF at a frequency of 510 MHz was added. The VCO, which covered a range from 510 to 900 MHz in the network analyzer, is extended to 910 MHz to provide a 0–400-MHz input frequency. The offset oscillator, which was originally heterodyned with the VCO to provide the receiver local oscillator in the network analyzer, is retuned from 495 MHz to 455 MHz by changing the programmable divider from 99 to 91. In addition, the mixer that provided the local oscillator for the receiver in the network analyzer becomes the second mixer for the spectrum analyzer. The second local oscillator is heterodyned with the first IF at 510 MHz and provides a second IF at 55 MHz.

The third frequency conversion to the 5-MHz IF is made with a simple crystal oscillator at 60 MHz.

The conversion of the network analyzer to a spectrum analyzer requires the addition of a first IF filter at 510 MHz, a second IF filter at 55 MHz, a third mixer, and a third local oscillator. These items do not represent a great expense.

Several expensive items are retained from the network analyzer, which justifies the necessary complication to allow the analyzer to serve both functions. All of the sweep voltage circuits, the VCO, the frequency readout, input RF connectors, attenuators, the CRT display, power supplies, etc., are retained. This represents a very large part of the cost of the spectrum analyzer.

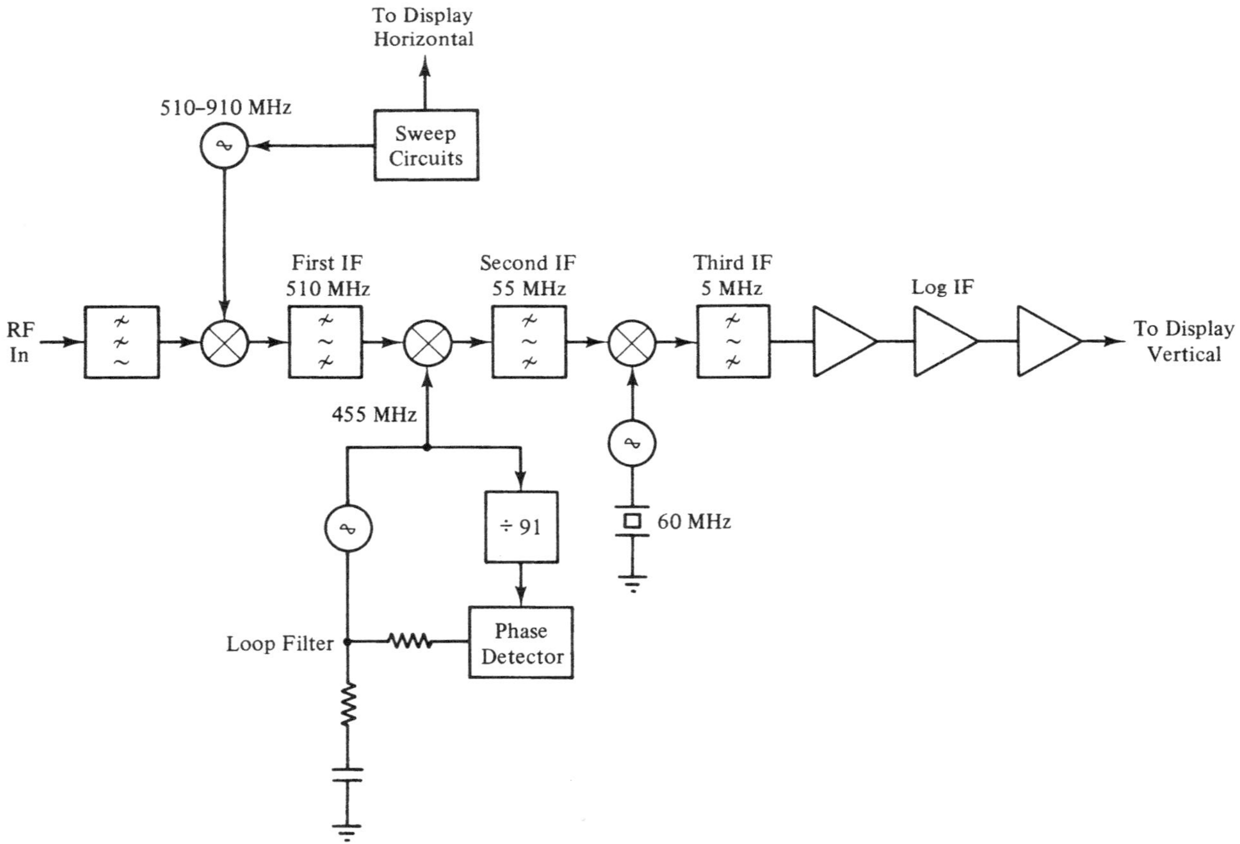

Figure 9-7
A block diagram of a network analyzer described in this chapter.

9.5 The Scalar Network Analyzer

The virtues of the vector network analyzer have been carefully extolled and the circuits thoroughly investigated. There are, however, advantages to the scalar network analyzer. The tracking generator/spectrum analyzer combination described in Chapter 6 was an inexpensive method of obtaining network analysis when a spectrum analyzer was available.

Other methods of network analysis are less costly than the vector analyzer. This is particularly true when the need for network analysis extends well into the millimeter wavelength range.

A number of important measurements may be made with the scalar network analyzer that are vital to the design of electronic circuits. Some of these parameters are listed here.

1. *Gain* This refers to the gain or loss of a circuit—not to be confused with transfer function, which is a vector quantity.

2. *Standing-wave ratio or VSWR* This is an indication of the impedance of the device under test.

3. *Reverse isolation* This parameter is essentially the same as gain except that the device under test is reversed.

These three parameters, with the measurement of standing-wave ratio applied to both the input and output ports of the device under test, making a fourth parameter, constitute the scalar equivalent of the four S parameters S_{11}, S_{12}, S_{21}, and S_{22}.

A very inexpensive method of scalar network analysis is shown in Fig. 9-8. Rather than a superheterodyne type of receiver, a diode detector is used as the receiver for this type of network analyzer.

There are advantages other than just cost to this type of network analyzer. First, the diode detector can be made to cover an extremely broad bandwidth. A reasonably priced detector with a small-geometry diode can be made to cover from nearly DC to 10 GHz or more. For millimeter wavelengths, diode detectors can be integrated into waveguide components and operated to more than 100 GHz.

One disadvantage of this form of scalar network analyzer is the lack of sensitivity. A well-designed spectrum analyzer can have a sensitivity of -115 dBm, whereas the sensitivity of a diode detector is typically on the order of -45 to -60 dBm. A typical maximum input before damage would be on the order of $+15$ dBm, which translates to a dynamic range of between 60 and 75 dB. This compares to a dynamic range of about 120 dB for the tracking generator/spectrum analyzer combination. There are many applications where 120 dB of dynamic range is not required and 60 or 75 dB would be sufficient.

The diode used for a diode-type detector is, typically, a device made specifically for high-sensitivity diode detection. The diode is a very small geometry Schottky diode that is fabricated to have a small barrier potential.

The diode is a nonlinear device. For large signal inputs, the output voltage is proportional to the input voltage. Below about −15 dBm, the output voltage is proportional to the square of the input voltage or is proportional to the input power. This is called the square-law region.

It is necessary to provide a signal processor circuit for the diode detector to produce either a linear display or a logarithmic display.

Another significant disadvantage of the simple diode-detector type of network analyzer is that the diode detector will be affected by harmonic content. This is not a problem when analyzing passive devices such as filters but becomes a factor for active devices such as amplifiers. If the analysis bandwidth does not exceed an octave, a low-pass filter may be included in the measuring setup to eliminate any harmonic energy generated. Linear passive devices do not generate harmonics and will not suffer these effects.

Usually, the diode detector type of network analyzer does not contain a signal source. In the vector network analyzer, it was an advantage to have the signal source contained within the instrument. The generation of the local oscillator signal for the receiver was easier with the internal signal source. In the case of the diode-type network analyzer, no local oscillator is required and therefore any sweeping signal source may be used.

The sweep width, frequency coverage, frequency readout, source level control, etc., are provided by a conventional sweep generator; the network analyzer provides the vertical drive for an oscilloscope or provides the oscilloscope display within the network analyzer. A ramp voltage from the sweep generator is provided for the horizontal drive for the oscilloscope.

The block diagram of Fig. 9-8 shows a simple diode detector followed by a DC-coupled amplifier for each of the two display channels. Some advantages are obtained if the RF signal source is modulated and passed through an AC-coupled amplifier and synchronously demodulated. This is a classic technique that has been used for many applications, most notably a chopper-stabilized amplifier. One of the more important advantages of this technique is the elimination of the DC-coupled amplifiers and thus the improvement of DC offset drift. Also, because the signal is synchronously demodulated, there is a reduction of the effects of noise.

To use the AC method, it is necessary to modulate the signal source. Some laboratory sweep generators are provided with an external amplitude-modulation capability for this purpose. Many sweep generators require an external modulator to make use of the AC signal source.

The AC signal source cannot always be used for analyzing networks. In general, any passive device may make use of the modulated signal source. An active circuit that has an AGC system, where the modulating signal may interfere with the proper operation of the AGC system, is one device that may not allow

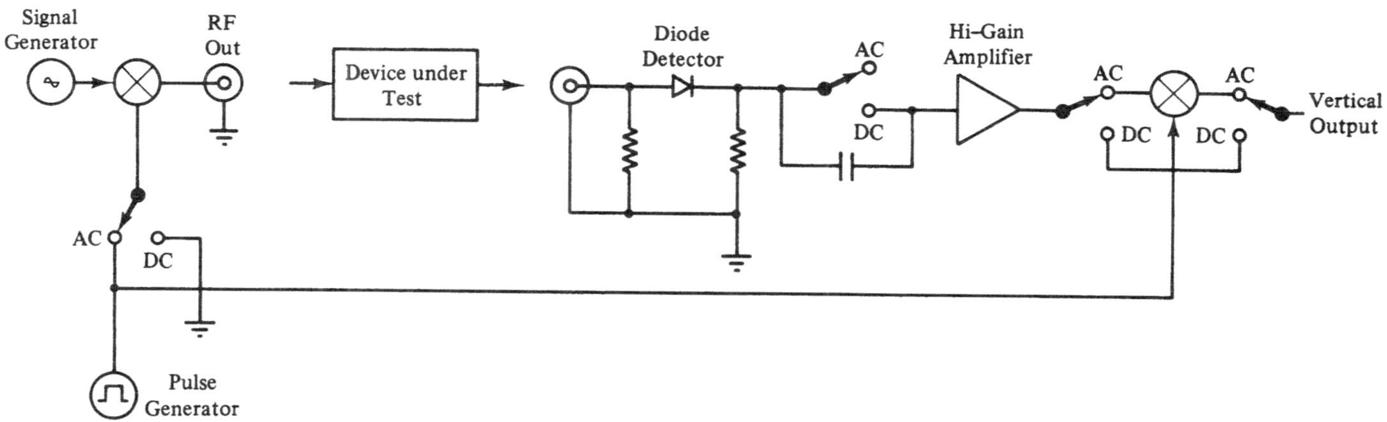

Figure 9-8
The block diagram of a scalar network analyzer with switchable AC or DC operation.

the modulated signal source. Another situation is an amplifier that has considerable gain at the modulating frequency. In this case, any leakage of the modulating frequency would be greatly amplified and then detected with the broad-band detector.

Because the modulated signal source is not always acceptable, many scalar network analyzers have a switched detection system, allowing the selection of either an AC or a DC system.

Review Questions for Chapter 9

1. What are some of the differences between a spectrum analyzer with a tracking generator and a network analyzer?
2. Why is the dynamic range of a network analyzer typically greater than the dynamic range of a spectrum analyzer?
3. What important characteristics are required of a power divider used for a network analyzer?
4. How does the length of the interconnecting cables used with a network analyzer affect the measurements?
5. What is the "reference plane"?
6. What purpose does a "line stretcher" serve?
7. How does the network analyzer measure the input impedance of a device?
8. What is group delay? How does this differ from group delay distortion? What type of electronic systems are sensitive to group delay distortion?
9. How does the network analyzer measure group delay?
10. What are the advantages of using AC detection in the scalar network analyzer? What are the advantages of DC detection?

Bibliography

Barett and Rayher. Spectrum analyzer gains synergetic partner: the tracking generator/counter. *EDN* (March 15, 1970).

Bloomfield, P. "Fourier Analysis of Time Series, An Introduction." Wiley, New York, 1976.

Bracewell, R. "The Fourier Transform and Its Applications." McGraw-Hill, New York, 1965.

Brigham, O. "The Fast Fourier Transform." Prentice-Hall, Englewood Cliffs, New Jersey, 1974.

Charest. Measuring wide bandwidth FM deviation. *EDN* (March 1, 1969).

Cooley, J. W., and J. W. Tukey. An algorithm for machine calculation of complex Fourier series. *Mathematical Computation*, **19**:297–301 (April 1965).

Cushman Electronics. "Using the Spectrum Monitor." Cushman Electronics, San Jose, California, 1978.

Engelson, M. Understanding resolution for better spectrum analysis. *Microwaves* (December 1972).

Engelson, M. Pinning down frequency stability. *EDN* (May 1969).

Engelson, M., and Breaker. Interpreting incidental FM specifications. *Frequency Technology* (February 1969).

Engelson, M., and Breaker. Spectrum analysis of FMing pulses. *Microwave Journal* (June 1961).

Engelson, M., and Long. Optimizing spectrum analyzer resolution. *Microwaves* (December 1965).

Engelson, M., and F. Telewski. "Spectrum Analyzer Theory and Applications." Artech House, Dedham, Massachusetts, 1974.

Geselowitz, D. Response of ideal radio-noise meter to continuous sine wave, recurrent impulse, and random noise. *IRE Transactions on RFI*, **RFI3** (1)(May 1960).

Gumm, L., and Engelson, M. Spectrum analysis of the TV and FM signal. *BME* (April 1973).

Hewlett-Packard. "EMI Measurement Procedure." Application Note 142. Hewlett-Packard, Palo Alto, California, 1972.

Hewlett-Packard. "EMI Measurement Procedure." Application Note 122. Hewlett-Packard, Palo Alto, California, 1968.

Hewlett-Packard. "The Fundamentals of Signal Analysis." Application Note 243. Hewlett-Packard, Palo Alto, California, 1985.

Hewlett-Packard. "Microwave Component Measurements." Application Note 345-1. Hewlett-Packard, Palo Alto, California, August 1986.

Hewlett-Packard. "Complete *S* Parameter and Distortion Measurement for Wide-Band Video Amplifiers." Application Note 357-2. Hewlett-Packard, Palo Alto, California, February 1988.

Hewlett-Packard. "Advanced Filter Evaluation and Limit Testing." Hewlett-Packard, Palo Alto, California, April 1988.

Koopmans, L. H. "The Spectral Analysis of Time Series." Academic Press, New York, 1974.

Linden. Improve the accuracy of spectrum analysis. *Microwaves* (June 1976).

Roth, P. Effective measurements using digital signal analysis. *IEEE Spectrum* (April 1971).

Roth, P. Digital Fourier analysis. *Hewlett-Packard Journal* (June 1970).
Tektronix Inc. "Noise Measurements Using the Spectrum Analyzer: Part One, Random Noise."
Tektronix Inc. "Noise Measurements Using the Spectrum Analyzer: Part Two, Impulse Noise."
Thomas, R. Making noise measurements with the spectrum analyzer. *TV Communications* (January 1976).

Index

Printed in Dunstable, United Kingdom

91897636R00127